Lincoln Christian College

D0893997

LONDON LIFE IN THE 14TH CENTURY

VIEW OF LONDON IN 1624
From a print in the Guildhall Library

LONDON LIFE IN THE 14TH CENTURY

BY

CHARLES PENDRILL

KENNIKAT PRESS
Port Washington, N. Y./London

LONDON LIFE IN THE 14th CENTURY

First published in 1925
Reissued in 1971 by Kennikat Press
Library of Congress Catalog Card No: 79-118495
ISBN 0-8046-1243-9

Manufactured by Taylor Publishing Company   Dallas, Texas

914.203
P39

CONTENTS

56311

LIST OF ILLUSTRATIONS

PREFACE

THERE *is* a Romance of Old London, attached not only to those few ancient buildings which the Great Fire and the heedless hands of unthinking vandals have left us, but also permeating every street and alley in the old part of the City ; but we can only feel this Romance fully if we know where the historic spots were situated and the circumstances which made them what they were. In this connection how often we speak of the Freedom of the City, its Liberties, its ancient system of apprenticeship, its Craft Guilds and Livery Companies, with their absurd quarrels supported by the arguments of sword and buckler rather than by those of reason ; and yet how often is our knowledge of what all these conditions involved quite inadequate. In the following pages I have endeavoured to explain the meaning of these things— the duties and responsibilities of citizenship, the methods by which trade was carried on, and the way in which the city was governed—and how these matters affected the lives of the citizens.

When studying the history of people of our own race it is well to start with the proposition that they were actuated by the same feelings and aspirations as ourselves, modified by those habits and customs which are a necessary phase of the slow and gradual acquisition of knowledge ; not only scientific knowledge such as medicine and sanitation, but more important still,

political knowledge. The highest form of such knowledge consists in the full realisation of that primary fact
of existence that injustice and oppression revert ultimately upon the heads of those who use them, while
fairplay engenders the kindliness and good feeling which
alone make life tolerable. While our modern political
quarrels prove that we are still far from a complete
understanding of this basic fact, we shall find that our
ancestors possessed it in a yet more elementary degree,
and its growth appears to be due more to the spread of
commerce than to any other cause. Thus we shall see
at one end of the scale the tyrant seizing all he can
while his power lasts, and at the other end the petty
rogue doing the same thing by fraud and chicanery,
and those who were neither tyrants nor rogues imposing
no restraint on the passions of the moment ; while
somewhere in the middle we shall see the honest merchant
preoccupied with the maintenance of his trade privileges, so that he can pursue his course in peace and
security. But the dawn of political knowledge will
be observed in that succession of enlightened Mayors
who compelled quarrelsome citizens to submit their
differences to arbitration, directed their utmost efforts
to the pacification of mutually jealous crafts, and when
on the Judgment Seat tempered firmness with mercy ;
by their public zeal making London the most renowned
city in Europe.

The origin of that financial pre-eminence which has
made London the money market of the world may fairly
be ascribed to a few of the homely virtues, such as
accuracy in accounting and the prompt payment of
debts ; and the same strain of carefulness in the national
character may be held responsible for the meticulous
care exhibited by the Londoners in writing up the day

to day transactions of the official centre of their city. So it is that from the 13th century onwards London possesses a series of records unequalled by any other city in the world, and but for such a fortunate circumstance the present book and many others of a similar kind would never have been written.

If we had no more than the splendid series of Letter-Books in which the business of the city was recorded we should still possess a wonderfully complete picture of life as lived in London in early times. The Letter-Books are so called because each is distinguished by a letter of the alphabet, starting at A and reaching to Z, and again from AA to ZZ ; but A to H are the only volumes relevant to the period here discussed. They are written on vellum, and were not distinguished by letters from their beginning, for in early times some among them were known as the " White Book," the " Red Book," the " Black Book," etc. It may be conjectured that the system of lettering was adopted shortly after 1350, for book G, dealing with the period 1352–1374, is the first of the series which has never been known by any other name than that of its letter. A tribute must be paid to the public spirit of the Corporation in having the first eleven of these volumes calendered and published, so making them available for all students.

Still preserved at Guildhall are other books of records dealing with the period but not included in the above series, among which the oldest is *Liber de Antiquis Legibus*. It consists of 159 leaves of parchment, bound in white leather, and contains many extracts from the chronicle of William of Malmesbury ; but the remainder, the part which concerns the history of the city in the 13th century, has been translated under the title of

Chronicles of the Mayors and Sheriffs of London, and bound
in one volume with a valuable French chronicle of
London covering the period 1259–1343. Another
book, *Liber Custumarum*, contains a homily, still very
much up to date, on the duties of rulers in general and
the Mayor in particular, quoted from an early Italian
writer, and a very complete account of the Iter at the
Tower in 1321, besides many facts relating to the London
crafts and incidents in the early history of the city.
Liber Albus, or the White Book of the city, is probably
the most valuable of them all for gaining an insight into
the methods of city government in the 14th century.
It was compiled in the early part of the 15th century
from the archives still existing at Guildhall, together
with others which have since disappeared, by John
Carpenter, the famous Town Clerk, and friend and
executor of Richard Whittington. Among these records
mention must be made of the Coroner's Rolls, which
constitute a source of extreme value for the habits
of the people in the 14th century, but unfortunately
they are very fragmentary. Starting with the year 1300
and ending in 1378, there are long intervals between
those dates for which no Rolls have survived, and
towards the end of the period the entries become very
sparse. This state of things may be accounted for
by the fact that whenever an Iter was held at the Tower
all such Rolls had to be delivered to the Justices for their
inspection, and probably many of them failed to get
returned.

In the course of the centuries some of these records
have not been without their misadventures and vicissitudes. Out of six books left to the city in 1328 by
Andrew Horn, a famous fishmonger and Chamberlain,
at least three have disappeared. Letter-Book E was

lost to the city for a long time, and was recovered in the reign of Henry VIII by the good offices of a Sergeant of the City and an expenditure of 20s. *Liber Custumarum* was perhaps the most unfortunate, for about the year 1550 or shortly afterwards it was lent to a borrower who neglected to return it, and when it was eventually recovered in 1608 a large part was missing, which found its way into the Cottonian Library at the British Museum, where it still remains. All the records had a miraculous escape from the Great Fire of 1666. The Guildhall itself was burnt, but the flames fizzled out on reaching the ground level, the vaults, where there is no doubt the archives had been conveyed, being left intact.

Besides the records kept at Guildhall, there are other chronicles containing valuable information concerning London in the early period. Among these may be mentioned Gregory's Chronicle, written by a 15th-century Mayor, and of course the incomparable Stow, whose Annals and Survey, with various odd notes which he has left behind, cannot be overrated for our purpose. As might be expected, many references to London and London doings are to be found in all the national chronicles of the period, none of which should be neglected by the student.

The reader will notice that at times I have strayed backward into the 13th century or forward into the 15th, but this has only been done when one of those periods supplied a better illustration of some custom of the times than could be found in the 14th.

I have refrained from burdening the text with a multiplicity of footnotes, because I myself have often been irritated by such things on occasions when I was quite willing to accept the author's judgment without requiring his justification ; but the reader can take it that every fact adduced can be vouched for, and I shall be happy to supply chapter and verse to any inquirer.

It only remains to express my deep appreciation of the unfailing courtesy of the officials of the Guildhall Library during my search for the illustrations, when they appeared to regard no amount of exertion as too great in seeking out and offering me anything in their possession which seemed suitable.

LONDON LIFE IN THE 14TH CENTURY

CHAPTER I

THE STREETS OF LONDON

THE narrow, winding lanes still to be found in the city of London must not be regarded as an indication that all the streets were of similar dimensions in early times, for it is certain that many of the main thoroughfares started their careers with a comfortable width. In Cheapside, for example, not only were there various erections in the middle of the fairway, such as the Great Cross and two water conduits, but right up to the time of Henry VIII tournaments were held in the street itself. From the 13th to the 16th centuries, however, many of the roadways were encroached upon by a process which had its origin in the habit of tradesmen, not content with the display they could make in their shops, of erecting stalls in the streets outside. The authorities at the Guildhall, so far from endeavouring to suppress this practice, drew in many cases an annual rent from the tradesmen, restricted the width of such stalls to $2\frac{1}{2}$ feet, and reserved the right to have them removed at any time. When, as sometimes happened, the administration of the city became very lax for long periods, the stalls would tend to become permanent structures built of wood, and

later, no notice being taken by the authorities, would
be rebuilt of brick and become a vested interest.

It is said that China possesses the most perfect code
of laws in the world, the only trouble being that they
are never carried out, and this was largely true of
medieval London. An instance of this state of things
is seen in the condition of the streets, notwithstanding
that a very complete system existed for keeping them
clean and in good repair. For this purpose four scavengers or " rakers " were appointed in each ward, chosen
at the meeting of the wardmote, and service in this occupation was compulsory. They drew their wages direct
from the householders, going round for this purpose
accompanied by the local beadle and constable, a necessary precaution, as exemplified by a case in 1390, when
a tailor was fined and imprisoned for assaulting one of
the constables of the ward of Bread Street while occupied
on this duty. It may be of interest to note how these
appropriately named " rakers " became in course of
time the modern scavengers. There was at one time
a toll called a " scavage " levied on all goods entering
the city, and the official whose duty it was to collect it
was called the " scavager ". Afterwards, when these
men had little work to do owing to most of the incoming
goods going direct to special warehouses where the
duty was collected, they were appointed to superintend
the work of the " rakers ", and in process of time their
name was transferred to the actual cleaners of the
streets. In addition to the work of these men, every
householder was responsible for the cleanliness of that
part of the street abutting on his home, and if it were
found dirty or covered with refuse the beadle could
fine him fourpence. If he brought out his household
rubbish and placed it in the street before the cart which

took it outside the city and dumped it at the places appointed was ready to remove it, he could be fined two shillings ; but if he placed it in front of a neighbour's premises the fine was increased to four shillings. Moreover, there were inspectors of nuisances in those days, appointed, not at the wardmote as were the " rakers ", but at the Guildhall by the Mayor and aldermen. There were four of them—two masons and two carpenters, and they were known as " the sworn masons " and carpenters of the city ". Their duties consisted in examining into any complaints of encroachments upon the streets, or " purprestures " as they were called ; seeing that no man laid his pavement higher or lower than that of his neighbour ; settling disputes as to boundary and party walls and divisions of land ; and surveying property for the purpose of allocating the dower of widows, who by the law of the city were entitled to a third of their deceased husband's property by way of " freebench ". For repairing the roads a toll was levied on horses and vehicles passing through the gates—one penny on every cart and a farthing on every horse carrying victuals or merchandise, threepence a week on carts bringing sand, gravel, and clay, a similar sum on carts bringing corn and flour from Stratford, a farthing on carts laden with brushwood, and a penny on carts bringing charcoal. Carts or horses carrying the victuals or personal belongings of private individuals passed free of toll. Further to stimulate the upkeep of the thoroughfares, many wealthy citizens left money by will for the purpose. If all these admirable arrangements had been carried out London would have been a healthier and more comfortable city to live in, but unfortunately the public spirit of the time was not equal to fulfilling them. It was on account of the depth of mud in the streets, especially at certain seasons of the year, that many people wore pattens, or wooden clogs supported on circlets of iron, and thus we have the Guild of Pattenmakers, mentioned for the first time in the Letter-Books under the year 1379. To add to the accumulation of rubbish in the streets, many tradesmen not only sold their goods out in the open, but carried on the actual work of their business in the public highway. Thus in 1310 tailors and fripperers were warned to cease from scouring fur in the streets during the daytime, but to perform that operation in the night, as it caused such great inconvenience to the nobles passing by ; while in 1366 poulterers were similarly warned not to pluck their poultry in the highways. It was the regular thing for the King, when he proposed passing through the city, to send warning ahead that all filth and obstructions should be removed from the streets before his approach, and it is recorded that on one occasion Edward III, passing along the river on his barge and noting the dirty condition of the streets leading down to the water, addressed a strong letter to the Mayor on the subject.

It was in order to take advantage of this situation that the pig-owners of the city, and there were many of them, allowed these animals to roam at will through the streets to pick up a living. Orders against this practice were issued time after time, and an official appointed to seize all such wandering pigs and to return them to their owners only upon payment of fourpence, or in default to kill them for his own use. Nevertheless, the practice continued all through the middle ages, and on one occasion in the year 1332 was the cause of a lamentable tragedy. It happened that a wandering sow strayed in at the open door of an unattended shop near Queenhithe, and severely bit on the face a month-old child which was lying there in its cradle. The mother, returning later, snatched up her child and tenderly nursed it until midnight, when it died ; but, as in most such cases at that period, the obvious precaution of summoning a doctor was disregarded. It was probably on account of their ferocity that wandering dogs were considered a nuisance, for in an order directed against them in 1387 pet dogs are excepted.

The houses in a street were not numbered as they are to-day, and consequently the directions in deeds and records reciting the position of buildings are remarkably vague, usually consisting of such unsatisfactory indications as " the tenement lately held by so-and-so ", or " the shop opposite the Great Cross near the end of " Wood Street ", and so on. Many houses in consequence adopted a sign by which the premises should be known, and these were hung out on poles projecting across the street, which, by reason of the exigencies of trade rivalry, tended to reach inordinate lengths, so that in 1375 it was found necessary to restrict them to 7 feet. Many houses were built of three or four stories, with outside stone stairways leading down to the street, and the upper stories overhung so far that often the view of the sky was almost excluded. Thus in 1379 a complaint was made that a householder in Cosynlane in the ward of Dowgate had built a kitchen which stretched right across the street, but upon the Mayor and aldermen going to view it and making inquiries upon the spot, they came to the conclusion that from old times there had been a building there which hung even lower. At first the houses were constructed of wood with thatched roofs, but as early as the time of Richard I, after the city had suffered from innumerable

" great fires of London ", the citizens were encouraged to build of brick or stone, and to tile their roofs. They became so scared of fire that the law as to roofs was rigidly enforced. In 1302 a man who had roofed his house in Candlewyck Street with thatch was summoned at Guildhall and compelled to undertake to tile it by a certain date, and in the meantime to be responsible for any loss occasioned to his neighbours in the event of his thatch causing a fire. All large houses were compelled to keep a long ladder and a barrel of water always ready, and every ward had to possess a large hook with a wooden handle, called the " ward-hook ", with two chains and two strong cords. When a house caught fire this hook was hurled to the roof and all hands joined in pulling down the burning building to prevent the conflagration spreading. A curious petition addressed to the Mayor by the inhabitants of the ward of Bishopsgate in 1314 is found in the Letter-Books, in which they crave permission to chop down an elm tree growing near the city wall and with the money obtained by the sale of the wood to purchase a new rope for their wardhook. In the 13th and 14th centuries it became increasingly customary to build with brick or stone, but Stow tells us that so lax had the law become that many of these structures when they required rebuilding were pulled down and re-erected of wood, with the consequence that in his time most of the city was built of that material.

If, by some transmutation of epochs, a modern Londoner could project himself into the 14th-century city his eyes would be confronted with scenes whose quaintness indicates the peculiar and often childlike mentality of our ancestors. It is true that his modern more sophisticated nose would experience difficulty in withstanding the objectionable effluvia from the reeking roadways and houses, for there was no drainage system in the modern sense either within doors or without, but perhaps it is well to pass lightly over this point. The first sight to attract the wayfarer's attention would be the gaudily coloured dresses of the men and women, lending to the streets a touch of brilliant colour reminiscent of the Orient. There he would see men of the better class wearing parti-coloured hose from the ankle to the waist, the violent contrast in tint of each leg producing a curious and bizarre effect. The combinations most favoured were black and white, blue and white, and red and black. At one time a contrast much affected by city officials was blue and mustard ! The upper part of the body was covered by a short coat often trimmed with fur, and with loose hanging sleeves, and many were the colours favoured for this garment. Besides such colours as green and scarlet, we hear of medley (a mixture of tints), ray, giving a striped effect, and applebloom, the precise shade of which must be left to the imagination. Around the waist was worn a girdle, made of wool, leather, or linen thread, and garnished with " latten ", copper, iron, or steel, or in the case of the very wealthy, with gold or silver. The use of lead, pewter, or tin for this purpose was forbidden. In the absence of pockets the pouch or purse, often made of velvet, was suspended from the shoulder by a strap. In 1370 a man was sentenced to stand on the pillory for cutting off a woman's purse in the Stocks Market, and it is not difficult to see in this 14th-century version of pocket-picking the origin of the term " cutpurse ". The foregoing articles of apparel were covered by a gown made in an array of colours as extensive as was the coat, and often with a

hood to match, which could be thrown back upon the
shoulders. Caps, however, were a favourite form of
headgear, and they ranged from beaver caps lined with
scarlet cloth or green velvet for the nobility, caps half
red and half green, caps of black, blue, red, and russet
for ordinary folk, down to the black shaggy caps known
as " hures " for the common people. In the latter
part of the 14th century many extravagant fashions
were brought over from Eastern Europe in the train
of Anne of Bohemia, the Queen of Richard II. These
included the long-toed boots which afterwards grew to
such extremes that they had to be tied to the knees,
and also the extraordinary custom of cutting the cloth
into small pieces and laboriously sewing them all together
again. William Langland, the author of the *Vision of
Piers Plowman*, says that it would take seven men
working for six weeks to sew all these pieces together
in sufficient quantity to make a suit of clothes, and
would cost twenty times the value of the original cloth.
These fashions are referred to in a poem of the period
as " Cuttede clothes and pyked schoone ". The sleeves
of the gowns and the hem of the clothes eventually
became so long that they often trailed the ground,
collecting in their course the mud and refuse which
littered the roads. The dirtiness of this fashion is
commented on by Chaucer, who also speaks of the great
waste of material in both men's and women's clothing,
and condemns the indecency of tight hose and short
coat, likening the back view of a fop of the time to a
" she ape in the fulle of the moone ".

The rulers of the city, although the dignified position
they occupied and their age prevented their vying with
the young bloods of the nobility in extravagance of
dress, were not without aspirations towards the display

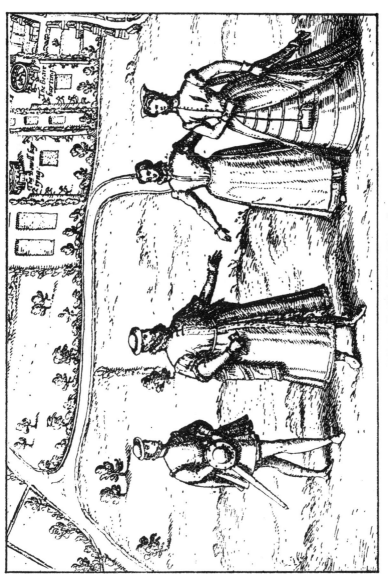

COSTUMES OF OLD LONDONERS, 1572

From a print in the Guildhall Library

of a certain floweriness of garb which in these days would be considered inconsistent with a proper gravity of demeanour. Stow thus describes the appearance of a sheriff of London in the 14th century : " His hair " rounded by his ears and curled : a little beard forked : " a gown, girt to him down to his feet, of branched " damask, wrought with the likeness of flowers : a " large purse on his right side, hanging from a belt " from his left shoulder : a plain hood about his neck " covering his shoulders, and hanging back behind " him ". The dress peculiar to an alderman may be understood from an order of 1382 dismissing one of them from office, in which he is forbidden from henceforth to wear " any robe of the livery of the Mayor, " aldermen, or sheriffs, new or old, to wit, any cloak " parti-furred with fur or lined with silk, on pain of " losing the franchise and all that could be forfeited ". The clergy themselves, so far as the secular arm was concerned, were not averse to the wearing of bright colours, for we read in 1323 of a chaplain who possessed a gown of red medley worth 20s. o. ; and even funerals acquired a giddy appearance if one may judge from the inventory of the goods belonging to the church of St. Mildred in the Poultry made at the time of the Dissolution, wherein are included three hearse cloths, one of crimson satin and gold, another of dark crimson satin embroidered in blue for men, and the third of similar satin " lyon colour " for children.[1]

The fine ladies of the period affected equally gaudy clothing, wore a great deal of fur, and were particularly distinguished by their headgear, in reference to which and to other newly acquired habits Stow remarks : " Also noble women used high attire on their heads,

[1] Milbourn's *History of St. Mildred's Church*, p. 7.

" piked horns, with long trained gowns, and rode on
" side saddles, after the example of the Queene who
" first brought that fashion into this land, for before
" women were used to ride astride like men ". But
the simple dress of the middle-class woman, with its
delightful contrast of black and white, relieved by the
merest touch of colour, must have exhibited a charm
unsurpassed in any age, if we may judge by the description
of the young wife of a carpenter found in the pages
of Chaucer. She wore a girdle of silk, a snow-white
apron full of many a gusset, a white embroidered smock
with a black collar, and on her head a white cap with
black ribbands. From her girdle hung a leather purse
studded with brass knobs and decorated with green
tassels, and her shoes were laced high up her legs.

As a foil to the bright colours of the people of position
—nobles, gentry, civic functionaries, and merchants—
might be observed the sober habit of the scholar, the
physician, and the professional man, consisting of a
plain black gown reaching from the neck to the feet,
buttoned closely at the throat and wrists. And for
background was the great throng of workmen and poor
dressed in suits of homely russet with which all the
colours of the superior classes mingled to produce a
bright and kaleidoscopic effect.

In order to gather an impression of medieval London
with its overhanging, ornately built houses, its motley
throng of nobles, ecclesiastics, merchants, and workmen,
its glamour and its dirt, let us direct our steps along a
typical thoroughfare—round St. Paul's and down Cheapside as far as the famous Tun upon Cornhill. Here
was perhaps the most historic part of the city, the scene
of its most important commercial activity, its public
gatherings, and many of its tragedies. A tribute to

VIEW OF OLD ST. PAUL'S, SHOWING PAUL'S CROSS
From a print in the Guildhall Library

the importance of Cheapside, or West Chepe as it was called, may be observed in the crucial matter of rent, for whereas at the commencement of the 14th century a warehouse consisting of a shed with perhaps one room above would fetch as much as £4 a year in that thorough-fare, at the same period two shops in Sopars Lane (the modern Queen Street), are recorded to have been let for £1. 8s. 0. and £2. 14s. 8d. respectively ; a shop in the parish of St. Mary Colechurch for £1. 13s. 0. ; and a house in Cornhill for £2. 10s. 0.

As we enter St. Paul's Churchyard from Bowyer Row (now Ludgate Hill), on our right is an ancient tower built originally for a bell tower, and afterwards known as the Lollard's Tower, on account of its use by the Bishop of London as a prison for heretics caught within the city. On the left or north-west corner is the Bishop's Palace, in the great hall of which many notable feasts were held to entertain kings, distinguished foreigners, and city magnates. Here Edward II, when Prince of Wales, held his court and called before him the chief men of London to concert measures for the good order and safekeeping of the city at a time when war with France was threatened. In the hall of the Palace was a cupboard of eight tiers covered with gilt plate consisting of cups, bowls, and flagons of enormous value, the property of the Bishop. A display of this kind was not at all unusual in city houses, for all citizens who could afford to do so took great pride in ornamenting their homes with an array of fine plate. Thus we see from the report of a burglary at the house of a cook in Bridge Street, near London Bridge, who, by his occupa-tion cannot be supposed to have been among the wealthiest of the inhabitants, that he possessed 18 silver spoons ; 7 pieces of silver ; 4 silver-mounted girdles ; 2 mazers,

or wooden cups, bound with bands of silver gilt ; a pair
of amber paternosters, or rosaries, one with a gold clasp
and the other with clasp of silver gilt ; and a gold ring.

The churchyard presents a scene of considerable
animation, for in addition to the comings and goings of
priests and of those whose business or devotion took
them to the Cathedral, it is evident that, to some extent
at any rate, commerce reared its head even in these
sacred precincts.   At one time in the early 14th century
the gardeners of the nobles had the privilege of
standing there and selling the produce of their masters'
estates situated in the suburbs without the city walls,
but were afterwards removed because of the obstruction
caused to the numerous prelates in their goings to and
fro between the Cathedral and the surrounding buildings.
On the south side of the church was a fine chapter-
house, which, however, was afterwards spoilt by cutlers
and other tradesmen, who were licenced by the corporation to erect sheds against it for the purposes of their
business.   Stow says that in his time these sheds had
grown into tall houses which quite obscured the view
of all but the top of the Cathedral.   On the north side
was a charnel-house, into which the bones of deceased
Londoners of generations past and gone were collected.
It must have been in the nature of a pit, for in 1282
a chapel was built over it which went by the appropriate
name of the " Chapel on the Bones of the Dead ".   The
benefice was in the gift of the corporation.   Both
chapel and charnel-house were done away with in 1549,
when it is said that thousands of cartloads of bones
were removed and re-interred in Finsbury Fields.   Over
the spot sprang up afterwards dwelling-houses, warehouses, and sheds.   In the same part of the churchyard,
but somewhat farther eastwards, was the famous Paul's

Cross, a pulpit cross of wood, from which sermons were preached, proclamations read, new statutes passed by Parliament rehearsed, bulls of the Pope recited, and on occasion various people publicly cursed. On one occasion in the 14th century, while a great prelate was preaching there on what should have been the Sabbath, his sermon was rudely interrupted by a shrieking crowd with blood flowing from their wounds, fleeing from a fight which was proceeding in Cheapside.[1] In the north-east corner was a belfry, in which was hung the Common Bell of the city, whose loud-tongued clangour was the signal for all the citizens to assemble. The belfry was surmounted by a gilt cross and ball erected in 1280. When in 1314 these were taken down to be repaired it was discovered that the pious founders had deposited within the ball a cloth of fine linen such as was used at Holy Communion, and wrapped therein a piece of the True Cross carved in the form of a cross ; a stone from the Holy Sepulchre, another from the spot where the Saviour stood when He ascended to Heaven, and another from Calvary ; also a purse containing a piece of silk in which were wrapped some bones of the eleven thousand virgins, and other relics the nature of which could not be determined. These were replaced and other relics added. The Common Bell was a very ancient institution dating at least from Saxon times, and was very useful in a clockless age, for its sound, which could be heard all over the city, summoned the inhabitants to assemble, not only in cases of sudden emergency, but for meetings of the Folkmoot, which from earliest times was held at this spot. Here the business of the city was transacted in public assembly, the new sheriffs elected each Michael-

[1] See chapter on Trade Fights.

mas, and courts held to decide civil actions and to issue probate of wills.   It was here that Henry III in 1245 summoned a meeting of the citizens to receive their formal permission to march into Wales—with his tongue in his cheek as we may suppose.   These meetings were discontinued after 1298, when the centre of city life gravitated to the Guildhall, but the Common Bell remained and continued to be used to summon the citizens to arms.   When at length the bell was removed four others were substituted which received the name of " Jesus' Bells ".   Stow relates that they disappeared in 1549 when Henry VIII staked them against £100 in a game of dice which he played with Sir Miles Partridge, and lost.

The churchyard was also used for assemblies other than official ones, such as trade meetings and love-days. The latter was a pretty custom of the middle ages. When a dispute arose between two bodies of people, such as two rival crafts, influential persons who aspired to the rôle of peacemaker would appoint a love-day, on which all interested parties were invited to meet and amicably discuss their differences, and there is no doubt that the very name by which they called these meetings must have had some influence in quieting the passions of the disputants.   A meeting of this kind was held in St. Paul's Churchyard in 1318 in order to effect a reconciliation between Edward II and his barons, which however proved to be of short duration.   However, it would appear, by the scorn which some old writers pour upon those who get up love-days, calling them " lorels " and other opprobrious names, that they were not always held for such benevolent purposes as the foregoing.   During the 14th century this spot came to be used for purposes even less consistent with its sacred character than public meetings, for certain people made a practice of holding wrestling matches there. These were expressly forbidden by proclamation from the Guildhall in 1411. It was a popular habit throughout the middle ages to play such games as wrestling, hurling, and leapfrog in the streets and churchyards in spite of the efforts of the authorities to relegate them to such open spaces as Smithfield.

Ecclesiastical doings naturally provided many sights in the churchyard. Solemn processions always formed a large part of Catholic ritual, and on occasions when the great prelates from all parts of the kingdom assembled at St. Paul's the scene must have been gorgeous indeed. Such assemblies occurred when a legate was sent from Rome to inquire into the conduct of the English Church and in the conclave of bishops to formulate new rules for its improvement. One event of this kind took place in 1237, when the legate caused a lofty seat to be built for him in the west end of the Cathedral, covered with tapestry and awnings, to which he was conducted by a long procession of bishops and abbots in full pontificals, the Archbishops of Canterbury and York leading the way bearing the Cross and lighted candles, the whole company reciting the litany as they walked. Other processions were of a grosser kind and illustrate the curious mixture of holy and profane things so characteristic of medieval catholicism. Stow relates that once every year the clergy of St. Paul's were presented with a fine fat buck. The body was sent to the kitchen to be roasted, but the head was cut off and fixed on a pole, and the Dean and Chapter, with garlands of roses on their heads, carried it round in solemn procession.

The fabric of the Cathedral itself was a mighty pile, the pride of the citizens and their most cherished possession. Stow, in some memoranda he has left behind, pronounces the following eulogy on St. Paul's : " A " Minster of such worthy, strong and costly building, " so pleasant and so delectable, it passed all comparison, " not only of Minsters within this realm, but elsewhere, " as sure as travel hath taught us in other realms either " Christian or heathen ".[1]   From the same indefatigable antiquary we learn that its length was 720 feet, its breadth 130 feet, the body of the church 150 feet high, and the steeple 520 feet high.   The steeple was surmounted by a weathercock in the form of an eagle made of gilded copper, whose length from head to tail was 4 feet, the breadth of its extended wings $3\frac{1}{2}$ feet, and its weight 40 pounds.   To defray the expenses of the Cathedral and of the Dean and Chapter many houses and parcels of land were given or bequeathed at various times both within the city and without.   In 1292 we hear of Henry le Galeys, a former Mayor, offering them some shops near the churchyard, but before these could be accepted permission had to be obtained from the King, who ordered Ralph de Sandwych, the Warden of London, to hold an inquiry to ascertain whether such gift would be prejudicial to the Royal interests.   All tenants of the Bishop of London, and of the Dean and Chapter of St. Paul's, were as free of tolls in London as were the citizens themselves, even though the property they held might be situated outside the liberties of the city.

Fugitive felons had a right of sanctuary in St. Paul's as at other churches.   As early as 1289 it is reported that one Walter Bacun took sanctuary there, and when the Coroner, in company of the Warden and other good men of the city, called to interrogate him, he

<hr>

[1] *Three* 15*th-Century Chronicles*, Camden Society.

claimed that he was a chaplain, and confessed to stealing sixteen silver dishes from a citizen named Barunchin. He thereupon surrendered the dishes to the Coroner, by whom they were handed over to the Sheriff, who, two days later, formally restored them to their owner at Guildhall.

It was not often that the sanctity of the Mother Church of the city was involved in the political troubles of the times. Such an event, however, occurred in 1326, on the occasion of the deposition of Edward II, when the London mob, after seizing and executing several of the King's favourites, got completely out of hand and were ready to indulge in any mischief. In this emergency the Chancellor thought it prudent to remove the King's treasure from the Wardrobe to St. Paul's, but this did not prevent the mob from invading the sacred building and looting it. Shortly afterwards, when Prince Edward arrived on the scene, all that was left were a few chests containing the Wardrobe accounts and some vestments, which he caused to be removed to the Guildhall.

Within the Cathedral porch the serjeants of the coif or serjeants-at-law stood awaiting employment by the citizens, each having his alloted pillar to lean against. These were the barristers of the period, and had the exclusive right of pleading in the Court of Common Pleas. They obtained their name from the custom of wearing on the head a white coif surmounted by a red cap. Chaucer, in his prologue to the *Canterbury Tales*, thus describes one of them who was numbered among the pilgrims :—

> " A serjeant of the law, war and wys,
> " That often hadde been at the Parvys,[1]
> " Ther was also ful riche of excellence."

> [1] Or churchdoor.

Within the Cathedral were many chapels, chantries, and tombs of the great, including that of the founder, St. Erkenwald, bishops of London, and early Saxon kings. In the 14th century the famous Sir John Pulteney, draper and four times Mayor, among many others, founded a chantry for the good of his soul, and by his will left the appointment of the officiating priest in the disposition of the Mayor for the time being. Upon one of the columns supporting the roof was marked a standard measure for the use of the citizens, a measure which was known as " feet of St. Paul ", and is so referred to in a statement concerning the metes and bounds of the Cnihten-gild, the ancient name for Portsoken Ward. It was not unknown for miracles to occur in St. Paul's. After Thomas Earl of Lancaster had been beheaded in 1322 crowds of people arrived to pray before a tablet which he had formerly erected in the church, at which time the crooked were made straight, the blind received their sight, and the deaf their hearing. Such a commotion was caused that the King, fearing a popular rising, ordered the tablet to be removed.

Emerging from the churchyard by the north-east gate towards Cheapside there stood in the 14th century an ancient cross known at one time as the " Duke of Gloucester's Cross ", but afterwards, on account of its dilapidated condition, as the " Brokyncross ". It seems to have possessed a certain religious significance, for in an indenture of apprenticeship of the year 1376 it is mentioned as the pledge and surety for the fulfilment of the contract in place of the usual personal security. Doubtless this was done in order to make the deed more binding on a superstitious mind, and point is given to this supposition by the fact that the indenture was a fraudulent one, executed in the name of a youth without the consent of his parents. The cross stood midway between the churchyard gate and the door of the church of St. Michael le Quern, so called because of a cornmarket, often referred to as the cornmarket " on the Pavement of Chepe ", which was held beside it. This church was peculiar in that a public right of way ran through it. In 1378 the rector stopped the passage by building a wall across the entrance, but was soon compelled by the Mayor to remove the obstruction. The Brokyncross was surrounded by stalls for the sale of various small goods, let by the corporation for 6s. 8d. a year each. On the occasion of the birth of Edward III a pavilion was erected nearby wherein a tun of wine was put on tap for anyone to drink who would. The cross was demolished in 1390 and a water conduit built on the spot, though Stow seems to think this conduit was not made until the reign of Henry VI.

We are now really in West Chepe, which, as its name implies, was a market place or " cheping ". It was lined on either side with warehouses or " selds ", many of only one storey, though some boasted an upper room known as a " solar ", or sun parlour. Stow, writing in the 16th century, says that by his time all these sheds had become tall houses of four or five stories, the upper ones overhanging the streets ; and the last of the ancient buildings, situated at the east end of the street and occupied by a woman who sold seeds, roots, and herbs, lingered on until a few years before he wrote. It must not be supposed, however, that in the 14th century all the houses in West Chepe were of this size or type. On many occasions we find mention of " The " Great Seld of Rohesia de Coventre ", which probably comprised a whole row of shops with a goodly frontage towards the street. In 1325 a shop within this seld is mentioned, while in 1317 a piece of ground in it was let for 20s. o. a year. Again, in 1341 there is mention of a new stone house in Chepe belonging to the Prior and Convent of Christ Church, Canterbury, a portion only of which they let to a vintner for £13. 13s. 4d. a year.

There were paviours in those days, but they did not lay pavements such as we know to-day. There was then no distinction between roadway and sidewalk, the entire surface being composed of the same cobble stones, with a channel, or gutter, running down the middle of the street to carry away the rainwater, or, in the wider streets, two parallel channels which divided the thorough-fare into three sections. Such was the case in West-chepe and Cornhill, where, from St. Paul's to Leadenhall, we have to imagine a continuous row of stalls placed between these channels and devoted to the sale, not only of victuals but of other commodities, such as shoes, old clothes, blacksmith's wares, and stationery, each class of tradesman located in his allotted section. From stray references in the records it is often possible to judge whether a street were wide or narrow from the number of rainwater channels which it possessed. Thus, while Westchepe and Cornhill were of sufficient width to require two of these channels, Newgate Street appears to have boasted only one, and that in the middle of the roadway, for it is stated that when the King's Justices came to St. Martin-le-Grand and held their sessions in the Great South Gate, abutting on Newgate Street, the prisoners to be tried had to be lined up on the opposite side of the road, because if they once succeeded in crossing the channel in the middle they could claim sanctuary in St. Martin's.

It was not so profitable to own a stall in Westchepe as in some other parts of the city, for it could never remain unmolested long enough to develop into a permanent structure, as happened at one time in Old Fish Street, where the stalls, growing into tall houses, converted what had formerly been one street into two. This being the main route through the city to Westminster, it happened periodically that the stalls were cleared away to allow free passage to the King or to other notables. An occasion of this sort caused some trouble in 1273, when the Mayor ordered the stalls of the butchers and fishmongers to be removed for the passage of Edward I, who was expected back from the Holy Land. The occupiers had paid rent for their holdings, and some of them a large sum of money for a life tenancy to the Mayor's predecessor. The dispossessed ones thereupon went to Guildhall in a body and publicly abused the Mayor, who pleaded that he was acting by the King's orders. The upshot was that the Mayor who had granted the life tenancies was degraded from his office of alderman, and it was probably due in part to this dispute that the Stocks Market was founded in 1282. Again, in December 1347 a writ was received from the King inquiring whether any ordinances existed in the city for suppressing the nuisance arising from the retailing of victuals and other merchandise in the highways of Chepe and Cornhill, and ordering that any such ordinance should be put in force. Accordingly in the following January an effort was made to clear the streets of these merchants and thirty-eight citizens were appointed to carry it out, among them apothecaries, mercers, pouchmakers, glovers, vintners, an armourer, etc. The duty thus imposed furnishes an example of the obligations to which freemen of the city were liable.

Immediately to the left on entering West Chepe, between Foster Lane and the next turning, Gutter Lane, was one of the spots where bread from Stratford was sold from the carts which brought it into London. This was an important supplement to the city's supply of bread, and was encouraged throughout the middle ages, but was not permitted to be sold in shops. The London bakers were strictly overlooked by the authorities, chiefly in the matter of the weight of their bread, but it was obviously more difficult to extend this supervision to the men from Stratford, because usually the man in charge of the cart was merely the baker's assistant, who, if caught, pleaded ignorance ; and because he could sell short-weight bread and escape before he could be detected. It was for this reason that a rule was made in 1392 that when any loaf from Stratford was found deficient in weight the whole cartload should be confiscated. Raids were frequently made upon these men by the officials, and on one such occasion in 1387, when the Mayor himself came to make an inspection, one of them hastily inserted a piece of iron into a loaf to increase its weight, but was detected and seized.

At the beginning of the century the north-west end of Chepe and round into Foster Lane was the home of the saddlers, and was known as the " Saddlery " or " Cordwainery ", while Foster Lane itself derived its name from the " Fusters ", or makers of wooden saddle-bows. There is an account in 1300 of a saddler who had his workshop in the " solar " or first floor room of a house situated between Honey Lane and Milk Street, and keeping a plank of wood projecting from the window on which to hang his saddles to dry, it fell down and killed a man who was passing in the street below. At the same end of the street was a tavern named " The Cock," the goodman of which was, in the year 1390, murdered in his bed, a crime for which his wife was burnt and three of his assistants drawn and hanged at Tyburn.

On the right, from Old Change to the corner of Bread Street, stretched the Goldsmithery, or Goldsmith's Row. In the 14th century this spot consisted mainly of low buildings of one or two stories, and had not attained the distinction which it acquired in after times. The portion near Bread Street was rebuilt in magnificent style towards the end of the 15th century, so much so that Stow boasts of it as the finest row of shops in England. The kind of articles in which these merchants dealt may be judged from the report of two burglaries, perpetrated in 1382 on the same night and by the same two men, one at a shop on the corner of Friday Street and the other on neighbouring premises. The haul included silver girdles braided with silk, ranging in value from 16s. 0. to 46s. 0., a silver-gilt chain 40s. 0., a silver chalice 38s. 0., two wooden cups known as " mazers " with bands of silver-gilt, 33s. 4d., six silver spoons 14s. 0., two gold rings set with diamonds £15, a gold and ruby ring 26s. 8d., three strings of pearls 70s. 0., six gold necklaces 100s. 0., and many other articles of value, including buckles, paternosters (or rosaries), and a knife called a " copegorge ", or cut-throat. The burglars would have been hanged had they not successfully claimed benefit of clergy by reciting their " neck-verse ". One such was hanged in 1340 for stealing at the same spot a silver-mounted glass cup valued at 8s. 0. The above-mentioned shop at the corner of Friday Street was still a goldsmith's in the 18th century, when it was occupied by one Stafford Briscoe. The famous Mermaid Tavern, where Shakespeare and others foregathered, was situated between Friday Street and Bread Street, and is first mentioned in 1462, and on the corner of Bread Street was a house belonging in 1342 to one Dame Isabella Godchepe, from which 100s. yearly was payable to the leper hospital of St. James de Cherryngge, which formerly stood on the site of the present St. James's Palace.

The little green plot on the left of Cheapside as one goes from St. Paul's, where grows the tree which is so familiar a landmark to Londoners, marks the churchyard of St. Peter, Chepe, or St. Peter, Wood Street, destroyed in the Fire of London and never rebuilt. In 1325 this church was the scene of a tragedy which displays the pugnacity of the people in those days, and also the curious method adopted by a wounded man to summon assistance. Three men had been quarrelling in a tavern known as the " Brokenselde," near the corner of Milk Street, when one of them pierced another through the body with a long knife called an Irish knife. The third man, to complete the work, thereupon struck the injured man on the head with his " misericorde ", a knife specially made, as its name implies, for dispatching a victim. Notwithstanding these injuries, he succeeded in reaching the church of St. Peter, Chepe, and commenced to ring the bells, but being overcome he soon fell dead. Many persons were passing to and fro in Chepe at the time, but curiously enough none of them attempted to interfere or to assist the wounded man, whose body was afterwards discovered by the sub-clerk of the church.

The shop which stands in front of the tree is an ancient encroachment upon the street. The original structure, known as the " Long Shop ", was built against the churchyard wall in 1401 by permission of the corporation, who received at first a rental of £1. 10s. 4d. a year for it, afterwards reduced to 13s. 4d. Near the end of Wood Street was yet another goldsmith's shop, let in 1381 for 4 marks (53s. 4d.) a year, and near the same spot a house called in 1349 " Bernselde ".

Almost opposite here in the middle of the street stood the famous Great Cross, a large structure of stone, probably Purbeck marble from the neighbourhood of Corfe Castle, erected in 1290 by Edward I in honour of his deceased Queen Eleanor, and elaborately decorated with her image and arms. Around its base were carved in relief figures representing the Virgin Mary, the Crucifixion, Edward the Confessor, etc., and it was surmounted by a cross of timber, covered with lead, and gilt on the outside. Sentiment in those days always gave way to material considerations, and so, like the " Brokyncross ", it soon became surrounded by stalls let by the corporation at a rental of 13s. 4d. a year to dealers in small goods, such as pens and ink. These stalls were known as the " Stations in Chepe ", and thus gave rise to the term " Stationer ", applied to dealers in similar articles. Among historic incidents which have centred round this spot may be mentioned one in 1326, when Prince Edward and his mother were attempting to depose Edward II. They caused an open letter to the citizens to be affixed to the cross begging assistance in their enterprise, a missive which so inflamed the people that they waited upon the Mayor imploring his interference on the Prince's behalf. The Mayor, fearing to compromise himself, issued a proclamation that all enemies of the King, Queen, and Prince should leave the city ; but the crowd, taking this as a move against the King's favourites, seized several of them, dragged them into Chepe, and there beheaded them.

From this point down to Sopers Lane, near where

Queen Street now stands, the tournaments were held.
Throughout the middle ages these martial festivals and
also single combats were often held at Smithfield, where
was a flat space eminently suitable for the purpose,
which makes it more difficult to understand why some
of them should have been staged in the comparatively
narrow and congested thoroughfare of Cheapside, and
even at times on London Bridge. In spite of the
awkwardness of the ground, a jousting was held at the
latter spot in 1396 between a party of thirty Scots and
as many English. These meetings were conducted
with all the pomp and circumstance which characterised
the high-water mark of the age of chivalry, and the
knights were often led from the Tower by chains of roses
held in the hands of gaily bedecked ladies, who preceded
them on horseback. When in 1329 Edward III held
a solemn jousting in Chepe, the roadway was carefully
sanded, the houses gay with bunting, and a noble archway
in form of a tower erected across the street, from which
the Queen and her ladies could view the passage of
arms. Unfortunately, when they ascended the archway
it collapsed in the middle, letting them down in most
undignified fashion upon the knights below, several of
whom were injured, though none seriously. The
carpenters who built it were on the point of becoming
victims of the King's wrath when the gentle Queen
Phillipa, with her usual magnanimity, interfered and
saved them from punishment. To avoid such accidents
for the future, the King built beside Bow Church a great
house of stone from which to view the tournaments.
It was called the " Crownsilde ", meaning the Royal
House, and was used down to the time of Henry VIII
for viewing the jousting and the annual march of the
watch on Midsummer Eve. The arrangements for

these affairs had to be paid for by the city, and we find from their accounts that a tournament in Chepe in 1331 cost them £88. 12s. 0.

The neighbouring church of St. Mary-le-Bow, so called because it was built upon arches or bows, was one of the most historic spots in London. An ecclesiastical court—the Court of Arches—originally met there and derived its name from the church. It was sufficiently famous to be mentioned in the national chronicles as early as 1091, when a violent wind lifted off the roof and, after whirling it about in the air, drove the roof beams, which were 27 or 28 feet long, so far into the earth that only an eighth of their length remained above ground. Again, in 1270 the steeple fell down, killing more than twenty people. In 1196 it withstood a siege. One Fitzosbert, known as " Longbeard ", a rebel in the city, barricaded himself in the steeple with plenty of munitions and victuals, and the citizens only succeeded in dislodging him by smoking him out. An atrocious murder committed at Bow Church in 1284 is instructive in showing the treatment meted out to suicides by our ancestors. One Laurence Ducket, a goldsmith, having wounded a man in West Chepe, fled to sanctuary at Bow Church, and ascended the steeple to pass the night. He was pursued by friends of the wounded man, who entered, slew him, and hung his body at a window to let it appear that he had taken his own life. The jury were completely deceived, and pronouncing a verdict of suicide, his body was dragged through the streets by the feet and thrown into a ditch outside the city walls. The truth came out by means of a boy who had accompanied him to the steeple, and the result was that sixteen men were drawn and hanged, and one woman, Alice Atte Bowe, burnt. The church was

placed under interdict, and the doors and windows
stopped up with thorns ; but the body of the murdered
man was taken from the ditch where it had been thrown
and decently buried in the churchyard. Attached to
the same church was one of the three earliest schools
founded in London, the others being St. Paul's and
St. Martin-le-Grand. It was mentioned by Fitzstephen
in the first description of the city extant, dating from
the 12th century. It may not be inopportune to note
here what was considered the necessary equipment and
maintenance of a schoolboy in the early 14th century.
In 1313 a guardian was ordered by the Mayor's Court
to provide for a boy whilst at school every year one
furred gown, a German or short coat with tunic to
match, four pairs of linen cloths, sufficient shoes, and
tenpence a week for board and lodging.

Who has not heard of the famous Bow Bells, cele-
brated in fairy tale and nursery rhyme ? The great
bell, when unaccompanied by his satellites, seems to
have had an element of doubt in his composition—

> " I'm sure I don't know, says the great Bell of Bow " :

But when all the bells spoke in unison they could exhibit
the abundant self-assurance characteristic of prophets
in all ages—

> " Turn again, Whittington, Lord Mayor of London."

Agreeably with these attributes the great bell was used
late in the 15th century as the Common Bell of London,
and the whole peal for ringing the curfew. In the
course of the century, or within a few years after, we
hear the names of several shops situated round about
this spot, either at the end of Bow Lane, known at that
period as Cordwainer Street, or at the entrance to the

churchyard. Such names occur as " Le Legge ", " Le Maydenesheed ", " Le Cage ", and " Le Crowne ". The latter was a mercer's shop near the church, and is of especial interest because it can be traced in one way and another through the centuries down to the 18th, when it became the " Crown and Glove," because it was occupied by a glover. The legend runs that in the reign of Edward IV the occupier, one Walter Walker, was executed for high treason inasmuch as he had promised his little son that he would make him heir to the " Crown ". Were it not that at that time the possession of the crown so often changed, and the succession to it was so uncertain, one might at once dismiss this tale as too obviously founded upon the name of the house.

Not far away, by the corner of Honey Lane Market, was an apothecary's shop, the property of London Bridge, let by the Wardens in 1363 for 7 marks a year, and near the same spot stood the Standard, a tall erection of stone, the origin of which appears to be unknown. It is first mentioned in the Letter-Books in 1337, and was probably intended as a supplementary water conduit. It may be regarded as the city's place of sacrifice, where not only capital sentences were carried out, but also those minor mutilations which form so barbarous a part of medieval justice. Among many instances, two fishmongers were executed here in 1340 for striking the Mayor during a riot ; Bishop Stapleton and several others were beheaded in 1326, though according to Stow this occurred at the " Brokyncross " ; in 1381 Wat Tyler executed several citizens at the spot, Jack Cade following his example in 1450 ; while in 1461 a man had his hand struck off here for assaulting another in presence of the Judges at Westminster. In the 16th century there is a record of a man who had illtreated a child being thoroughly whipped at this spot by the " beadles of the beggars ". Here also it was the custom to publicly burn any fraudulently made goods which had been seized, or the nets of Thames fishermen which had been confiscated for having too small a mesh. In 1269, because the foreign merchants refused to weigh their merchandise at the official " beam," their scales were seized and burnt at the Standard, and the parts which were non-inflammable were smashed with hammers. Here also the heads of rebels, crowned with ivy, were often exposed to public view before being taken to the Tower or London Bridge. At the same spot stood the pillory, or rather one of them, in which the makers of fraudulent goods and other swindlers were confined and subjected to public scorn. How good to be a small boy it must have been in those days, for what can more delight the juvenile heart than the privilege of throwing stones and mud at people without receiving unwelcome attentions from the police ? In olden times this amiable idiosyncracy could be indulged by a visit to the pillory.

On the right of Chepe, from Bow Lane to the corner of Bucklersbury, stretched the Mercery, a long row of shops kept by the mercers, where the poet Lydgate, riding through London,. says that he was offered for sale fine lawn, Paris thread, cotton umble, and linen. But the mercers of those days sold a much greater assortment of goods than these. Their stock included mirrors, brushes, combs, gold and silver rings, pearls, and bracelets, and among the haul made by burglars at this spot in 1340 are to be found such items as one dozen girdles of Paris, value £4 ; 30 pieces of velvet, £3 ; 20 dozen purses, £2 ; 8 pieces of cloth of different colours, £3 ; and other goods to the value of £20.

In 1330 we find some shops in the Mercery let for
£10 a year, and in 1320 a single chamber in a seld at
the same spot, fitted with chest and cupboards, let to
a mercer for 13s. 4d. a year. It must not be supposed
that the whole of Cheapside was divided between
the goldsmiths and the mercers. In 1365 we find
grocers, pepperers, and apothecaries domiciled in the
street, and at other times are mentioned a cutler, from
whom sixty-three knives valued at 6s. 8d. and other
goods were stolen ; a cheesemonger, and various taverns.

At the end of the Mercery, where Cheapside finishes
and the Poultry begins, stood the Great Conduit, the
most imposing water supply of the city. It contained
a great leaden cistern supplied with water by underground pipes from Tyburn, which gushed out through
brass taps from pipes passing through the handsome
battlemented stonework which formed the exterior.
The springs at Tyburn and the water tower adjoining
were given to the city in 1237 by the owner of the
ground, Gilbert de Sanford, and in the same year the
merchants of Amiens, Corby, and Nesle, in France,
having been accorded certain trading privileges in
London, displayed their gratitude by subscribing £100
towards the expense of running the pipes and building
the Conduit. These merchants were engaged in the
export of woad to England, the dye used for imparting
a blue colour to cloth. It is the same dye which was
worn by the Ancient Britons, without, however, the
interposition of clothing. In 1354 the city received
a welcome addition to the facilities at Tyburn, when
Alice, widow of William de Chabham, granted them a
parcel of land 24 feet square to serve for a fountain head
to the Conduit, the parcel to be selected by the Mayor
and commonalty from all her land at " Cherchend "

in the vill of Tyburn, together with the right to dig,
lay cisterns, and make subterranean ways under 40 feet
of her land adjacent to the said parcel.   It often happened
that citizens left money by will for the upkeep of the
Conduit.   Thus, in 1328, 10s. 0. a year was bequeathed
for this purpose, to be paid out of the rent of a house
in Ironmonger Lane ; in 1378 the executors of Adam
Fraunceys gave 500 marks for repairing the Conduit
and for carrying the water up to the cross-roads on top
of Cornhill ; while in 1385 a widow, having £20 to
expend in charity under the terms of her husband's will,
gave £10 to the same object.   According to Stow and
other chroniclers the Conduit was erected about the
year 1285, but mention is made of it at least ten years
earlier by a contemporary annalist,[1] and in the city
Letter-Books under the year 1282 we meet with such
personal names as " Thomas de Conduit " and " Elias
de Conduit ", from which it may be inferred that the
Conduit was no new thing at that date.   In the 14th
century officials were annually appointed to administer
the accounts, to receive the incomings, and to pay for
repairs, and at the end of their term to submit their
balance sheet to the Mayor at Guildhall.   Under these
officials, or " wardens " as they were called, was a keeper
who held the keys, so that water could not be obtained
unless he were present.   In 1350 the receipts amounted
to £11. 15s. 4d., and after various repairs had been
paid for the balance remaining was £2. 1s. 6d., out of
which their remuneration had to be paid.   In 1337 the
wardens were convicted of rendering false accounts
and keeping back lead and money belonging to the
city to the value of 10 marks.   In 1368 the Conduit
with its profits was let to two men, a knight and a cutler,

[1] French Chron. of London, p. 237.

for a period of ten years at an annual rent of 20 marks, they to keep in repair all work above ground, while the city repaired all underground work. A clause in the agreement provided that the sheriffs and aldermen were to have their water free of charge, others paying as of old accustomed.

In 1337 the London brewers were found to be drawing so much water from the Conduit that everyone else had to go short, and accordingly their use of this supply was henceforth much curtailed ; but afterwards they rented certain pipes for their exclusive use. At that time a great deal of the London beer was made from the none too savoury water of the Thames, and if more came to be used from this source owing to the restrictions placed upon the brewers at the Conduit, the citizens certainly made a bad bargain. An idea of the bad condition of the Thames water and the lack of realisation of its danger on the part of the people may be gathered from an ordinance of 1366 touching Dowgate dock, from which it appears that while some people emptied dung and rubbish into it, others came and filled leathern bottles with water, taking it away by the cartload. In 1382 the inhabitants living near the same dock petitioned the Mayor for permission to build stairs down to the river for the double purpose of drawing water and voiding refuse. There were also latrines on the banks of the Thames, for in 1393 an order was issued for the removal of one, and on its site was to be built a house for the accommodation of butchers, where they could cut up carcases and take the offal out to midstream and there consign it to the deep. It is true that a certain amount of water was obtained from the wells which existed in many large houses, but whenever an accident occurred in connection with one of them, such as a person killed

by falling down the shaft, the sheriffs would cause it
to be closed up.

Among the inhabitants one of the chief pleasures to
be derived from occasions of festivity resolved itself
into a matter of free drinks, and at such times it was
customary to cause the Conduit to run with wine instead
of water for all who cared to partake. This was done
in 1274, when Edward I brought his Queen to London
for the first time; but in 1299, on the occasion of bringing
in his second wife, he went one better by erecting two
large towers near by for the same purpose.

Not far away, on the left of the street, on the spot
where Mercer's Hall now stands, was the church or
chapel of St. Thomas of Acon, or de Acres, which in
the early part of the century possessed the unique distinction that the hour of prime, rung upon its bells, was
the signal for all the gates to be opened for the admission
of travellers. At the same period curfew was rung
upon the bells of St. Martin-le-Grand, when gates
were closed, taverns put up their shutters, and markets
were discontinued for the night. In the latter half of
the century, however, we find curfew rung upon the
bells of four churches—St. Mary-le-Bow, Allhallows,
Barking, St. Bride in Fleet Street, and St. Giles, Cripplegate, and towards the end of the period, due perhaps to
an increase of clocks, definite hours are mentioned for
the closing of the gates and taverns, such as nine or ten
o'clock. A variation of the usual order may be observed
in 1376, when taverns were called upon to close as the
tenth hour was sounded on a bell called " la clocke ",
hanging in a tower of the church of St. Pancras, Soper
Lane, of which all that now remains is a deserted grave-
yard in Pancras Lane, behind Queen Victoria Street.

We have now arrived in the Poultry, which, as its

name suggests, was in early times the poultry market. But by the 14th century it was much more than that, being crowded by the stalls of butchers and fishmongers, and by the year 1345 the congestion from this cause became so great that foot passengers found the greatest difficulty in getting through. When complaints of this state of affairs reached the authorities they removed all these tradesmen to the Stocks Market, and some of the butchers who tarried too long over their departure had their meat confiscated. On the west corner of Old Jewry stood the church of St. Mary Colechurch, destroyed in the Great Fire and never rebuilt, at whose font are said to have been baptised St. Edmond, the King and Martyr, and St. Thomas à Becket ; and somewhat farther eastward was the church of St. Mildred, demolished during the 19th century, beside which ran Scalding Alley, where the butchers cleaned and dressed their meat. Near the church was a cutler's shop bearing the name of " Le Castell on the Hope ", and a little to the east of Grocer's Hall Court stood one of the Compters or prisons belonging to the sheriffs, which in later times acquired the name of " the Hole ".

The next object of interest is the Stocks Market, or, as it is termed in early documents, " Les Stokkes ", which was founded in 1282 by the Mayor, Henry le Gales, or Walleis, but was intended less as a convenience to the citizens than as a source of revenue for London Bridge, the rents accruing from the letting of the stalls being devoted to the upkeep of that fabric. It was situated where is now the open space in front of the Mansion House. There was no Mansion House in those days ; each newly elected Mayor selected some large house in the city in which to hold his term of office. The site so occupied to-day was then the church

and churchyard of St. Mary Woolchurch Haw, on the
north wall of which the market abutted.   This church
was so named because within its haw or yard stood the
Great Beam or weighing machine for wool, tin, and other
commodities which were bought or sold in bulk.   The
market, according to Stow, derived its name from a
pair of stocks which from ancient times stood upon
the spot, and in its turn gave name to the neighbouring
church of St. Christopher-le-Stocks, known before that
time as " St. Christopher in Brade Street ward ", of
which the only vestige now remaining is the garden
plot so familiar to Londoners within the Threadneedle
Street entrance of the Bank of England.

At first the entire market was let to a body of seven
men for the term of their lives, with the right to demise
their holdings to whom they pleased, but afterwards
when any stalls became vacant the wardens of London
Bridge had the letting of them.   The city governors,
in the interests of the bridge, endeavoured to make this
the principal market for fish and an important one for
meat.   They issued regulations from time to time
ordering that no fish should be sold elsewhere except
in those places where the fishmongers had sold their
wares from ancient times, and many prosecutions were
instituted against those who, in defiance of orders,
ventured to retail fish from shops or stalls in any other
spot.   In 1323 and 1324 one obstinate fellow was
summoned to the Guildhall and warned again and again
not to sell his fish elsewhere than at the Stocks Market.
Several times he promised not to offend again, once he
denied it and demanded a jury, who promptly pronounced
him guilty, and at another time he had the effrontery to
come to court and admit having done it, and declared
his intention of continuing to do so.   Next he came up

and voluntarily renounced the freedom of the city, and was ordered henceforth to be treated as a stranger. Afterwards he apologised, and was readmitted to the freedom, but again transgressed and lost it, and this was intended to be final. Nevertheless he interested the Prince of Wales himself on his behalf, and at the latter's request he was reinstated once more. In 1325 we hear of him being in trouble again from the same cause. The loss of the freedom here referred to would not absolutely prevent him from trading, but reduced him to the position of an outsider, or, as it was called, " foreign " fishmonger, when he would be required to pay various tolls and suffer other restrictions.

In order to formulate the rules of the market the citizens had to get a special charter from the King, but it was even then so difficult to enforce them that in the next reign they obtained from Edward II a confirmation of his father's charter, and armed with this the Mayor went in person to the market, and calling the fishmongers around him, read it aloud as a warning to them all.

Though thus compelled to use the market, the position of the fishmongers was not in other respects altogether a happy one. They were obliged to bring their fish already cleaned so that they should not deplete the valuable water supply from the neighbouring conduit in Chepe. They also suffered from the competition of the foreign fishmongers, who, although they were not granted stalls, had certain spots assigned to them where they could stand with their fish. These latter were compelled to cease business at curfew, and could not take back with them any fish which remained unsold, a rule intended to compel them to dispose of it cheaply.

The wardens of London Bridge were also not without their difficulties in administering the affairs of the market.

In 1365 the parson of Woolchurch Haw claimed the
right to let the stalls and collect the rent, and threatened
to excommunicate the wardens if they persisted in
usurping his functions. His victims only escaped the
dread anathema when the Mayor obtained a letter from
the King forbidding the parson to carry out his threat.

Stow informs us that at first the market was let for
£46. 13s. 4d. a year, and only after it was rebuilt in the
15th century with chambers above did the receipts
increase until by 1543 they amounted to £82. 3s. o.
However, an entry in the Letter-Books shows that during
the latter half of the 14th century it already yielded
over £60 a year.

Turning from this spot, which from early times, as
it is to-day, was a centre from which streets radiated in
every direction, cartwheel fashion, we are close to the
Tun on Cornhill, which stood in the middle of the road
near what is now the Royal Exchange. It was built
by the Mayor, Henry le Gales, at the same time as the
Stocks Market, as a temporary prison for night-walkers,
suspicious characters, and women of loose morals caught
by the watch, and received its name by reason of its
round shape, which was supposed to resemble a wine
tun perched on end. It is believed to have been the
origin of the term " round-house " as applied to a prison.
According to Stow, common women were shut up there
for the night, and the following day their heads were
shaved and they were led through the streets to the
sound of trumpets and pipes. Certain it is that the
authorities throughout the 14th century used their
utmost endeavours to clear the city of these people, as
may be seen from the stringent regulations made against
them. So soon after the erection of the Tun as 1297
it was resolved at a meeting of the Court of Aldermen,

with the Mayor presiding, that it should cease to be used as a prison, and yet throughout the following century it continued to be used for its original purpose. This is a good example of the methods adopted by the citizens to circumvent the interference of outsiders with their system of administration. The above resolution was arrived at in obedience to an order from the King, but content with recording what amounted to no more than a pious opinion, they quietly continued to carry on as before. In addition to night-walkers, people were imprisoned in the Tun who were convicted of using insulting expressions of or to the Mayor and aldermen. It was repaired in 1332, when an entry is found in the accounts of the Chamberlain of London of £40 spent for repairs to the city walls and the Tun. Beside it stood a pillory in which swindlers of various sorts were exposed to public derision.

Near the Tun was held a market for the sale of " frippery ", or second-hand clothes and furniture, which had attained such considerable proportions by the early part of the 14th century that its activities were not too small a matter to engage the attention of the King's Justices sitting at the Tower in 1321, and later in the same year of the King himself. The fripperers were accused of conducting an " evecheping ", or market continued after curfew, which became the resort of thieves, cutpurses, and other bad characters, and was accordingly ordered to be closed at sunset, when warning was given by the ringing of a bell which hung upon the Tun. This admonition producing no effect, the King sent his writ to the Mayor and aldermen directing them to arrest and punish the offenders, mentioning forty-seven of them by name. Among these names are to be found " Roger Panyfader de Houndsditch "

and " John le Bribour de Houndsditch ", indicating the
early connection of that famous thoroughfare with the
trade in second-hand clothing. Many of these men
were tried and convicted at Guildhall, but in the end
very little was done to them. This was another place
where bread from Stratford could be sold from carts,
and the blacksmiths also had the right to stand there
and sell their goods. Opposite the pillory was in early
times a bakehouse, which in 1318 was let to a fishmonger
for 60s. o. a year, probably as a storehouse for his fish
owing to its proximity to the Stocks Market. The Tun
was pulled down in 1401 and replaced by a conduit,
which, like that in Chepe, was fed by the Tyburn springs.
Stow says that the cistern was afterwards covered over
with planks and a cage of timber erected over it, wherein
was placed a pair of stocks, with a pillory on top of
the cage.

Perhaps sufficient has now been written to give a
general idea of the crowded streets of Old London,
with the curious structures that often adorned them,
with the very roadways utilised for the purposes of
business or pleasure, to the obstruction of the traffic
for the transit of which they were originally intended ;
and we may pass on to the consideration of the curious
customs and ways of life of the 14th-century city.

CHAPTER II

PAGEANTS AND PROCESSIONS

OUR present sophisticated age requires something more to impress it than the emblematic cars which are dragged through the streets to make a Lord Mayor's Show, although its interest is readily aroused by the pageants, so popular in recent years, which depict the glories, the great deeds, or even the manners and customs of ancient times. The annual progress of the city's chief magistrate is regarded as essentially the children's day, while their elders who take them often look on with amused contempt rather than with reverence. But what constitutes to-day a juvenile pleasure was with our ancestors the delight of the whole populace, and when a victorious king or his newly-crowned queen entered the city, their simple minds chose this method of giving their sovereign a royal welcome. One difference, however, is to be noted in the arrangement of such pageants, for whereas to-day the emblematic structures with their mummers form part of the procession, in the middle ages they were usually stationary at intervals along the route, and delivered their addresses or displayed their inscriptions to the approaching cavalcade.

Many were the opportunities afforded the citizens in the course of a year of indulging this love of pageantry. In addition to Lord Mayor's day they held similar celebrations at Easter, Whitsuntide, Midsummer, and

on Saints' days ; and even the conveyance of a prisoner
from one prison to another was made the occasion of
pompous display instead of being conducted by means
of the more discreet " Black Maria." Thus in 1295
a traitor named Sir Thomas de Turberville was seized
and brought to the Tower, from whence he was afterward
conveyed through the streets of London to his trial at
Westminster. The principle that an accused man must
be regarded as innocent until he is tried and convicted
was not so well appreciated then, and the authorities saw
fit to vent their mordant humour by making his journey
a public spectacle. Dressed in a striped coat and white
shoes, his head covered with a hood, they mounted him
upon a sorry hack, his feet tied beneath the animal's
belly, and his hands tied behind him. Behind him on
the same horse rode the hangman holding a halter in
his hand. Around him rode six torturers dressed to
represent the devil, one of them holding his rein, and
in this manner they proceeded to the place of trial.
After his condemnation they drew him on a fresh bull's
hide at the tails of six horses from Westminster as far
as the Conduit in Chepe, the executioners riding beside
and reviling him all the time, and from thence they
returned to the gallows, probably at Smithfield, where
they hanged him. Even in cases of minor misdemeanour
the citizens loved to make the culprit a general laughing
stock. On one occasion the parson of the church of
St. Mary Abchurch, being caught under compromising
circumstances in the company of the wife of a prominent
grocer, was seized and conveyed through the streets to
Bridewell with his breeches hanging about his knees
and his clerical hat and gown solemnly borne behind
him.

The annual progress of the newly elected Mayor from

London to Westminster was always a popular celebration. It had its origin early in the 13th century when King John made a law that the Mayor, after his election, should appear at Court for the approval either of himself, or, in his absence, of his ministers. At times when neither the King nor his ministers were available owing to their absence in Scotland or foreign parts it was customary for the Mayor to be received by the Constable of the Tower. For this purpose the latter sometimes journeyed to Westminster, but more often performed the function at the Tower, when, as that fortress was claimed by the King as his personal property, the Mayor was not allowed inside, and the ceremony took place outside the outer gate. This event occurred on the 29th of October, and so remained until the reform of the calendar in 1752. At first it was a simple visit of the Mayor and his friends to Westminster, but soon developed into a procession of first-rate importance, the aldermen and members of the various crafts participating, mounted on superb horses and dressed in brand new suits of bright colours embroidered with the emblems of the crafts. According to most of the old chroniclers the first Mayor to go to Westminster by water was John Norman in 1453, accompanied by the chief men of the city in state barges, and in celebration of so notable an event the Thames boatmen made and sang a song beginning with the line " Row thy boat, Norman." However, in reality this was probably the first time that the water procession was made with such state, for the Liber Albus, or White Book of the city, which was compiled in 1419, states that in early times the Mayor went to Westminster either on foot by land or by boat on the river, and indeed one old chronicler notes that Hamo de Chigwell, Mayor in 1321, performed the journey by the latter means as a novelty. A small part of the route was, of course, always covered by land, the returning concourse landing at Paul's Wharf, from whence they rode on horseback to the Guildhall.

The newly elected sheriffs were also under obligation to present themselves at Westminster for approval, an event which took place on the 29th of September, and these were also accompanied by the crafts in their liveries. This being only a month before the Mayor's own procession, many members of the misteries bought their new suits for the first occasion, and in consequence the sheriff's progress to Westminster tended to eclipse that of the Mayor, a state of things intolerable to the chief magistrate of the city. Accordingly, on the 13th of October, 1389, the election day of the new Mayor, the aldermen were called upon to debate this momentous question, and as the result an ordinance was made that " whereas men of divers misteries were accustomed to " be clothed in a new suit of clothing and to hire horses " and incur other expenses at the presentation of the " sheriffs before the Barons of the Exchequer on the " morrow of St. Michael, and again to incur similar " expenses shortly afterwards when the Mayor rode to " Westminster on the morrow of SS. Simon and Jude " the sheriffs in future should only give clothing to the " city's officers and their own serjeants, and that they " should no longer ride, but go to Westminster by water " or on foot, and that those of the misteries who were " willing to accompany them should go in their last " clothing and not have new clothing given to them, " under penalty of 100 marks to the Chamber." [1] On the day of the Mayor's procession in 1415 an incident arose which furnishes another example of the determina-

[1] Cal. Letter-Book H. 347–8.

tion of the Mayor to maintain the dignity and importance
of his position on these occasions.   Early in the morning
the joyful intelligence arrived of the victory of Agincourt.
Promptly all the bells were rung, the *Te Deum* sung,
and at nine o'clock the news was publicly proclaimed at
St. Paul's.   The circumstances afford a curious parallel
to those of August 1914, for the city had been full of
rumours of disaster to the tiny English army in France,
with consequent anxiety among the populace ; and in
view of this it was resolved that the Mayor's procession
for that day should be turned into a pilgrimage of
humiliation and thanksgiving to God at Westminster.
Accordingly the Queen mother, the bishops, all the
barons who were in London, with the Mayor and aldermen and a vast concourse of the people set out on foot
to the Abbey, chanting the litany as they went.   But
afterwards, as it was more consistent with the high
position of the Mayor that he should go on horseback
rather than afoot, he took occasion to proclaim that his
unaccustomed pedestrianism on that day should not be
regarded as a precedent.   It was customary for the Mayor
and aldermen, on the day of this procession, to dress in
parti-coloured cloaks and hoods of red, scarlet, and white,
the red on the right side.

The election of the Mayor, which took place at Guildhall on the 13th of October, was not without its due share
of ceremony.   The proceedings started with a mass solem-
nised in the presence of the Mayor and aldermen in the
chapel attached to the Guildhall.   The chief men of the
city, assembled at the Court of Husting, chose two
aldermen, both of whom had served the office of sheriff,
and submitted their names to the retiring Mayor, who
with all the aldermen proceeded to an upper chamber
to decide which of them should be appointed.   When

they had made their choice they descended into the
courtyard where the people were assembled, with the
newly elected Mayor on the right of the retiring one,
the Recorder of the city announcing their decision.
There was also a Lord Mayor's banquet in those days,
but it was held either at the Tailor's Hall or the Grocer's
Hall.   The Guildhall was then merely a small house
in Aldermanbury, and only in 1411 did they start to
rebuild it in stately and becoming fashion, finishing the
work about twenty years later.   Kitchens were added
in 1501, and in that year the Mayor, Sir John Shaa,
held his feast there for the first time.

The visits of kings and queens to London gave better
opportunity to the citizens to exhibit their inborn love
of scenic display than was afforded by the Mayor's
progress to Westminster, and also furnished excuse
for subsequent revelry in the form of singing, dancing,
and drinking.   It was on these occasions that the
Londoners let themselves go—decorating and illuminat-
ing the streets and houses and dressing in their finest
clothes, and carrying the ceremony through with the
greatest solemnity.   Moreover, they never gave their
sovereign the mortification of riding into his capital
unattended ; a procession some hundreds strong, consisting of the Mayor, aldermen, and citizens in rich
clothes embroidered with gold and the marks of the
various crafts on their sleeves, mounted on the finest
horses the city could produce, went out to meet him,
usually at Blackheath.   An early example occurs in 1255,
when the wife of Prince Edward (afterwards Edward I)
came to England for the first time.   She was received
with processions, illuminations, ringing of bells, and
singing, and the place of abode assigned to her was
decorated with palls of silk tapestry like a temple, and

1. A GROUP OF MINSTRELS
2. MUSICAL INSTRUMENTS
From Wright's "Domestic Customs and Sentiments"

even the floor was covered with arras in order to remind her of her Spanish home. Matthew Paris says that laughter and derision were caused among the people by such excessive pride, but this popular attitude is to us merely an indication of their unfamiliarity with carpets at that time, when, except in the houses of rich merchants, it was more usual to cover the floors with rushes. In the following century carpets became more frequent in the homes of the citizens, as may be seen from the inventory of the goods and chattels of a man and woman apparently of no particular social position, accused, indeed, of a sordid murder, wherein are included two carpets valued one at 16 pence and the other at 10 pence. Nevertheless, throughout the 14th century great quantities of rushes were brought to the city, so much so that special regulations had to be made to insure that the river and the streets were not littered with them at the spots where they were unloaded from the barges.

A gorgeous pageant in honour of Richard II in 1392 had a curious origin, no less than the loss of the city's freedom and the efforts of the citizens to regain it. It appears that the King had demanded a loan of £1,000 from the citizens, who not only refused it, but attacked and nearly killed a Lombard who was willing to lend it himself. Others say that the trouble started with a riot in Fleet Street occasioned by a dispute over a loaf of horsebread. Be this as it may, the Mayor, sheriffs, and influential citizens were ordered to appear before the King at Nottingham, where the Mayor and sheriffs were deposed, sent to various prisons, and a Warden appointed to rule the city in their stead. The citizens, in order to regain their liberties, offered the King the sum of £10,000, but instead of accepting this immediately, he announced his intention of paying them a visit in person. On the day of his arrival he was met at St. George's Church in Southwark by the Bishop of London and all the clergy of the city. At London Bridge he found awaiting him a great concourse of citizens —men, women, and children—who presented him with two white horses trapped in cloth of gold, hung with silver bells. Crossing the bridge, he passed through the city streets, which were decorated with cloth of gold, silver, and silk, to Westminster. The Conduit in Chepe ran with wine both red and white, and here he and the Queen were presented with golden crowns by a child representing an angel. Other gifts offered to them were a tablet depicting the Trinity in gold worth £800, to the King, and another of St. Anne to the Queen in remembrance of her name ; also horses, trappings, gold and silver plate, cloth of gold, silver, and velvet, gold basins and ewers, gold coin, and priceless jewels. Upon this, and no wonder, the King restored the liberties, and gave permission for the election of another Mayor. However, he did not forget their previous offer of £10,000, which he now took care to collect.

It is no doubt natural that great soldiers should always be the darlings of the people where others who perhaps render them more permanent benefits are often little regarded, and so it is no matter for surprise that the victory of Agincourt wrought the citizens to a pitch of excitement which was not allayed until they had given the conquering hero a rousing reception on his return to London. The Mayor, sheriffs, aldermen, and the crafts, in parti-coloured red and white hoods, rode out to meet him at Blackheath, and returning, they were met at Southwark by a procession of the city clergy.

All these people with the King and his prisoners rode into London, where pageants were arranged at all the conduits, and at the Great Cross in Chepe, with an array, as we are told, of angels, archangels, patriarchs, prophets, and virgins, singing and playing instruments in his honour, while the Great Conduit in Chepe ran with wine instead of water that day. At St. Paul's he was met by fourteen mitred bishops singing *Te Deum Laudamus* in thanksgiving for his victory. As great a welcome was accorded to the Black Prince when he entered London in 1357, if it is possible to judge by the fact that it took him from nine in the morning until one in the afternoon to ride from London Bridge to Westminster.

For the most complete account of such a pageant which has been handed down to us we have to go to a slightly later period—1432—the occasion of the entry of Henry VI into London, and the reason is that the corporation, realising its importance and historical value, employed the poet Lydgate to compose a detailed metrical description of the proceedings. The event was of such peculiar significance because Henry VI, though a mere boy, was returning from his coronation in France—the first King of both countries—and in the breasts of the citizens was the hope that this was to mark the inauguration of a permanent Anglo-French Empire. It would be hardly possible to give here the full details as recorded by Lydgate, but a few points from his narrative will suffice to convey a general idea of the whole. The Mayor, with his usual following, rode out to Blackheath to meet the King, and there delivered an address pointing out the greatness of the occasion. The Mayor's robe was made of crimson velvet, with a great velvet hat trimmed with fur, a golden girdle about his waist, and about his neck a golden baldric which trailed behind him. His three

henchmen mounted on great coursers, wore suits of red
spangled with silver, the aldermen in scarlet gowns
and hoods, and the commoners in white gowns and
scarlet hoods, with the signs of the crafts on their sleeves.
In the middle of London Bridge was a tower draped with
velvet, cloth of gold, silk, and tapestry, from which
emerged three ladies with flowing hair and coronets of
gold, representing Nature, Grace, and Fortune, and
bearing written inscriptions announcing that they conferred upon him all the virtues. These were accompanied by seven golden-haired maidens dressed in white
to represent angels. In Cornhill was a pageant of the
Seven Sciences, and farther along at the Tun was a
beautiful child on a throne with Mercy on his right and
Truth on his left. The Conduit in Chepe ran with wine,
presided over by a person representing Bacchus. At
this spot was also arranged a greenery with trees bearing all manner of fruits, domestic and foreign. Farther
along Chepe was a castle of green jasper with two genea-
logical trees adorned with leopards and fleur-de-lys,
and showing the King's descent from St. Edward and
St. Louis, and on the side facing St. Paul's another tree
illustrating the descent of Christ from Jesse. At the
Little Conduit near St. Paul's (the old Brokyncross) was
a pageant representing the Trinity surrounded by angels.
All these pageants bore upon them inscriptions explaining their meaning and purpose. After visiting St. Paul's
the King was conducted by the Mayor and citizens
to Westminster, where the Abbot came out and presented
him with the sceptre, which he carried up to the High
Altar.

The passion for pageantry sometimes induced the
citizens to organise what may be termed gratuitous
shows, not to welcome any royal visitor, but when news

arrived of the birth of a prince, or, as is recorded on one
occasion, when a prince, being in the vicinity of the city,
they marched out for the purpose of entertaining him.
It was in 1377 that Prince Richard (afterwards Richard II),
staying at his palace of Kennington, was visited on a
Sunday night by 130 men of the city, who rode on horseback in masquerade dress representing a Pope, twenty-
four Cardinals, knights, and esquires.   On obtaining
admission to the palace the mummers played dice with
the Prince, taking care that he always won, and afterwards
danced with him and all the other lords there present.
When news of a victory arrived in London the citizens
had their own methods of " mafficking " which may
compare favourably with our own ; they arranged processions of the crafts through the streets bearing strange
devices representing each particular mistery.   Thus we
are told that in 1293, upon receipt of news of a victory
in Scotland by Edward I, a procession of the kind was
held in which the most conspicuous figures were the
fishmongers, who had four gilt sturgeon on four horses,
four silver salmon also on four horses, followed by
forty-six knights on horseback made up to represent
fish, and finally a knight representing St. Magnus,
the patron saint of the trade, with 1,000 horsemen.   These pageants were such a frequent feature of
city life that large quantities of " properties " were
constantly kept in stock.   They were warehoused,
together with the city's arms and engines of war, in the
chambers over Leadenhall Market, which was, for this
reason, the usual place of assembly for those taking part
in the pageants, and often for the citizens when the
necessities of the times called them to arms.   It was
here they assembled in 1326 in support of Edward III
at the deposition of his father.

The tournaments which were held in London were preceded by magnificent processions of knights and ladies to the lists, which were a source of joy to the beholders, and would easily outshine anything that can be seen to-day at coronations or royal weddings. In 1390 a body of sixty knights on horseback in full armour was led by sixty gaily dressed ladies mounted on palfreys, each of whom led a knight by a golden chain from the Tower to Smithfield, with bands playing on trumpets and other instruments of the period. In after times, however, the spectacular part of these affairs grew to such proportions as almost to eclipse their primary purpose, which was, of course, the display of martial prowess. Thus, at the marriage of Arthur, eldest son of Henry VII, with Catherine of Aragon, a solemn, not to say pompous, jousting was held on the waste ground surrounding the Palace of Westminster, when Westminster Hall itself was used by the combatants as a dressing-room, from which they issued surrounded by trappings each of which was a pageant in itself. It will perhaps be sufficient to mention two of them, the Duke of Buckingham, who rode out surrounded by his servants dressed in black and red silk, who held over him a great chapel draped with white and green silk, and surmounted with turrets and pinnacles of curious workmanship, set full of roses ; and the Earl of Essex, who had a great green mountain borne above him with trees, stones, and marvellous beasts upon the sides, and a beautiful maiden seated on the summit.

In view of the simple piety which characterised the minds of the people in the middle ages, it will not be surprising to find that religion played a conspicuous part in processions, rejoicings, and feastings. Christianity was never an esoteric religion, and its leaders from

DRUM, FIFE, AND DANCING IN THE MIDDLE AGES

Nuremberg Chronicle, 1493, from a copy in the Guildhall Library

the earliest times participated in the lives of the people, not attempting to suppress their ancient customs and pleasures in favour of a devout austerity, but rather taking such matters into their own hands and directing them into purer and less materialistic paths. It was a metamorphosis of this kind which overtook the pagan feasts of Midwinter, and to a lesser extent Midsummer. The former, being adopted by the Church as the nativity of the Saviour, it was possible to endow it with a greater religious significance than the latter, the best they could do for which was to assign it as the feast of St. John the Baptist. It is thus that we find the pagan festival of Midsummer Eve lingering on into 14th-century London as the noisiest celebration of the year, when the wildest doings, so long as they did not degenerate into criminality, were tolerated in the streets, and the most imposing displays were made by the citizens. On this night the march of the watch through London was a famous event, and kings and queens, with their royal visitors from abroad, did not disdain to come to the Crownseld in Chepe to view it. In preparation for this pageant it was the duty of the alderman of each ward to select the most reliable from among the inhabitants to form the watch, for the double purpose of preserving order in the streets and of forming the grand procession. On the night part of this body were stationed singly at selected spots to perform police work, while the remainder, armed with bacinets and gauntlets of plate, covered with red and white cloaks, assembled at Smithfield at nine o'clock in the evening. This contingent was about 2,000 strong, and formed up by wards, each ward being distinguished by a differently coloured lance. A portion of their number marched beside them carrying cressets or long poles surmounted by grated pans of blazing fire, while others accompanied them bearing fuel to replenish the flames, and in this order they marched through Chepe and the principal streets to the east end of the town.   In the meanwhile every house hung out a lamp which burned all night, and in other streets bonfires were lighted, each neighbour joining in to throw on more logs, while others danced around them in fancy dress, disguised with masks and false beards.   The houses were decorated with garlands of flowers and branches of trees, and at the doors of many of them the inhabitants spread tables with victuals and drink to regale their friends, inviting any with whom they had been at variance to come and compose their quarrel on the auspicious occasion.   This festival lasted until the time of Henry VIII, who was himself a frequent participant in the revels, but was abolished after the Reformation.

Christmas Eve exhibited more of the decorum which we associate with it at the present day.   During the days preceding the festival public sports were held such as wrestling and running at the quintain, but on the Eve the inhabitants were warned to keep within their houses after curfew ; watches were formed in each ward to enforce this rule, and taverns and cookshops were compelled to close early.   As at Midsummer, each house hung out a lantern which burned all night, and this was compulsory, being instituted less on account of the festive season than to enable the watch to maintain order.

Other religious festivals, such as Easter and Whitsun, or Pentecost, as it was called, although made the occasion of further pageantry, were conducted with greater solemnity, the Church taking an official part in the proceedings.   Of these the chief was Whitsun, and the principal day Whit-Monday.   Between nine and ten in the morning of that day a procession, headed by all the

rectors of the city churches, started from St. Peter's
Cornhill to march to St. Paul's. After the rectors came
the liverymen of the sheriffs, followed by those of the
Mayor, and the rear was brought up by the Mayor,
Recorder, and aldermen. They passed through Chepe
and entered St. Paul's Churchyard by the north gate,
where they were met by the officials of the Cathedral,
and passing out by the south gate they entered St. Paul's
by the great west door. They came to a stand in the
nave, when the organ played and a hymn was sung,
while an angel censed them with holy water from above ;
after which the Mayor and aldermen approached the
High Altar, made their offerings, and returned home.
The ordering of this procession was not without its
troublous aspect, for a dispute continued for long between
the parishioners of St. Peter's Cornhill, St. Magnus the
Martyr, and St. Nicholas Cole Abbey, as to which of
their respective rectors should take precedence on the
occasion, each contending that the place of honour,
which curiously enough was in the rear, should be
occupied by their own pastor. After this contention
had lasted many years the Mayor and aldermen resolved
in 1417 to settle it themselves in favour of the rector of
St. Peter's on the ground that that church was reputed
to be the oldest in London, having been founded in
A.D. 199 by the British King Lucius, and remaining the
metropolitan church of England for several centuries.
This day and the day of the Mayor's procession were
the only two occasions during the year on which the
Mayor and aldermen were accustomed to be clothed
exactly alike ; the rule as laid down in the Liber Albus
is as follows : " *item*, the Mayor, Sheriffs, and Aldermen
" were all accustomed to clothe themselves alike twice
" a year, **viz.**, at the riding of the Mayor to take his

" oath at Westminster, that is to say on the morrow of
" the feast of the apostles Simon and Jude, when such
" clothing was made with honest furs. They were again
" accustomed to clothe themselves alike against the
" feast of Pentecost, the lining being of silk."   In reference to this custom a curious ordinance was made by
the Mayor and aldermen in 1358 to the effect that none
should alienate the gowns worn on these occasions
within the year under penalty of 100 shillings, and if
one of them died within the year his executors should
be under a like penalty not to alienate his gown during
the same period.   " Clothing themselves alike," on
Whit-Monday resolved itself into gowns of green cloth
lined with green taffeta, a drastic change from the
favourite red and white of the Mayor and aldermen, and
in 1382 led to a grave breach of the proprieties by the
alderman of Walbrook Ward, who arrived at the place
of meeting in a gown without a lining. The outraged
feelings of the Mayor were only assuaged by the solemn
trial of the culprit, who was sentenced to entertain him
and all his fellow aldermen to dinner at his house on the
following Thursday " at his own proper charges," and
the court further announced that in future this should
be the regulation penalty for the same class of offence.

On Tuesday in Whitsun week the Mayor and aldermen
went in procession from the church of St. Bartholomew,
through the gate of Newgate, past the church of St.
Michael le Quern, and so through Old Change to St.
Paul's, and on this occasion they were accompanied
by the men of Middlesex. On the next day, Wednesday,
with the people of Essex they marched from the church
of St. Thomas of Acon to St. Paul's, and on each of these
occasions the same ceremony was observed inside the
Cathedral as on Monday. It was customary on each

of these days for the Archdeacons respectively of London, Middlesex, and Essex to give a gratuity to the serjeants-at-mace of the Mayor and sheriffs, but perhaps " gratuity " is hardly the proper word to use, for it appears that if the amount was not forthcoming the Archdeacons were distrained upon by the officers of the city.

Another important ceremony of the kind occurred on Corpus Christi Day, which is the Thursday after Trinity Sunday, and falls in May or June, being dependent on the date of Easter. It was a considerable festival in London, when the churches were decorated with flags and garlands of flowers, and the parishioners dressed in fancy costume to illustrate New Testament history. It was also the day appointed for the annual procession of the Guild of Skinners, who marched through the streets with a hundred torches burning and over two hundred priests singing, and accompanied by the Mayor and aldermen. It was either with this pageant or a similar one that a fracas occurred with some drapers on Corpus Christi Day in 1389. The procession claimed the right by immemorial usage to pass through the middle of a house in the parish of St. Mary Abchurch, but in the year mentioned the householder, a draper, resenting this invasion of his privacy, together with some fellow members of his craft, resisted the invaders by force of arms and turned them aside. Afterwards at the Guild-hall he was fined £15 for this obstruction and one of his followers £5.

There was seen in London at times another kind of procession, which, in its mingled pathos and sordidness, is a reminder of that mixture of the primitive, the magnificent, and the bizarre which characterises the outward manifestations of the working of the medieval mind.

These reflections arise when considering the system of
" penance " inflicted in many cases of wrong-doing,
rather as a mitigated penalty and an act of mercy.   Not
all such cases were concerned with offences against
religion, but the city fathers, copying perhaps the methods
of the Church, saw a fitness in this method of purgation
where the crime committed was a flouting of or a lack
of reverence for authority.   Justice as administered by
the Mayor and aldermen was generally mild.   They
had no love for inflicting the death penalty, and were not
anxious even to keep offenders in prison, and it is
astonishing, considering the barbarity of the time, how
often an apology and a promise not to offend again
made at the Guildhall would ensure forgiveness.   An
instance of the infliction of " penance " occurred in 1387,
and two more are recorded in the following year, all of
them imposed for assaulting or insulting the aldermen.
In the first case the culprit was ordered to walk from
the Guildhall through Chepe and Fleet Street, carrying
a lighted candle three pounds in weight and to deposit
it on the High Altar at St. Dunstan's Church.   The
second had to walk from his house through Walbrook,
Bucklersbury, Cheapside, and Old Jewry with a lighted
candle weighing two pounds and place it upon the altar
in the chapel of Guildhall.   The third, after serving six
months in Newgate, had to carry a candle from the prison
to the same chapel by way of St. Nicholas Shambles,
Chepe, and Old Jewry.   As a mark of contrition and
perhaps to add to their discomfort they had to perform
their penitential journey with head, legs and feet bare.

Notwithstanding the instances just cited, " penance,"
when applied in secular cases, usually bore a very different
meaning, as will be explained in a subsequent chapter.
In the sense we are now considering it was more often

a religious penalty, inflicted not only for heresy, but for any offence of a sacrilegious kind against the Church. Two interesting cases of the kind may be given here. The first occurred in 1303, and was the outcome of the famous burglary of the King's Treasury at Westminster in that year, in which the sacristan of the abbey, several monks, and some of the King's servants, were implicated. One of the culprits named Podlicote, or Podyngtone, took sanctuary at the church of St. Michael Crooked Lane, when two city bailiffs, in defiance of the privileges of the Church, dragged him out by force and handed him over to the sheriff. For this offence they were compelled to walk barefoot, with nothing on but shirt and breeches, and carrying lighted wax candles, from Bow Church to Newgate, and from Newgate back to the church where the offence was committed. Even then the outraged church had not quite finished with them, for next day they had to walk from London to Canterbury without girdles or hoods. The second case, in 1417, concerns actual sacrilege in the church of St. Dunstan's-in-the-East, a little below London Bridge. During divine service a quarrel started between Lord Strong and Sir John Trussell, and the bone of contention is said to have been their wives. Drawing their swords to attack each other, a fishmonger who happened to be present stepped between them in an endeavour to separate them, and met the common fate of peace-makers, being killed in the attempt. The church was suspended, and Lord Strong, who was held to be the aggressor, was on the following Sunday cursed in every church in London with bell, book, and candle. He afterwards escaped the consequences by doing penance through the city streets. It may not be inappropriate at this point to explain in what a 14th-century public cursing actually consisted, when its dreadful effect upon the superstitious mind will readily be realised, and the celerity with which, in many well-known instances, the culprit was brought to heel, will be understood.   There could be no peace upon this earth and no mercy expected by any luckless individual who drew upon himself the excommunication of Mother Church.   The priest, ascending the pulpit with lighted candle in hand, pronounced a curse of which the following is a specimen : " By the authority of " the Father and of the Son and of the Holy Ghost " and of Our Lady Saint Mary God's Mother of Heaven, " and all other Virgins, and St. Michael and all other " Apostles, and St. Stephen and all other martyrs, and " St. Nicholas and all other confessors, and of all the " Holy saints of Heaven ; we accurse and warn and " depart from all good deeds and prayers of Holy Church, " and of all these saints, and damn into the pain of " Hell all those that have done these articles beforesaid, " till they come to amendment ; we accurse them by " the authority of the court of Rome, within and without, " sleeping or waking, going and sitting, standing and " riding, lying above earth and under earth, speaking " and crying and drinking ; in wood, in water, in field, " in town ; curse them Father and Son and Holy Ghost ; " curse them Angels and Archangels and all the nine " orders of Heaven ; curse them Patriarchs, Prophets, " and Apostles, and all God's disciples and all Holy " Innocents, Martyrs, Confessors, and Virgins, monks, " cannons, hermits, priests, and clerks, that they have " no part in Mass nor Matins nor of no other good " prayers, that be done in Holy Church or in any other " places, but that the pains of Hell be their mead with " Judas that betrayed our Lord Jesu Christ ; and the " life of them be put out of the Book of Life till they

" come to amendment and satisfaction made. Amen."
After reciting this, the priest dashed down his candle,
spat on the ground, while at the same time the bells
commenced to toll as for a funeral.[1]

This account may fittingly be closed with the well-
known case of Eleanor Cobham, Duchess of Gloucester,
convicted in 1441 of heresy, meddling with witchcraft,
and attempting the King's life by sorcery. She was
tried by the King's Judges and sentenced to perform her
penance three times on three different days, taking on
each occasion her barge from Westminster and landing
in various parts of London, and at each spot she was met
by an assemblage of the Mayor, sheriffs and crafts. On
the first day she walked hoodless and carrying a lighted
candle from Temple Bar to St. Paul's ; on the second
day from the Swan in Thames Street to Christ Church,
Newgate Street, by way of Bridge Street, Gracechurch
Street, and Leadenhall ; and on the third day from Queenhithe to St. Michael's Cornhill. The chronicler adds
that she performed all this with so meek a demeanour
that all the onlookers were filled with compassion.

[1] *Instructions for Parish Priests,* p. 23.

CHAPTER III

THE FREEDOM OF THE CITY

THE freedom of the city was much sought after and highly prized, not only for the privileges it involved, which were accompanied by corresponding duties, but for the prestige it conferred upon its holders, especially when travelling away from London ; and upon many occasions kings and great nobles requested the honour for their favourite servants. Among the more substantial advantages to be derived from possession of the freedom was the facility it promoted in mercantile operations, and the reason for this is apparent from a remark of Blakstone : " Market overt (or free and open " market) in the country is only held on special days, " provided for particular towns by charter or prescrip- " tion : but in London every day except Sunday is a " market day. The market place or spot of ground " set apart by custom for the sale of particular goods " is also in the country the only market overt ; but in " London every shop in which goods are exposed publicly " for sale is market overt, for such things only as the " owner professes to trade in." [1] In short, trade was free or practically free in London, whereas in other parts of the country it was fettered by all sorts of restrictions, both as to time and place, mainly for the benefit of over-

[1] *Romance of the Law Merchant*, p. 40.

lords, who were accustomed to exact tolls and fees on most commercial transactions.

The citizens, because they had to bear the burdens of citizenship whilst enjoying its privileges, were jealous of any attempt by strangers to come and live among them without taking up the freedom. Such strangers could not embark in business on their own account except as retailers of food, and then only under severe restrictions. They were not allowed to purchase or hire premises in which to sell or store the foodstuffs they brought in, but were compelled to bring them in daily from outside, and not to take any back with them which remained unsold. This is illustrated by the prosecution of two poulterers in 1381, who attempted to remove from the city eight capons and nine geese of which they had failed to dispose, and which, in consequence, were confiscated. Their presence, indeed, was only permitted at all for the sake of bringing cheap food to the people, and apart from this concession no stranger was allowed to remain in London beyond a few days without obtaining a citizen to stand security for his good behaviour. Consequently, people living in London without becoming freemen were mostly workmen—employees of the craftsmen, who stood as their guarantors. An alien merchant, bringing his goods to London from foreign parts, was allowed forty days in which to remain for the purpose of disposing of them, unless he were a member of one of those continental trading communities who were accorded special privileges from time to time. He was permitted to hire a warehouse for storing his merchandise, but could not buy or rent a house in which to live ; he was compelled to lodge at a hostel owned by a freeman of the city. Severe measures were often taken against strangers coming into the city and usurping the functions

of freemen, as may be seen from a complaint made in
1345 by the brokers of wool and drapery to the effect
that non-freemen were buying and selling the goods of
these trades on commission.   The Mayor thereupon
ruled that any money so taken should be forfeited and
divided, half going to the city and half to the brokers,
and subsequently several such seizures were made.

A disadvantage under which a non-freeman laboured
was the lack of protection afforded to his children should
he die during their minority, whereas in the case of
orphans of freemen the Mayor was legally their guardian
and carefully studied their interests.   This may be
observed in the case of a minor who was heir to a brewery
and seven shops in the parish of Woolchurch Haw.
The Mayor appointed him a guardian, who afterwards,
without permission, sold his wardship and marriage to
another.   This being contrary to the law of the city and
the interests of the boy, his person was taken from the
custody of the new guardian by the Common Serjeant,
whose duty it was, under the Mayor, to look after the
interests of orphans.   In ordinary cases this would have
meant new arrangements for his guardianship, but when
it was proved that his father had by some means succeeded
in living and acquiring property in the city without
obtaining the freedom, the boy was given up again to
his new guardian, and no further interest was taken in
his fate.   As has been said, the wardship of orphans of
freemen appertained to the Mayor, who appointed the
nearest relative, but one who could not inherit in case of
the orphan's death, as guardian, and placed his property
in the hands of some responsible person to take charge
of and to trade with until the orphan's majority.   The
mother, if living, was usually chosen as guardian, and if
she married again, her new husband was joined with

her in that office. It was necessary for each person concerned with the custody of the infant's person or his money to obtain several citizens to stand as surety, who, in their turn, were responsible to the extent of all their possessions should the principals default. There are several instances where fathers were appointed as guardians of their own children because property had been bequeathed to them by a third party. Thus in 1394 one John Tiddesbury was appointed guardian of his two daughters, both, curiously enough, named Johanna, on account of £40 bequeathed to them by their uncle, the stipulation being made that the father should neither apprentice nor marry them without the consent of the Mayor and aldermen. Afterwards, in 1408, a man was fined 40s. 0. for marrying one of them without such consent obtained. Again, in 1387 a maid servant whose employer bequeathed 10 marks to her by his will, is referred to as an orphan notwithstanding that her father is alive. Quite apart from the responsibility of managing the orphan's estate, the guardianship of an infant might, in those boisterous times, prove more onerous than was altogether pleasant. Thus in 1325 one Gilbert de Mordone, a fishmonger, who also possessed a brewery in Crooked Lane, near London Bridge, lived there with his wife and family, and a ward named Emma. One evening a certain Walter de Benygton, a tailor, came there with seventeen associates for the purpose of carrying her off, their hoods full of stones, and armed with swords, knives, and other weapons. Entering the brewery, they ordered four gallons of beer, which they proceeded to drink. The fishmonger, his brother, and other inmates of the house, knowing full well for what purpose they had come, begged them to go away quietly, but they replied that they would stay whether wanted or not, as the house was public. They then proceeded to throw stones, which they took from their hoods, at their unwilling hosts, and the fishmonger's brother, being hurt thereby, rushed out of the house shouting, pursued by the tailor holding a knife in either hand. Hearing the hubbub, several neighbours then appeared on the scene and endeavoured to pacify the disputants, when one of them, being attacked in his turn by the tailor, felled him with a blow on the head from his staff. The too ardent tailor, although not quite dead, was dragged to the end of Crooked Lane, left out in the open all night, and the following morning, taken to a neighbouring house, where he breathed his last.

There were three ways in which the freedom could be obtained—by birth, by apprenticeship, and by redemption, or purchase. The son of a freeman had a prescriptive right to become one himself in due course, but this was not always to the good, as privileges too easily obtained tend to be taken rather as a matter of course ; and so we find in 1313 members of all the guilds coming before the Mayor and complaining that many young free citizens were totally uninstructed in the ancient laws, franchises, and customs of the city. It was accordingly resolved that all these customs, together with the duties of the various bailiffs, or city officers, and the rules of the various guilds, should be enrolled in a register and once or twice a year publicly read. However, most sons of freemen obtained their admission by the second method—apprenticeship—when they had to serve a master for a term of years, usually seven, though in the Letter-Books they are found serving for all periods between three and sixteen years. The apprentice, at the end of his term, had to go before the Mayor accompanied by his employer, who had to give assurances as to his character and faithful service before he could be admitted to the freedom. If his employer were dead, he had to bring many neighbours to testify to these things, and when this happened before his full term had expired he was either transferred by the Mayor to a new master or charged an extra fee for admission. Both the commencement of his apprenticeship and its termination, known as his " ingress " and " egress," had to be enrolled at Guildhall, and on each occasion he had to be accompanied by his master and pay a fee of 2s. 6d., unless he were apprenticed to the Mayor, sheriffs, or aldermen, when this was remitted. If, as was often the case, the employer had neglected to enroll the apprenticeship at its commencement, a year's grace being allowed for this purpose, it naturally followed at the end of the term that the court possessed no documentary evidence of such apprenticeship, and could only accept the master's word that it had been fully served. Consequently, an extra fee was demanded, sometimes as high as 22s. 6d. ; but if the omission were discovered during the term of apprenticeship, the employer would be. summoned, fined, and compelled to make the enrollment. Although there are many instances recorded of such prosecutions, the rule appears not always to have been adhered to, for there are other examples where apprentices, though not enrolled until years afterwards, were yet charged no more than the usual 2s. 6d. In the same way, when an apprentice allowed a long period to elapse after completing his term before enrolling his " egress " and claiming the freedom he was again charged extra, but it may be suspected that such cases usually refer to those who were found established in business without possessing the freedom, but were nevertheless able to prove having served their apprenticeship.

During the period of his service the apprentice was

regarded as a mere servant—both a body servant and a business servant, and sometimes indeed as no more than a chattel. He was the personal property of his master, and could be dealt with much as any other property. In 1311 a citizen bequeathed his apprentice to his widow, and on her re-marriage he became bound to her and her husband jointly. One testator released his apprentice by his will, whilst another was bequeathed by a merchant to his son ; but in the latter case the young man redeemed the remainder of his term by a payment of 6 marks to the heir. In 1320 the apprentice of a potter was sold with the business, while in 1312 there is a case of one being sold by his master to another for the remainder of his term, and in the same year one was given away because his master could no longer afford to keep him. But notwithstanding this position of apparent servitude, apprentices were officially regarded merely as junior members of the craft, and treated with the consideration due to people of honourable position. Thus in 1351 we find the Mayor granting the guardian-ship of a boy four years old to the two apprentices of a fishmonger, while in 1349 another so appointed was entrusted with the entire possessions of his ward, which he wisely handed over to his master for safe keeping. The Mayor's solicitude for the safety and the humane treatment of apprentices is evident from the manner in which he dealt with a complaint made in 1398 to the effect that hurers, or makers of the shaggy caps worn by the lower orders, were in the habit of sending their apprentices " down to the water of Thames and other " exposed places, and amid horrible tempests, frosts, " and snows, to the very great scandal, as well of the good " folks of the said trade, as of the city aforesaid ". It appears also that these young people quarrelled with the pages of the lords, who had been sent to the same spot to water their horses—" and they are then on the " point of killing one another ". The Mayor's decision upon this complaint was that for the future any hurer so offending should be fined 2s. o. the first time, 3s. 4d. the second time, 6s. 8d. the third time, and after that should be liable to a physical penalty, which would probably take the form of the pillory.

It sometimes happened that an apprentice was released by his master before his term had expired, and again in this case he would be charged extra, sometimes as much as 20s. o. There are various cases of apprentices being charged from 5s. o to 12s. 6d., because they had started trading before their term was up, and one 5s. o. because he had been apprenticed before his master had been admitted to the freedom. Another, when his master died, finished his term with the executors, and yet was charged 13s. 4d. before he could obtain the freedom. Another duty of the apprentice at the time of his " ingress " was to swear to be faithful to his new master. In 1332 a youth who refused to take the required oath was committed to Newgate by the Mayor and aldermen, which caused him quickly to repent, and in a chastened frame of mind to come next day into the Court of Husting and duly swear. Only two cases appear in the Letter-Books where the amount of premium paid to a master for the apprenticeship is mentioned, one in 1359, when a girl was apprenticed for 40s. o., and the other in 1374, of a boy indentured to a skinner for eight years on payment of 46s. 8d.

There are many examples of girls taken as apprentices and not always into trades which seem specially suitable for their sex. Indeed, that the apprenticeship of girls was part of the regular order of things is shown by an

ordinance of 1393 where " male and female " apprentices are mentioned.   As early as 1276 mention is found
of a girl who was apprenticed to a paternosterer, or
maker of rosaries, and afterwards released by her employer
for 14s. o.   In 1346 a girl was apprenticed to a corder,
or ropemaker ; one in 1381 to a draper, and in 1382
another to a grocer.   In a case in the latter year the
particular work to be taught is specified—the art of a
" thredwomman."   In this instance the employer's
trade is not mentioned, but it appears that her guardian
was a draper and her father had been a woolmonger.
In other cases the girl was bound to the tradesman and
his wife ; in 1392 we find one apprenticed to a tailor
and his wife, in 1395 one to a broderer and his wife, and
in 1394 another to a mercer and his wife.   There does
not, however, appear to be any record of such girls
fulfilling their term and claiming the freedom.   There
are instances, both in 1310 and 1311, of women being
admitted to the freedom, but in no case do they seem to
have passed through a period of apprenticeship.

   In the 14th century there is little evidence of common
action by the apprentices, but in the following century
they were, on occasion, able to cause serious trouble to
the authorities.   Among other examples may be cited
an affray in 1456 between the apprentices and the
Lombards.   It began with the action of a young man
in taking a dagger from a foreigner and breaking it,
in consequence of which he was arraigned before the
Mayor at Guildhall and committed to one of the sheriffs'
counters.   Afterwards, as the Mayor went home to his
dinner, he was held up in Chepe by a crowd composed
principally of apprentices of the Mercers, who would
not allow him to depart until their fellow had been
delivered up to them.   Encouraged by this preliminary

success, and attracting to their number all the bad characters of the city, they proceeded later in the day to attack and despoil the Lombards in their own homes. Some of the rioters were arrested and confined to Newgate, but when the King's Justices attempted to bring them to trial the situation in the city became very menacing. It was rumoured that the people were arming secretly and purposing to ring the Common Bell, at that time Bow Bell, as the signal for a general rising, in consequence of which the Judges thought it more prudent to retire from the city.   Notwithstanding that eventually two or three who had actually committed robberies were hanged at Tyburn, the position remained so unsettled that the King and Queen left London for a time.   Again in 1493 the Mercers' apprentices made an organised attack upon the merchants of the Hanse at their house known as the Steelyard, approximately on the site of the present Cannon Street station.   The attack, however, proved abortive, for the merchants had sufficient warning to enable them to keep their gates fast shut.   As many as eighty arrests were made over this affair, among whom, as the chronicler says, " there was not one householder, " but all servants, apprentices, and children ".

The freedom of the city by redemption, or purchase, was granted by the Court of Mayor and aldermen to approved applicants, who had to make their application through the medium of the trade they intended to follow, six reputable members of which had to guarantee their character and their capability.   The method may be understood by the following extract from the ordinances of the Pouchmakers, or " Tasse-makers ", as they were sometimes called, dating from about the year 1349 : " That no foreigner (or outsider) hold shop nor trade in " things appertaining to the mistery before he be made

" free by the officers and examined by the masters of
" the mistery whether he be fit for that mistery and
" estate or not ".   In a charter of Edward II, where this
condition is laid down, it is added, " especially an English
" merchant ", words which are found repeated in subsequent charters.   This is an example of the system of
" Englishry ", by which men of native or Saxon origin
were discriminated against even so long after the Norman
conquest.   In early times it was compulsory for a freeman to continue in the trade through which he obtained
admission, but in 1326 it was ordained that a citizen
could change his trade at will.

The system of approval by the trades led to the appearance of intermediaries who, in return for a fee, would
introduce the would-be citizen to the trade through
which he intended to obtain the freedom.   This fact
is elicited by a case in 1382 of fraud on the part of one
such go-between who was employed by a cutler from
York to introduce him to his fellow craftsmen in London.
The agent presumably was not *persona grata* with the
Cutlers, or Bladesmiths as they were called, and therefore introduced the unsuspecting countryman to the
" Bladers ", a name which in London referred to the
Cornmerchants.   Not satisfied with this piece of decep-
tion which by itself was sufficient to debar the Yorkshire-
man from obtaining the freedom, he proceeded to charge
him the sum of £4 on the excuse that he had been obliged
to " tip " an alderman and a clerk half a mark each and
had paid £3 to the Chamberlain for the entrance fee.
As a matter of fact he had paid only 20s. o. for the latter
purpose and had given no gratuity to anyone.   When
prosecuted at Guildhall he was fined £3 and compelled
to repay his victim 18s. o., but it does not appear that
the latter obtained the freedom he sought.

Fraudulent means were at times employed by the applicants themselves, and took the form of obtaining the freedom through some other trade than that they intended to follow. The reason for this is to be found in the difference in amount of the fee charged, which varied in proportion to the importance and prosperity of the particular mistery. Several such cases were tried before the Mayor in 1385. In one, two men had been introduced by the Haberdashers, six of whom stood as surety, whereas the applicants were really mercers, their stock-in-trade consisted of mercery, and from the first they had practised no other trade than that of mercers. Moreover, at their admission they swore that they were poor men and could not afford to pay more than 20s. 0d., whereas they were both fairly well off, one of them possessing more than £200. It was stated that had their real position been known they would have been charged £20 or £40. The complaint was brought into court by the Mercers, and both delinquents forfeited their newly acquired freedom, as did also one of their sureties who was proved to have been in league with them. Another man, a draper, had been admitted as a weaver, and afterwards confessed that the only weaving done in his house consisted of the cloth that his wife made for domestic purposes, and that he had traded as a draper from the first. The Drapers also complained of a man who had been admitted as a tailor, and in this case not only he but all his sureties lost their freedom as accomplices. In later years, however, a more lenient view appears to have been taken of such conduct, for in 1395 we find two broderers, one of them a foreigner, explaining that through ignorance of the customs of the city they had been admitted as tailors, and begged to be transferred, a prayer which was readily granted on security of good men of the Broderers and a payment of £3. Two years later a more flagrant case reached as mild an ending. Two men who had been apprenticed, one as a pewterer and the other as an ironmonger, and admitted through those trades, afterwards confessed that not only they, but their masters before them, had always been grocers ! Their transfer was agreed to, with the permission of the Grocers, on payment of 20s. o. and 40s. o. respectively.

The authorities appear to have been somewhat chary of admitting foreigners to the freedom, and the reason becomes apparent from a writ of the King in 1312 ordering them to admit several aliens, in reply to which they quote instances of foreigners so admitted who had turned out to be swindlers, and reciting the harm such men had done to the city. Later in the same year, at a public meeting presided over by the Mayor, it was resolved that in future no alien should be admitted except in full Husting and with the consent of all the people. It is to be noted that when the freedom was conferred upon a foreigner, not only was he charged a higher fee than others, sometimes as high as £5, but he was also required to bring well-known people as sureties to guarantee the city against loss. An unusual condition was attached to the admission of a merchant of Toulouse in 1284. He was required to obtain a letter from the governors of his native town, with whom the Londoners had had some trouble, to the effect that London citizens should not in future be molested there. In default of obtaining this he was to forfeit his newly acquired freedom, and also the 40s. o. fee which he had paid. Many citizens also considered it derogative to the dignity of the city that any strange merchant should be admitted merely on account of his wealth, and a

1. GOLDSMITH'S SHOP
2. MERCER'S SHOP
From Cutts' "Scenes and Characters of the Middle Ages"

question of this kind caused a breeze between the Mayor and the Common Council in 1378. The latter accused the former of admitting a man as a fishmonger without their consent, simply because he was known to be rich and powerful. The Mayor adopted a conciliatory attitude and explained that he had no idea the man was rich, that he was recommended by six members of the fishmongers, and that he (the Mayor) did not realise that the Common Council would require to be consulted. After some more argument in a similar vein he succeeded in obtaining a majority of the Council to agree with him, and so the incident closed.

The admission of bondmen to the freedom was also a subject which exercised the minds of the citizens, for it must be remembered that the condition of serfdom still lingered on in England throughout the 14th century. The subject is somewhat obscure, for although it seems to be established that a bondman remaining in the city unmolested for a year and a day could thereby obtain not only his emancipation from the condition in which he was born, but in some cases the freedom of the city as well, yet in other cases it is just as certain that the freedom was forfeited upon it becoming known that the holder had been born in serfdom. A case in point occurred in 1305, when four men were deprived of the freedom when it was discovered that they held land by tenure of villeinage of the Bishop of London at Stepney. Be this as it may, a new rule was adopted in 1387 to the effect that no stranger should be received as apprentice or admitted to the freedom unless he should swear that he had not been born in serfdom. If any such should obtain the freedom under false pretences he was to be fined and lose the freedom, but if, " which God forbid ", any such should become Mayor, alderman, or sheriff, he was to be fined £100 as well as suffering the same deprivation. This law, however, was not to affect the right of asylum in the city. There is, indeed, an example in the early part of the century of an alderman of London born in the state of bondage, who, on revisiting his native village, was arrested as a fugitive serf. In consequence, he brought an action against the lord of the district for false imprisonment, which he appears to have lost ; but how this affected his position in London is not apparent.[1]

Men who were granted the freedom at the instance of the King, great nobles, officials of the Treasury whose favour was of value to the city, or civic functionaries, were usually admitted at a reduced fee, and often for nothing. In 1310 the King's Treasurer recommended his clerk for the freedom, and he was not only admitted without charge, but was given an annuity of 40s. 0. for life as well. The system of computing the fee seems to have been quite haphazard, or rather there seems to have been no system at all. It is difficult to understand why in 1310 a certain Sir W. de Carleton got his servant admitted for nothing while a retainer of the Earl of Gloucester, though recommended by his master, was charged 13s. 4d. The King's farrier was admitted free, but his horsedealer, William of Toulouse, being a foreigner, had to pay 22s. 6d., the Mayor and aldermen themselves standing surety for him. In 1311 a man was admitted without charge at the instance of the Bishop of Worcester, the Chancellor, of whom the citizens had a wholesome dread since the occasion when he attempted to fine them £100 for not appearing before him at his command. The cook of the sheriffs, who had worked for several of these functionaries in succession, was admitted

---

[1] *Chief Justice Sir W. Bereford*, by W. C. Bolland, p. 28.

free of charge, as was also the Mayor's cook ; while in
1310 the Friars Minor, or Carmelites, obtained the
grant of the freedom for their cook, but he had to pay
13s. 4d. An apprentice for his ingress and egress was
charged 2s. 6d. on each occasion, and this seems to be
the fee expected by the city for enrolling the transaction
in the books kept for the purpose at Guildhall ; the
larger sums charged for redemption appear to be in
reality a special charge added to this enrollment fee.
This view is borne out by the odd amounts usually levied,
such as 22s. 6d. (£1 plus 2s. 6d.), 15s. 10d. (1 mark
plus 2s. 6d.), 12s. 6d. (10s. 0. plus 2s. 6d.), 9s. 2d.
(½ mark plus 2s. 6d.), or 29s. 2d. (2 marks plus
2s. 6d.). Each case, however, seems to have been decided
upon its merits or at the whim of the aldermen present,
and in cases where a round sum was charged, such as
5s. 0., 6s. 8d., 13s. 4d., etc., it may be surmised that it
was the enrollment fee of 2s. 6d. which was waived.
The receipts from these sums formed no mean part of
the city's income, for it is recorded that from September
1309 to December 1312 they netted from the ingress
and egress of apprentices and from redemptions of
freedom no less a sum than £498. 13s. 0.

Workmen employed by the craftsmen were not usually
freemen of the city, but there are instances where they
obtained enfranchisement at the request of their masters
after long and faithful service. In a case in 1311, in which
the applicant was most probably a workman, it was stated
that he had stood well in the city for thirty years and had
for long undertaken the burdens of the city. The burdens
referred to not only included the payment of taxes, but
personal service in many directions, such as the office of
beadle or constable of the ward, collector and assessor
of taxes, or even of raker or scavenger. For the purpose

of appointing men to these duties every citizen had to
attend the meetings of the wardmote in the ward in which
he lived, where, under the presidency of the alderman,
local business was transacted, and complaints received
and dealt with.   Once every year, on Plow Monday, the
first Monday after the Epiphany (6th January), the
" Great Court of Wardmote " was held at the Guildhall
before the Mayor, at which any matters which the aldermen had been unable to settle at their wardmotes were
presented.   Service on juries and inquests of various
kinds were also no light burden, especially when it is
realised that often as many as thirty or forty jurors would
be called to investigate a case of homicide or accidental
death.   It was not until reaching the age of seventy
that citizens could obtain exemption from any of these
obligations.

This brings us to the condition of Scot and Lot, terms
the exact meaning of which has been much discussed.
" Scot " was the necessity of paying taxes, and contri-
buting towards other money payments, such as loans and
grants to the King, while " Lot " refers to the citizen's
obligation to fill any office in the service of the city.
Even such positions as those of Common Councillor,
alderman, sheriff, or Mayor, ornamental and dignified
as they were, were nevertheless obligatory, and a citizen
was not at liberty to refuse election to any of them.
Not that any attempt at evasion was common ; they
were generally as much sought after then as they are
to-day, but many citizens, as might be expected, were
not anxious to fill the minor posts.   Thus in 1333 a
saddler obtained a special charter from the King to the
effect that he should not be obliged to serve on assize or
jury, or as Mayor, escheator, sheriff, coroner, or other
office.   The determination of the city to see the obliga-

tions of citizenship fulfilled is evinced by a case in 1313 when the King had exempted certain foreign merchants from the payment of all talages because they were his money-changers. Two of them wishing to obtain the freedom, it was stipulated that notwithstanding this exemption they should undertake to contribute to all the city's charges. In 1321 a different temper was exhibited by a poor freeman who came voluntarily before the Mayor and explained that he was not in Scot and Lot as other freemen were, apologised for this, and offered ½ mark, all he could afford, to the city. In consideration of his poverty and helplessness the Mayor accepted this contribution and forgave him his " trespass."

Another obligation of citizenship was that of service with the armed forces of the city, to which every able-bodied man between the ages of sixteen and sixty was liable. By the terms of the city charters the citizens were not liable to serve with the King's armies abroad, notwithstanding which we find them furnishing contingents for the wars in France and Scotland over and over again in obedience to the demands of the King. In spite of the adroitness of the city rulers in dealing with attempted inroads upon their liberties on many occasions, it must be confessed that successive Kings got the better of them in this respect, granting them each time Letters Patent to the effect that the aid so given should not be regarded as a precedent. But precedent or no precedent, the King renewed his demand on each occasion that he required their aid, and the city had to agree. Thus time and again during the acute period of Edward III's wars in France they provided at their own expense companies of men-at-arms, light horsemen, and archers to swell his armies. In 1369 one such force cost them 30s. 0. per man to equip, and in wages 1s. 0. a day for men-at-

arms and 6d. a day for archers, all citizens being compelled either to go or to pay. In the same way all the
inhabitants had to join in the city's defence on any occasion when trouble threatened, either from foreign invasion
or domestic disturbance, and a good example of the
method employed may be observed in 1377, when, on
the death of Edward III, an incursion of the French was
expected. Each gate was kept locked, ordnance for
throwing stones and shot was mounted on London Bridge,
and the defence of each section of the wall and ditches
entrusted to the men of a particular ward, under the
command of their alderman. The latter was the military
leader of his ward as well as its civic head, and had his
pennon borne before him, emblazoned with his arms in
relief. Leaving the other wards to their duty of guarding
the walls, the men of Chepe, Cordwainer Street, Bread
Street, and Cornhill wards assembled at the Standard in
Chepe ready to march to any spot where the attack might
be made, having with them six serjeants well armed and
mounted to report to the Mayor how things were going.
For the purpose of this mobilisation each alderman drew
up for the information of the Mayor a complete list of
those in his ward capable of bearing arms, those among
them possessing arms, those who could pay a weekly
sum towards the city's defence, those who could give a
day's labour every three weeks, and those who, being
too poor to purchase arms, were to be provided by the
authorities with " pavises," or large shields, that they
might act as shield-bearers to the others.

It was in order to prevent any escape from these lia-
bilities that residence in the city by freemen was insisted
upon in early times, and the enforcement of this rule is
of frequent occurrence. In 1312 a man was admitted
on this express stipulation, and afterwards two men

had to come to court and testify that the condition had been fulfilled ; while in 1311 a freeman found living outside the bounds of the city " contrary to the liberties " of the city and to his oath ", was fined 4s. 0. and compelled to undertake to take up his residence in London by a definite date. However, in course of time this rule was somewhat relaxed as it came to be realised that the more substantial merchants of other cities could be admitted to the trading rights of London with mutual advantage to the city and themselves. Thus in 1346 we find merchants of Hull, Norwich, Northampton, and Coventry free of the city, in which year, by reason of their status in London, twelve of them assisted the citizens with contributions amounting to £48 towards a loan of 3,000 marks to the King. By 1380, owing to the greatly increased numbers of these outside citizens, and in order that they should participate equally with other citizens in the expenses of the city, it was determined that they should be assessed, not in the wards as residents were, but by the Mayor and aldermen at Guildhall. For this purpose a list of such citizens was drawn up, by which it may be seen that they were located in all parts of the kingdom, and even in Calais.

In guarding the dearly bought liberties of London the citizens acted with severity towards any of their own number who by their conduct placed those liberties in jeopardy, and punished them by withdrawing the freedom. There are many cases of men so deprived for raising tumults in the city, or assaulting any of the officials, or for too freely criticising the Mayor and aldermen, because any widespread disaffection put the city to the risk of being taken into the King's hand. Many incurred this punishment for selling the goods of non-freemen as their own, thus defrauding the customs ; while in

1299 another suffered the same for impleading a fellow citizen in the court of the King's Marshal, thereby establishing a precedent which might prove dangerous to the liberties. In the same way, in 1370 a mercer who had married the widow of a pepperer, and had received certain instructions from the Mayor touching a legacy of the deceased, appealed to an ecclesiastical court, because it was customary for that court to have the first scrutiny of wills. On this becoming known the Mayor deprived him of the freedom, which he only recovered after five years, on payment of a fine to the city.

In the latter half of the century the value of the freedom, from one cause and another, had somewhat diminished, engendering grave dissatisfaction among the citizens, many of whom migrated to other towns. One reason for this was the Statute passed by the Parliament at York in 1351, which gave to foreigners equal trading rights with citizens. In the succeeding years many petitions were addressed to the King praying for the repeal of this act, the unfairness of which consisted in the fact that the foreigner was able to escape most of the obligations of payment and service to which the citizens were liable. The favouritism shown at this time to foreigners resulted in many attacks upon them by exasperated citizens, as shown by the numerous writs from the King warning the people against molesting them in any way. In 1359 a murderous attack is reported upon several Lombard merchants by mercers in the Old Jewry, where it is said that they " did wound, beat, and maltreat them, and, " against the peace of our Lord the King, commit other " enormities against them ". Such foreigners residing in the city did not always behave themselves as they ought, and in such cases it was often impossible for the citizens to obtain redress. In 1355 a merchant of Florence, living in the ward of Langbourne, complained to the King of a levy of 5s. o. which had been made upon him by the city as a contribution towards their expenses due to the war with France, and for which, in default of payment, they had distrained upon him. After some correspondence with the King they definitely refused to refund the 5s. o., giving as their reason that the foreign merchant lived regularly in the city and traded as fully as a freeman, and so they thought he ought to pay like any other inhabitant. In 1369 another foreigner, a Lombard, was accused of having, during a period of five years, exported gold and silver to the value of £1,000, contrary to statute, defrauded the King of customs duties by avowing the goods of another Lombard as his own, enhanced the price of silk by his method of retailing it, and " forestalled " various articles of merchandise, thus taking an unfair advantage of other merchants. He also owed money to several citizens which they were unable to recover. He was imprisoned in Newgate, and his goods and chattels seized, but, on his making fine of £200 to the King, the city was ordered to release him, and restore his property.

Another sore point was a law passed in 1363 by which each merchant was to select one trade or mistery and practise that only. This was an outcome of the activities of the " Grossers," familiar to-day as the Guild of Grocers, who " engrossed," or bought up wholesale such commodities as wax, almonds, soap, thread, dates, fruits, oil, leather, salt fish, canvas, and even copper and iron, with a view to storing them against a rise in the market. The term as originally used was almost equivalent to our modern " profiteer." As a slight modification of this law vintners bringing wine from Gascony were

permitted to buy cloth and herrings to take back with
them, but this was merely with a view to keeping money
in the country.

In 1364 the growing dissatisfaction resulted in a
petition for redress from the commons of the city to the
Mayor and aldermen, in which they stated that a freeman
of the city ought to be allowed to trade wholesale in any
goods out of which he could made a profit ; but as regards
his retail shop he should confine himself to selling goods
of his own mistery. They also advocated the old law that
foreign merchants should only be allowed to remain in
the city with their goods for forty days, a law dating back
to the days of King Alfred. Other matters were raised
regarding points in which the ancient laws as to the
freedom had fallen into disuse, with suggestions for their
revival and for bringing them up to date. Those who
possessed the freedom by right of birth ought not to be
charged anything for admission, but at the age of twenty-
one ought to be sworn in, because there were many such
living and trading in the city who were under the impression that, never having been sworn in they were not
bound to observe the franchises. Also they thought
that at least one day a month should be set aside for the
aldermen and the rulers of the misteries to meet and
discuss the affairs of the commons, and on this day only
should apprentices who had served their time receive
the freedom. These days should be called " Gildedaies," and apprentices then admitted should be charged
not less than 60s. o., those who could not afford so much
remaining as servants, for it would be better so than that
the number of masters should be multiplied unduly.
Consistently with the habits of thought of the period
they do not forget to add that these suggestions are
offered, not only for the good of the city, but also for the

Glory of God. The Mayor's reply was generally sympathetic ; he agreed with most of the proposals submitted, including the revised charge of 60s. o. for admission, but he thought that the " Gildedaies " should be held at his discretion rather than on a fixed date. Regarding the liberty to deal in any kind of goods he thought it best to postpone a decision, the matter being rather a question for parliament. This law was repealed shortly afterwards, but the clause giving equal privileges to foreigners was retained ; in fact English merchants appear to have been discriminated against, for the act of repeal makes an exception that English merchants shall not export wool, woolfels, or gold and silver in the form of plate or money. The question remained a burning one for many years afterwards, and the objections of the citizens to foreigners appear to have been concerned less with their wholesale trading than with their participation in retail business. When, in 1368, the King sent his writ to the Mayor ordering him to make proclamation that all merchants, foreign or denizen, were equally at liberty to trade in the city both by wholesale and by retail, the Mayor quietly put the writ away and took no notice ; while, as an indication of the soreness aroused, it is recorded that in 1371 a blacksmith who had spoken too freely upon the subject was sentenced to the pillory.

So far as the fee of 60s. o. for admission, which from this time was regularly charged, is concerned, it was found in the course of time that it militated rather against the prosperity of the city. It prevented many people who might have proved worthy citizens from becoming freemen because it was exacted at the period when they could least afford it, and so they settled in Southwark or Westminster instead, leaving many houses in the city vacant. The arrangement was therefore altered in 1381, and a new rule adopted by which it should be lawful for the Chamberlain and two aldermen to admit any fit and proper person for a fee suitable to his estate, and no master, surveyor, or warden of a mistery should be allowed to exact any fee for recommending applicants on pain of being fined double the sum so received in addition to making restitution. However, this fee was once more reimposed in 1383 when a Mayor belonging to the opposite party in city politics was in power.

CHAPTER IV

TRADE AND FINANCE

FREE trade is quite a modern idea, and even so, it seems to be almost entirely confined to this country. Our ancestors knew it not, but on the contrary had a passion for regulating everything and everybody. They tried to supervise the manufacture of an article from start to finish, to say who should sell it and where, and at what price ; and they thought they were doing all this for the public benefit, not realising that free competition would probably have been more advantageous for everybody. The civic authorities, under the protection of royal charters from successive kings, either encouraged or compelled each trade to become a close corporation, so that no new-comer could practise without the permission or the recommendation of members of the particular craft ; and thus starting on the slippery path of trade regulation, soon discovered that a close corporation is the very thing to keep prices up and quality down. The result was that very soon it became necessary to stipulate what materials should be used in craftmanship, what size or measurements articles of manufacture should possess, where imported goods should be landed, how their weights should be tested and by whom, and at what price many articles should be sold ; but the frequent repetition of these ordinances and the many prosecutions under them are indications of the difficulties encountered in their enforcement. The rulers of the city in the middle ages were very human ; they did not exercise unnecessary brutality. If a man erred in ignorance or through a lack of understanding of the rules, and amply apologised to the Mayor, he was dealt with quite leniently ; but in the case of a flagrant offender who transgressed intentionally they were very stern, and put him in the pillory for an hour, or sometimes even drew him through the principal streets fastened to a hurdle ; and if he were able to tolerate the humiliation involved, nothing much worse happened to him. Even at the third time of offending the worst they would do was to conduct him to one of the gates, and compel him to abjure the city for ever.

Each craft or mistery was compelled to formulate its rules or " articles " and present them to the Mayor for his approval, after which they possessed the force of law, and any member of the trade who disobeyed them was liable to punishment. Wardens, or supervisors, were then chosen from among the more prominent men of the craft. They had to serve for one year, and it was their duty to see that all points of the articles were fulfilled, and to bring any breach of the rules to the notice of the Mayor. The articles in question bear a close similarity one with the other, consisting for the most part of rules for confirming the exclusiveness of the guild, for the taking of apprentices and the good order of the servants of the craftsmen, and for maintaining the quality of the goods produced ; the latter involving the prohibition of Sunday and night work, of female labour, and of mixing old materials with new. There are to be found, however, a few rules which are peculiar to one trade while wanting in the others. The Heaumers, or helmet-makers, succeeded in getting the better of their foreign competitors by obtaining confirmation of a rule that no helmets imported from abroad should be sold until they had been inspected and approved by members of the craft. This was on the plea that many great men of the realm had been killed by reason of wearing armour of inferior quality. Some drastic clauses existed in the articles of the Tawyers, a trade subsidiary to that of the Skinners, for whom they dressed certain kinds of fur. They were not allowed to perform any work for Easterlings (or Germans), Flemings, or for anyone but free Skinners ; they were not permitted to buy or sell any skins on their own behalf, under penalty of forfeiture, fine, and fourteen days' imprisonment ; they were forbidden to cut the head off any skin entrusted to them to dress, in order to render it easy for the owner to recognise it again. The Skinners in their turn had a self-denying clause in their ordinances, approved by the Mayor in 1365, to the effect that if any person bought a fur which was fraudulent by reason of being made up of new and old fur mixed, or of inferior fur to that which had been paid for, the masters of the mistery should supply the complainant free of charge with a new fur of the quality required. The mixing of old and new fur, or of fur of different kinds, was a serious offence, but one frequently committed and as often punished. The usual sentence was fourteen days in Newgate and a fine of £1, two-thirds of which went to the city and one-third to the trade, in addition to which the furs were confiscated. A curious rule was made among the Bowyers in 1394 to the effect that if any one of them bought more than 300 bowstaves he should divide them with the other members of the craft.

Cloth was another product which was carefully supervised by the authorities, not only for the purpose of maintaining its quality, but also because there was a subsidy due to the King on every piece sold. An official called an " Aulnager " was appointed by the King for this purpose, and no cloth was permitted to be sold until it had been measured and sealed by him. Afterwards, when this practice was discontinued, a serjeant of the Chamber of Guildhall was appointed to test the measurement of all cloth made in the city, receiving a fee of twopence for every whole cloth and a penny for every smaller piece sealed, but in 1386 this was reduced to a halfpenny for every piece. Fullers of cloth were ordered to full by hand and not with the feet. In 1376 there were forty-one of them in the city, and their mills were situated at Wandsworth, Old Ford, Stratford, and Enfield. No undyed cloth was allowed to be sent out to any of these mills to be fulled, and one dyer caught doing so was fined 10s. 0. and immediately appointed and sworn to see that nobody else did the same. In any dispute as to the measurement or quality of cloth the fullers were summoned to the Guildhall to decide the merits of the case, and it is an indication of the number of these actions that at one time they complained that the frequency of such summonses left them no time to attend to their business. Another safeguard against fraud was the rule that wherever possible manufacturers should have their trade mark imprinted upon the article produced. This was the case with swordsmiths, cutlers, workers in pewter, and turners, or makers of measures for wine and ale. In the same way the " Scriveners ", or writers of court hand, whose business it was to make out wills, indentures, and other deeds for the citizens, were compelled to sign their names to all such documents in order to prevent unauthorised persons practising their craft. One cause of the production of goods of inferior quality in a city of such well-organised trades as London is explained in the articles of the Glovers, submitted to the Mayor in 1349, in which the craftsmen complain that persons totally unconnected with the trade entice away their servants and take them into their houses, where in secret they make gloves from inferior or rotten leather, with a view to selling them to wholesale buyers coming into the city, thereby obtaining a bad reputation for the genuine glovers.

The modern habit in obedience to which people with similar views or aims form themselves into societies was almost universal in the middle ages, so much so that it is safe to assert that there was scarcely an inhabitant of London who was unconnected with one or more of these guilds and fraternities. Moreover, they were established not only for the furtherance of trade and manufacturing interests, but also for religious and social purposes, as, for instance, praying brotherhoods attached to the churches and chapels. Besides the well-known guild of Parish Clerks, who performed the plays at Skinner's Well which became so famous that even kings did not disdain to grace them with their presence, there was a community of Parish Chaplains, comprising the rectors of the city churches, formed chiefly for charitable purposes. It is recorded that the rectors of St. Mary Woolnoth, St. Benet, Gracechurch Street, St. Andrew, Undershaft, and St. Olave, Silver Street, had at one time and another served as " pittancer ", or distributor of alms, to the community.

Another remarkable feature of 14th-century craftsmanship was the minute subdivision of labour at a time when machinery and mass production were alike unknown. To produce such a simple article as a bow required a bowyer and a stringer ; while as to bows and arrows, the makers—Bowyers and Fletchers —had early agreed to part company. In 1375 a man who had practised both crafts was compelled to come before the Mayor and solemnly promise to work only at that of a fletcher for the future, and afterwards, inter-meddling once more with the trade of the Bowyers, was, on their complaint, prosecuted and fined. Again, to produce a saddle required the services of Saddlers, Loriners, Painters, and Joiners ; a knife necessi-tated Cutlers, Bladesmiths, Hafters, and Sheathers ; while to supply the public with a piece of cloth required Weavers, Fullers, Dyers, and Shearmen, besides the Drapers, Mercers, Haberdashers, and Corders who sold it.

An interesting outcome of the formation of traders and craftsmen into guilds was their habit of becoming segregated into distinct parts of the city, and it seems that when the location of a trade was changed it involved the migration of an entire craft. Thus, Bow Lane was originally called " Cordwainer Street " because it was occupied from early times by men of that trade, but afterwards, when they all removed elsewhere and the Hosiers took their place, it was renamed " Hosier Lane ". So famous did the streets identified with particular crafts become, that it is said that at the annual fair held at Stourbridge, in Cambridgeshire, each row of booths allocated to one trade was named after the corresponding street in London occupied by the same craft. A famous instance of this habit of segregation was that of the cooks, settled in Bread Street and Eastcheap. They owe their existence as a trade to the custom among

Londoners, especially when entertaining friends, of sending out for their dinner ready cooked, notwithstanding that in the 14th century a house of any size was equipped with a kitchen. These houses were also eating-houses, where people could be served with food as in a modern restaurant; but it would be a curious experience to-day to find all these places clustered together in two spots in the city. Lydgate describes how the cooks of Eastcheap cried hot ribs of beef roasted and pies well baked, with clattering of pewter pots, minstrelsy, and no greater oaths than " yea by cock " and " nay by cock " ; while there is a record in 1382 of a cook of Bread Street who supplied conger eel to a party of five countrymen which was unfit for human food. He was prosecuted, and twelve of his neighbours called as a jury, who deciding that the fish was bad, the unfortunate cook was compelled to return the money paid, and to stand on the pillory while the fish was burnt beneath him. At times the price of each article they sold was fixed by the Mayor and aldermen, from a roast pig at 8d. to ten roast finches for a penny. It is interesting to note that the price for cooking a capon, when the bird was the property of the customer, was three-halfpence, or in the case of a goose twopence, the order stating that this fee is for the " paste, fire, and trouble ", indicating a method of cooking poultry unusual at the present day. In 1379 the Piebakers, who appear to have been a branch of the Cooks, were forbidden to make and sell rabbit pies or giblet pies, because so many had been sold in a stinking condition, a prohibition also extended to the preparation of " venison " pies made of beef. One can imagine the kind of beef which it was possible to sell as venison.

Many of the London streets still bear in their names the original trade that settled in them, while in others

it can be traced with slight difficulty.   Such names as
the Poultry, Ironmonger Lane, Paternoster Row, Bread
Street, Milk Street, and the districts known as the
Ropery and Vintry speak for themselves ; while more
remotely indicating their origin are Cannon Street,
originally Candlewick Street, where the tallow and wax
chandlers lived ; Budge Row, from the Skinners who
sold a fur known as " Budge " ; Foster Lane, from
the Fusters, or makers of the wooden parts of saddles ;
Friday Street, from the fishmongers who did their
principal trade on that day of the week ; and Tower
Royal, from the foreign merchants of La Riole, importers
of wine.

Strangers bringing their goods into the city were not
allowed to sell them in shops, where they might change
hands more than once before reaching the public, thus
enhancing their price ; they were allotted various spots
where they might stand and sell, and were charged a
toll on the goods they brought.   If a man brought
poultry on his back, or corn on horseback, and disposed
of it without allowing it to touch the ground, he paid a
reduced toll, or, if he were a freeman of the city, nothing.
It was most probably the competition of these strangers,
combined with the fact that some of the craftsmen lived
in back streets where business was difficult, that induced
so many traders to desert their shops and sell their
goods from boxes and crates in the streets.   The
authorities were constantly endeavouring to cope with
the congestion thus caused, and many were the ordinances issued directing the dealers where to stand, and
a few examples may not be without interest.   Blacksmiths, when selling their products away from their
shops, were ordered to stand either at Grascherche (the
modern Gracechurch Street), St. Nicholas Shambles

5 6 3 11

in Newgate Street, or near the Tun on Cornhill ; non-freemen poulterers had to stand at the " Carfeux " near Leadenhall (the present cross-roads formed by Grace-church Street and Cornhill), but were afterwards ordered into Leadenhall Market, while the freemen poulterers had to stand by the wall of St. Michael's Church, Cornhill ; fishermen who caught Thames fish were not allowed to sell it to dealers, but only direct to the public, and had to stand by the wall of St. Margaret's Church near London Bridge, or by the wall of St. Mary Magdalen in Old Fish Street, a part of Knightrider Street ; while the Cordwainers were allowed to sell their shoes at one spot only, between Soper Lane and the Conduit in Chepe.

So far as the dealers in uncooked foods were concerned—butchers, fishmongers, and corn-merchants—the custom of selling away from their shops was not only encouraged, but enforced, for it was a cardinal principle with the rulers of 14th-century London that the necessaries of life should be sold, not in shops, but in open market, where their price and quality could be regulated and overseen. It is a truism that markets are not made but grow, and this was the case with all the city food markets except one—the Stocks Market—and in order to enable them to retain their pre-eminence it was granted by charter of Edward III that no market should be held within a radius of seven miles around the city. The food markets comprised Billingsgate, Gracechurch Street, Leadenhall, Cornhill, the Poultry, Old Fish Street, St. Nicholas Shambles, Smithfield, and the Stocks Market. Billingsgate was then, as now, the wholesale fish market, Old Fish Street was a retail fish market, Gracechurch Street was the market for corn and oats, Leadenhall, Cornhill, and the Poultry

Lincoln Christian College

were devoted to poultry, while the Stocks Market and
St. Nicholas Shambles were of a composite character.
Fish was landed at Billingsgate, not in wooden trunks
as it is to-day, but in baskets called " dorsers ", adapted
to be carried on the back ; and a custom of one fish
from every dorser was exacted for the use of the sheriffs.
From this impost some fish, such as turbot, dorey,
conger, and a few others were exempt, but nevertheless
had to pay a fee of twopence for " strandage ", or the
privilege of beaching the boat.   These customs, so far
as fish belonging to freemen was concerned, were
abolished in 1376.   There were fish-porters in Billingsgate market then, just as there are to-day.   This fact
is elicited by a case tried by a coroner's jury in 1336
in which two of them, assisted by a chaplain, rescued a
homicide from the custody of the beadle who had
arrested him.   Special arrangements were made for
the sale of sprats ; they were not allowed to be landed
in bulk and sold to the fishmongers, but had to be sold
to the public direct from the boats.   In 1379 it was
ordered that they should no longer be sold by the dish,
pan, or handfull, but by legal measure, such as bushel,
half-bushel, peck, or half-peck.   It must be remembered that, next to bread, fish was the chief article of
food in the city, not only on account of the weekly
fish day and the innumerable saints' days on which to
eat it was obligatory, but because it was cheap and
plentiful, reinforced as was the supply by the fish at that
time caught in the Thames, and so it is not surprising
to find that even such a small matter as the price of
herrings was sufficient to engage the attention of the
Mayor.   It is related that in 1382 a dealer had a ship-
load of salted herrings in the Thames, and started by
selling them to retailers at five a penny, so that they

could resell to the public at four a penny. When the
Mayor heard of this he thought it an unconscionable
price, and sent word to the dealer that he must revise
his terms. The dealer then lowered the price to six
a penny, the retailer to sell at five a penny ; but later it
leaked out that the owner of the herrings had sold some,
no doubt in large quantities, to a man who was sending
them out of the city, at the rate of ten a penny. Here-
upon the Mayor sent for the merchant in great anger
and told him it would be worse for him if he did not
further reduce the price to the citizens, and after a deal
of haggling he agreed to sell the remainder at nine a
penny. In 1379 an order was issued by the Mayor
that any fish which had gone bad was to be sent to
Newgate by the surveyors of the mistery, but an answer
to the intriguing question as to what was to happen to
it there is denied us. It must be borne in mind that
in the 14th century there was at Newgate no court at
which putrid food might have been condemned and its
owners punished, and it cannot reasonably be supposed
that the object in view was to place such fish under
lock and key. The only alternative is that it was intended
as food for the prisoners there, bestowed as an act of
charity. Prisoners in Newgate were not fed at the
public expense ; they had to provide their own food
or receive it from their friends, and those without means
were dependent on charity. For this reason many cases
are recorded of the prisoners dying of starvation.

The market of St. Nicholas Shambles extended from
the church of St. Michael le Quern, near the north-east
gate of St. Paul's churchyard, for some distance along
Newgate Street ; corn, meat, fish, poultry, and leather
were sold there. In 1309, two plots of ground there
on which to build their market were leased to the curriers

of leather for forty years at a rental of 4 marks a year, while in 1373 several vacant plots of land under the wall of the church were let to various poulterers at 4d. per foot per annum. The butchers of this market were always in trouble over the matter of slaughtering, and the consequent messiness of the surrounding streets. It is recorded that in 1343 the Mayor and aldermen leased to them, on payment of a boar's head annually, a piece of land and a quay beside the Fleet River, described as being near the Fleet prison, " where the Thames ebbs and flows ", for the purpose of cleaning their offal in the water. In 1354 the King received a complaint from the Prior of the Hospital of St. John of Jerusalem (situated in Clerkenwell, and of which St. John's Gate is the sole surviving relic) that the ground in question was his property from which the Mayor had ousted him, and that the stench arising from the operations of the butchers was so abominable as seriously to endanger the health of the prisoners. The Mayor protested that the ground had never been the property of the hospital, but at last giving in, transferred the butchers to a quay on the Thames near Baynards Castle, which became known as " Bochersbrigge ". To this spot the butchers carried their offal from St. Nicholas Shambles and dumped it in the river, the blood dripping on to the roadway of the streets and lanes through which it was carried. This produced a whole crop of complaints from the inhabitants, and resulted in more than one peremptory order from the King to the Mayor to remove the nuisance, under a penalty of £100. By 1370 " Bochersbrigge " had been demolished, but the butchers still continued to carry their offal to the Thames, although the King had instructed the Mayor to arrest and punish any caught doing so. Finally in 1371 slaughtering was forbidden at St. Nicholas Shambles, and the butchers were ordered to find some spot outside the city for the purpose. Non-freemen butchers were allowed to bring meat to the market for sale, but under the restriction that none might be cut up after " none " rung upon the bells of St. Paul's, and any meat in cut at that hour to be sold by Vespers, and any remaining unsold not to be taken away.

One trade which, by its nature and the requirements of its customers, could never become segregated, was that of the sellers of strong drink, and so we find these merchants in almost every street of the city. They were of two kinds—taverners and brewers—for a tavern was a place where wine was sold, and a brewery one where ale was brewed and sold. The universality of beer as the popular beverage at a time when tea, coffee, and cocoa were unknown, and the popularity of wine, will be realised when it is stated that in 1309 the city contained 354 taverns and 1,334 breweries. These figures must be considered in relation to the population, which, according to the statistics in connection with the poll tax of 1380, numbered 20,397 persons over the age of fifteen ; and so, providing there had been no material variation during the intervening years, we have the astonishing result of one drink shop to every twelve inhabitants. The ale of the period was made from malt, being quite innocent of hops ; and the practice of using the latter was introduced from the continent only towards the end of the century. Mention of " hoppyngbeer " is found for the first time in the Letter-Books under the year 1391. No beer was permitted to be sold until it had been examined and tasted by men called " ale-conners " who were appointed for the purpose, and it was the duty of the brewer to call them in each time he had completed a fresh brewing. The usual price of ale was three-halfpence a gallon for the best and a penny a gallon for the second quality. As to the wine trade, if it were a question of that only, one would not form a high opinion of the commercial morality of the time, for the number of warnings and admonitions addressed by the Mayor and aldermen to the taverners is astonishing, and far outnumbers any instructions issued to anybody else about anything. Adulteration of wine seems to have been the chief trouble. One trick of the taverners was to put the dregs of all the wines, no matter what the kind, into a cask lined with pitch or cobbler's wax, which gave it the colour and something of the flavour of " Romeny ", and under this name they sold it.   Poetic justice was meted out to one of these gentry in 1364, when he was solemnly sentenced at Guildhall to drink a quantity of his own wine and have the remainder poured over his head.   At the beginning of the century the Gascon and Rhenish wines then in vogue were worth about 3d. a gallon, rising later to 10d.   But towards the middle of the century, when Vernage, Malvoisie, Romeny, Candy, etc., the so-called sweet wines, came in, priced at from 16d. to 32d. a gallon, the temptation to mix off a certain quantity of the cheap with the dear proved too great to be resisted.   At first the authorities contented themselves with issuing proclamations denouncing the practice and threatening penalties. This proving unavailing, was followed by orders that sweet and other wines should not be kept in the same cellar, and that the cellar door should be kept always open so that customers could see from whence their wines were drawn. The latter clause was frequently evaded by the expedient of hanging a curtain in front of the open door, and this fresh offence had to be legislated against. The next stage was to forbid a taverner to sell both kinds ; he had to choose one or the other. All these efforts proving equally fruitless, an attempt was made in 1365 to prevent sweet wines being sold anywhere except in three taverns set aside for the purpose, one in Chepe, one in Lombard Street, and one in Walbrook. In these frequent inspection was to be made by officials appointed for the purpose, the price of the wines to be fixed by the Mayor at the beginning of each year, and the profits to be devoted to repairing the city walls, cleaning the ditches, etc. In the same year they were let out to farm to one Richard Lyons, a goldsmith, for a period of ten years at an annual rent of £200. Yet even this venture must have proved as unsuccessful as any of the others, and appears to have been abandoned after a few years, though in 1373 a fresh attempt of the sort was made when by Letters Patent from the King a monopoly for the sale by retail of sweet wines was granted to another merchant for a period of five years, a grant afterwards annulled by Parliament. In the articles of the Vintners and Taverners, formulated and submitted to the Mayor in 1370, no mention is made of the matter, and by 1377, or shortly afterwards, sweet wines were again being sold in the ordinary taverns, for in that year is found a return to the previous state of things in an order that sweet and other wines were not to be kept in the same cellar, and by the appointment of six vintners to go round to all the taverns and place a distinctive mark on every cask of wine indicating its kind and value, Malvoisie being particularly mentioned as a wine which must not be sold as such until it had been marked by the examiners. In the city courts wine was frequently exacted as a penalty or as surety for good behaviour in cases where the delinquent had attempted to stir up trouble against the authorities, or as damages in cases of libel or defamation.   In 1284 a tun of wine was paid as damages for killing a dog.

Of all the imports brought into the country from abroad, wine was one of the largest and perhaps the largest, and came from such far-away parts of the world as Greece and Cyprus.   It gave origin to the expression " tonnage " in respect of the capacity of ships, a word which in early records is spelt " tunnage ", and referred to the number of tuns of wine a ship would hold.   On arrival in the Port of London it was landed at Queenhithe and stored in cellars in the neighbourhood, and from this circumstance the district acquired the name of Vintry ward, which it still bears to-day.   Here the foreign wine merchants lodged and had their cellars, one of which, of very large capacity, was known as the " Four Gates ".   As the wine ships passed under London Bridge a toll of 2d. was levied on every cask for the repair of the bridge, and on a sale taking place each cask had to be gauged by an official gauger, who received for his trouble a halfpenny for every tun from both the buyer and the seller.   Carters to carry it away were also appointed by the authorities, and the arduousness of their task was recognised in an official order from the Guildhall to the Master of the carters in 1301 that he must not attempt to handle a tun of wine without twelve assistants.

If wine, so far as bulk is concerned, was the greatest article of importation, it was by no means the only one, and a list compiled in 1315 for purposes of levying murage shows that the ends of the known world must have been ransacked to supply London with merchandise.   It includes lead, wax, almonds, rice, pepper, ginger, cinnamon, frankincense, quicksilver, vermillion, verdigris, cummin, alum, sugar, licorice, aniseed, turpentine, gold pigment, sulphur, resin, copperas, figs, raisins, cloves, nuts, muscatels, mace, saffron, silk, brass, tin, glass, numerous kinds of fur and cloth, cloth of gold, leather, woad, honey, wine, salt, wood, steel, and many others. Even cokernuts were imported, and the shells often made into drinking-cups with stem and rim of gold or silver. The two chief ports for foreign trade were Billingsgate and Queenhithe, the customs levied at the former being paid to the King, and those of the latter, at any rate in early times, to the Queen. Later in the century Woolwharf, where the Custom House now stands, also became a thriving port. Large quantities of salt were imported from Poitou and landed at all these ports, where it was met by officials called " meters ", whose duty it was to measure and cart it on behalf of the merchants who bought it. At Billingsgate or Woolwharf they charged 2½d. for measuring a sieve of large salt containing 5 quarters and 6 bushels, or, including carriage as far as Bread Street or similar distance, 8d., while for measuring a sieve of small salt, containing 5 quarters only, the charge was 2d., or with carriage 6d. In the case of Queenhithe the price for measuring was the same, but as that port was considerably nearer to Bread Street than the others the prices including carriage were respectively 6d. and 4d. All imported goods had to be disposed of within forty days of landing, and were not allowed to be sold by private treaty, but openly where they were landed, or at the " seld " where they were stored. In the case of leather and cloth special places were appointed where they could be sold ; for the former a seld in Friday Street, and for the latter, by an order of 1387, the Stocks Market,

" the house where lives John Yonge, grocer, near the
" church of St. Antholin ", or a place opposite the
churchyard of the same church ; but by 1399 " Bakwelle-
halle ", or Blackwell Hall, near the Guildhall, was set
aside for this purpose. It was forbidden for one
foreigner to sell to another, as this would tend to enhance
the price of the goods, and it was regarded as a particularly
serious offence if a freeman conspired with a foreigner
to assert that goods, really owned by such foreigner,
were his own, freemen being allowed a reduction on
the various tolls charged.

It was usual for a foreigner to accompany his goods
to London for the purpose of their disposal, and his
life could not have been an easy one ; often he must
have been left wondering what he had to pay next.
After settling the port dues, tolls were exacted at various
times under such names as scavage, murage, pontage,
pavage, and strandage. Scavage was a toll which was
regularly paid on the display of the goods for sale, but
the others appear to have been levied only at particular
times. In 1396 the Italian colony in London embarked
upon the hopeless task of endeavouring to repudiate
the payment of scavage. They complained to the
Mayor that the sheriffs had levied this toll on their goods
coming from Southampton to London by land, and
asserted that they had not been accustomed to pay it
for the last twelve years. The sheriffs maintained that it
had always been payable on goods belonging to foreigners,
and observed that the Italians paid it on heavy goods
of little value reaching London by water, but objected
to pay it on light goods of great value which they trans-
ported by land. The Mayor took the trouble to examine
the old city records on the subject, and as a result declared
that in future they must pay scavage **on** all goods,

whether coming by land or by water. The right to levy murage for the repair of the city walls was granted by the King in 1338 for a period of five years, and again in 1386 for a period of ten years, besides other occasions during the century. In 1386 a long schedule of charges on every conceivable article of importation was issued, ranging from a farthing on a lamb or calf and 4d. on a millstone, to 2s. 0. on a thousand of " best grey work ", a species of fur. The median rate appears to have been about twopence in the pound *ad valorem*. The corporation was in the habit of letting out to farm any tolls or customs which they had the right to collect, and even then the money they received was not necessarily devoted to the purpose for which the toll had been imposed. In 1331 and 1332 the murage was let to one John Vyncent, he paying the city £235. 13s. 4d. for the period. As the King, however, frequently exonerated from payment of murage the merchants of various towns both English and foreign, the lessee took care to stipulate that any more such exemptions during his tenure should entail a corresponding reduction in his payment to the city. In the course of the two years this allowance amounted to £20. Of the remainder, all the city walls received was £40, and even that sum included repairs to the Tun on Cornhill as well. £193. 1s. 4d. of the money was devoted to buying presents for the King, Queen, and great men of the realm ; £27. 19s. 6d. was spent on repairs to the Chapel of the Guildhall, and £2. 10s. 0. was given to two messengers who had carried letters to and from the city. In 1338 they let the murage to farm district by district, which affords an opportunity of observing the relative commercial importance of various parts of the city. Thus, while they were able to charge 13s. 4d.

a month for the murage of Smithfield ; £25 a year for that of Billingsgate ; and 66s. 8d. a year for Leadenhall ; the murage of Chepe yielded 13s. 4d. a week, afterwards raised to 16s. od.

When cases of smuggling occurred the authorities were even more drastic in their action than they are to-day ; they would seize the whole cargo in reprisal for one small item which had failed to pay duty. In 1356 two merchants sent a cargo of woad and Spanish wax from Flanders to London, and on arrival some fresh skins which had not paid duty were found on board by the " scrutineers " of wool and other merchandise liable to custom, and in consequence they estreated the whole cargo. The two merchants appealed against this to the King on the ground that the skins were put on board at Faversham without their knowledge. The King thereupon instructed the Mayor to inquire if this were true, and if so to return the confiscated cargo, and a jury being summoned, decided in favour of the merchants.

The exports from the Port of London were as important as the imports, and included wool, leather, woolfels, lead, tin, worsteds, cheese, butter, feathers, gall, honey, felt, and tallow, but the greatest of them all was wool, which was turned into cloth by the weavers of France and Flanders. But in the first half of the century the ancient weaving industry of England having largely fallen into decay, foreign weavers were encouraged to settle in London in an effort to revive it. These people, however, besides having their disputes with the native weavers, could not always agree among themselves. An order from the Mayor is recorded in 1370 commanding the Flemish weavers to hold their guild meetings in the churchyard of St. Lawrence Pountney, and the

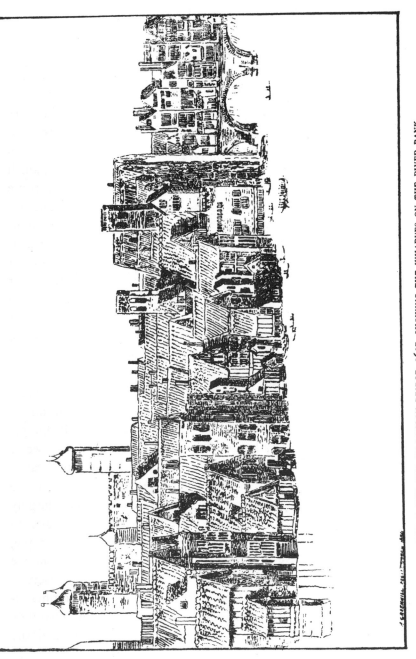

THE NORTH END OF LONDON BRIDGE, 1627, SHOWING THE WHARVES ON THE RIVER BANK

From a print in the Guildhall Library.

weavers of Brabant to hold theirs in the churchyard of
St. Mary Somerset, because when they held a joint
meeting it always ended in a fight. The great quantity
of wool passing outwards through the Port of London
may be gauged from the account of a loan of £5,000
made by the city to the King in 1370, repayment of
which was arranged to be made out of the customs on
wool, woolfels, and leather, granted to the King by the
Parliament of the previous year. The entire sum was
repaid between 16th June, 1370, and 1st January,
1371. After this time it became customary for the
city to recoup itself for loans to the King in this way,
but during Richard II's reign he used to deposit the
crown jewels with the citizens as additional security.
Thus we find him in 1377 for a loan of £5,000, which
was repaid between 6th October and 1st March following,
depositing two hoods embroidered with rubies, diamonds,
sapphires, and pearls ; two coronets to be worn on the
King's bacinet ; one girdle of gold ; one coat of cloth
of gold, buttoned with golden bells and embroidered
with large pearls around the collar and sleeves ; a
doublet of tawny satin, the sleeves similarly embroidered ;
circlets and silver plate. These were contained in two
" standardz ", two coffers called " panyars ", fifteen
leather cases, a wooden coffer bound with iron, and a
square coffer covered with black leather and bound
with iron ; all of which were locked and sealed with
the seals of the Bishop of London, the Bishop of Exeter
(Lord Treasurer), the Earl of March, Lord Latimer,
and Roger de Beauchaumpe. On another occasion,
towards the end of 1381, the King having borrowed
£2,000, and deposited a similar quantity of jewels,
begged for their return for the purpose of celebrating
his wedding, and offered in their place a " palet "—

probably a kind of headpiece—embellished with precious stones and known as the " palet of Spain ", valued at £1,708, which was accepted. On offering in 1383 one of the royal crowns as pledge for a loan, it is recorded that, before acceptance, the careful citizens appointed three expert jewellers to decide if it were of sufficient value.

In 1357 it was enacted by Parliament that a sack of wool was to contain 364 pounds, and at the same time the prices below which it might not be sold were fixed for the various counties, and ranged from 5 marks in Northumberland, Cumberland, and Westmorland, to 12½ marks in Hereford, the average being about 8 marks.

It was the custom in the middle ages for groups of merchants belonging to one district or country to trade as a company—working in co-operation—while each member dealt in his own goods and realised his individual profit. Many of these groups at various times were accorded special trading facilities in London, receiving permission to remain longer than the usual forty days and to live in houses of their own, and allowed certain remissions on the tolls usually exacted. Among these was a group composed of the merchants of three towns in France—Amiens, Corby, and Nestle—who paid an annual subsidy of 50 marks to the city, with which, however, they were frequently in arrear. Others were Italian merchants from Florence, such as the Scali, the Bardi, and the Peruzzi. The Scali had their house in the parish of St. Mary Woolnoth, and the Bardi theirs in the parish of Langbourne. These corporations often lent money to the King, and in this respect took the place of the Jews after their expulsion from England late in the 13th century. It is recorded that in 1345 the Bardi, as well as the Peruzzi, were brought to

bankruptcy owing to repudiation on the part of
Edward III.

Perhaps the most famous of these trading companies
was the Hanse, or Hanseatic League, who had their
headquarters at the "Steelyard", on the site of the
present Cannon Street railway station. They had the
right to elect their own alderman, and in 1381, during
the mayoralty of Sir William Walworth, they paid him
the compliment of electing him to that office, which he
accepted. They were engaged in the importation of
woad, timber, herrings, cheese, and horses. They paid
a duty of threepence on every tun of woad imported,
half of which went to the city, and half to the freemen
keeping hostel at which they lodged. In return for
their privileges they had the duty of keeping Bishopsgate
in repair and supplying part of the guard there. They
were, however, amenable to the ordinary law of the
city so far as the regulations relating to the quality and
make-up of goods were concerned. In 1378 one of
their number, with the appropriate name of Henry
Hydynghous, was found with false beaver skins, consisting of bellies mixed with half-bellies, hidden in his
cellar. Mixtures of this kind being contrary to the
rules of the mistery of Skinners, and to the law and
custom of the city, he was haled to the Guildhall, where
he protested that purchasers knew as well as he did how
the skins were made up. In consequence of this plea
he was spared imprisonment, and only part of the skins
were confiscated. But in those times the merchants
of the Hanse, equally with others, found it necessary
jealously to guard their privileges, for fear that otherwise
they might easily be lost. In 1386 they are found
expelling one of their own number for paying a larger
custom on merchandise than was right or necessary.

It may be that the citizens thought that such a man could ill be spared from their midst, for they promptly recompensed him by conferring on him the freedom of the city. When a foreign merchant owed money to the King, the latter claimed preferential treatment by forbidding other creditors of the merchant to proceed against him until his own claims had been satisfied. This was effected by letters of protection, which were issued to the foreigner by the King and had the effect of staying any action which might have been started against him.

In 1335 it was enacted by Parliament that all restrictions upon foreign traders should be removed throughout the Kingdom, any charters granted to cities and towns notwithstanding ; but two years later the King found it necessary to issue Letters Patent to the effect that London should be exempt from the application of this law because it was contrary to a clause of Magna Carta asserting the right of London to retain all its ancient rights and privileges unimpaired. This was not the end of the matter, for the controversy on this point raged throughout the rest of the century, with petitions to the King, fresh Acts of Parliament, civil commotion, and attacks on foreigners ; the citizens sometimes succeeding in asserting their rights, and at others being compelled to acquiesce in their temporary abeyance.

Trade between foreign and native merchants was conducted by the intermediary of brokers, who were elected by the members of the mistery they were to serve and presented to the Mayor for his approval. They were sworn not to trade on their own account, but only to introduce buyer and seller ; to faithfully convey money from one party to the other ; to warn the members of the trade of any false goods coming under their notice which were about to be offered for sale ; not to act for one alien selling goods to another, a form of trading strictly forbidden in the city ; not to accept commission in excess of the amount fixed by the Mayor ; not to permit any usurious bargain to be made ; and to faithfully guard in every way the interests of the trade they served. They were not allowed to " fore-stall ", or to go on behalf of their principals outside the city to meet and purchase goods on their way to London ; and if a broker introduced as buyer a person of no standing, on the latter's default he was responsible for the debt. If anyone not appointed ventured to act as a broker by introducing buyer and seller, even though it might concern a deal in goods of the trade to which he belonged, he was liable to lose the freedom of the city. Sometimes foreign merchants were appointed as brokers, and in this case they had to pay 40s. o. a year for the privilege, as against 20s. o. paid by freemen.

All goods brought into the city by foreigners had to be weighed at the official " beam ", or weighing machine, except such goods as corn, salt, or coal, which were considered more suitable for measuring ; but so far as transactions between citizens were concerned this does not appear to have been necessary, providing that the scales they used had been properly tested and sealed with the seal kept at Guildhall. There were two kinds of beam—the Great Beam or " Tron " for weighing heavy goods, such as wool, wax, almonds, rice, ironmon-gery, copper, tin, etc., and the Small Beam for lighter articles, such as spices and silk. Many other towns possessed similar weighing machines, and it had been the rule from Saxon times that all such scales, wherever located, should agree with the standard of London, where they were made, tested, sealed with the city's mark, and sent to any town which required them. Thus in 1298 the King ordered a Tron to be made in London for the town of Lynn in Norfolk, and again in 1307 one for Hull, for weighing wool. In the city an official weigher was appointed to operate the Great Beam, taking for his trouble a tariff of one penny for every ten hundredweight weighed, which he handed to the sheriffs for the benefit of the city, and one farthing a hundredweight as his personal fee. The Small Beam was usually let to farm, the weigher paying at first 10 marks annually for the privilege, afterwards increased to £10, and when the official complained of his inability to pay so much, reduced to £5, and later still to 50s. 0. It was customary to carry the Small Beam from place to place, wherever its services were required, but the Great Beam was, at the beginning of the century, situated in the churchyard of St. Mary Woolchurch Haw, and later removed to Woolwharf, and by 1392 it is found kept in a house called " la Herber " in Walbrook.

There was often considerable ill-feeling in the city between the foreign merchants and the buyers on account of the manner in which the weighing at the Great Beam was conducted. In early times, in the absence of any definite rules as to the number of pounds constituting a hundredweight, the weigher apparently could record almost any weight he pleased, and naturally the foreigners complained that favouritism was always shown to the citizens. At length, in 1257, at a great meeting of over 500 citizens, it was decided that 4 pounds in the hundred should always be given in favour of the buyer, an overweight which came to be known among the foreign merchants as the " courtesy of London ". Still, however, they continued to complain of unfairness on the part of the weigher, inasmuch as, by keeping his hands upon the machine, he would often

WEIGHING GOODS IN GROSS
From Cutts' "Scenes and Characters of the Middle Ages"

make the difference considerably more. In 1305, in answer to their representations, Edward I sent his writ to the Mayor, ordering him to see that in all such transactions the Beam should balance exactly, showing favour neither to one nor the other. The Mayor declined to accede to this, claiming the 4 pounds overdraught as one of the city liberties ; but in 1309, at a meeting of Mayor, aldermen, and merchants both native and foreign, it was agreed that a hundredweight of heavy goods should consist of 112 pounds, and a hundredweight of light goods weighed by the Small Beam of 104 pounds, the weigher removing his hands from the machine so that the balance should be exact.

In 1393 further trouble occurred with the foreign merchants, this time concerning the condition, or, as we should say, the " standardisation " of their goods. The grocers, who were, as their name, originally spelt " grossers ", implies, the great wholesale dealers of the period, petitioned the Mayor, praying that, on account of merchant strangers bringing to the city and selling in an uncleaned state such goods as pepper, ginger, cinnamon, etc., a rule should be made and enforced that no such merchandise should be sold until it had been " garbled " or sifted by a man appointed for the purpose by the grocers, and anyone selling such goods before " garbling " should forfeit to the Chamber double the weight of powder and dirt found therein. They further asked that no wax should be sold until it had been cleaned, under similar penalty. Later in the same year the foreign merchants came before the Mayor and suggested that if their spicery was to be garbled the same should apply to all merchants ; that the garbler should not be an interested party, either as buyer or seller ; and that, in the case of large consignments, a few parcels should be garbled and the amount of waste estimated accordingly for the bulk. All these requests being refused, the Grocers proceeded to present three of their number, from whom the Mayor chose one for the office, allowing him to take for his trouble for every bale of merchandise garbled 4d. from the vendor, and one penny for every piece of wax cleaned.

When one business man owed money to another, they came, under the law known as the Law Merchant, to the Guildhall before the Mayor and a clerk appointed by the King, though the presence of the latter seems often to have been dispensed with, and made recognisance of the debt, by which the debtor undertook to pay by a date named. This recognisance was enrolled in the city books, and a fee of twopence in the pound on the amount of the debt was charged. This practice, universal in early times, appears to have greatly diminished towards the end of the century, judging from the Chamberlain's receipts under this head. From Michaelmas 1365 to Michaelmas 1366 they amounted to only 7s. 6d., and the same in the following year. In 1367-8 they rose to 25s. 0., but in 1368-9 were down to 17s. 6d., and the following year to 10s. 0. If the debtor failed to pay by the date named, it was the duty of the Mayor to cause the sheriffs to seize and imprison him. After he had been in prison for some months and still failed to pay, the sheriffs appointed a jury of citizens to inquire into and value his goods and landed property. The former were confiscated to pay his creditors, and if they were insufficient his land or tenements were placed in possession of the creditors until the income derived from them had satisfied the debt. If the debtor had alienated any of his property after the recognisance of debt had been enrolled, such lease or sale was null and void, and the buyer or lessee was condemned to lose it ; but if the debtor had died in the meanwhile and his property had descended to a legal heir under age, it could not be touched, because a minor was considered incapable of defending his rights.   As debtors were in the habit of making over their property to others and flying to sanctuary, the Parliament of 1379 passed an Act by which they should be summoned at the church door once a week for five weeks, and failing to appear, their property should be seized for the benefit of the creditors, any collusive deed of gift notwithstanding.

In 1311 we have an early form of a Bill of Exchange, when a cordwainer, owing money to a draper, passed on to him a bond for £10 which he had received from another man, and registered the transfer at Guildhall. An enrollment of a recognisance of debt at Guildhall could be treated in the same way, the original creditor assigning it to others to whom he was debtor.   Promissory notes given by London merchants to foreigners in payment for goods purchased were sealed with the Common Seal of the city.

Next in order to the wholesalers came the retailers, great and small, from the opulent goldsmith to the poverty-stricken cobbler.   Notwithstanding the wealth amassed by some of the shopkeepers, such as goldsmiths, drapers, mercers, tailors, and fishmongers, it is surprising that some of the smaller fry succeeded in making a living. Whereas in 1398 we hear of a jeweller's shop on Cornhill the stock of which was valued at £600. 3s. 6d., in 1322 the entire possessions of a shopkeeper, trade not stated, in Bread Street, appraised on oath, consisted of two small pigs, valued at 3s. 0. ; one " shippingboard ", 3d. ; a broken chest and a table, 6d. ; a pair of worn linen sheets, 4d. ; and a blanket and a worn linen cloth, with other small articles, 2s. 9½d.   In the following year the possessions of a barber whose shop was situated near St. Dionis Backchurch, consisted of a brass bowl and pot, 2s. 6d. ; three old pans, 1s. 3d. ; a basin and ewer, 1s. 4d. ; a tin pitcher, 6d. ; five small dishes, 3s. 6d. ; four towels, 2s. 4d. ; a shirt, 4d. ; three old sheets, 1s. 6d. ; three blankets, 4s. 0. ; two silver rings, 2d.; three razors and a pair of forceps, 6d. ; a coffer, 8d. ; a chair and buffet, 9d.; and 7d. in cash ; while the entire stock-in-trade of a brewer was 100 flasks of beer worth 5s. 0., and a quarter of brewing barley, 4s. 0. ; and that of a cobbler, a piece of ox-leather valued at 10d., and twelve pairs of shoes made of inferior sheep's leather or " bazen " worth 4s. 6d.   Consistently with these figures, we find in 1383 a man starting a glover's shop on London Bridge with a capital of considerably less than £20.

The names of some of the retail trades connoted, in the 14th century, a somewhat different stock-in-trade to that of their representatives to-day.   The Mercers are a case in point, for they sold a list of articles more consistent with the modern trade of drapers, their ancient name now, though rarely used, being confined to dealers in silk.   " Jeweller " appears to have been the later name for the earlier " Paternosterer ", and their stock consisted largely of rosaries made of amber, jet, or silver gilt, with wooden or bone ones for the children ; and crucifixes.   Consistently with the custom of the times we find in 1375 a jeweller holding a stall beneath the gate of Ludgate, for which he paid a rental of 40s. 0. a year to the city.   The Merchant Tailors were originally known as Tailors and Linen Armourers, the latter department of their trade being a thriving one, as linen armour was universally worn by archers and light-armed troops. They received their charter from the King in 1390, granting them the right to elect a master and four wardens as often as they pleased ; but it was not until 1503 that the word " Merchant " was added to their title by Letters Patent.

Below the shopkeepers came the hawkers, or birlsters, who sold bread, beer, and most kinds of fish from door to door. The hawking of bread and beer was principally in the hands of women, and in the case of the former the baker allowed them thirteen loaves to the dozen, the odd one constituting their profit ; hence the term " baker's dozen ". Any kind of Thames fish could be sold from door to door for the convenience of the poor, while it was compulsory to sell in this way oysters, mussels, and salt fish. Eels were carried round the streets in buckets, from which they were sold. In 1326 there is an instance of a tragedy being caused in Cordwainer Street which started with the protest of an apprentice against the action of one of these hawkers who threw the slippery eel skins on to the pavement.

Lowest in the scale, perhaps, came the costers, who walked the streets with their cry of " costard apples for sale ", precisely as in the 18th century " Cries of London ". This appears from a case as early as 1301, when two men attempted to steal five apples from a coster in Gracechurch Street, and on being remonstrated with by a countryman, pursued him with jeering and abuse as far as Fenchurch Street, where, in exasperation, he turned and felled one of them with his staff.

An opportunity is occasionally afforded of viewing the actual profits resulting from business in the 14th century, and it will be observed that these fluctuated considerably according to the circumstances of the time. It was usual in the case of orphans under age for the

Mayor to entrust the money left to them to some substantial citizen with which to trade, an account having
to be rendered when the orphan came of age.   In 1374,
when a mercer presented such an account, it was found
that the profit on the original capital of £300 amounted
to 20 per cent. per annum, and after the expenses of
the youth's maintenance and education had been paid
the capital had nearly doubled in thirteen years.   By
the custom of the city the merchant was rewarded with
half the profit for his trouble.   In contrast with this a
case is recorded in 1354, only a few years after the
Black Death, which had ruined business for the time
being, where no merchant could be prevailed upon to
undertake the administration of the money of a minor.
Again, in 1335, a cry curiously reminiscent of one often
heard to-day comes to us, when, on the King requesting
the city to provide him with some troops at their own
expense, the sheriff replied expressing their willingness
to do so " notwithstanding trade being so bad ".

The banking system, as we understand it to-day, did
not exist in the 14th century, and a wealthy man usually
kept his entire floating capital in a locked chest in his
bedroom, from which fact it may be readily appreciated
that the punishment for the crime of burglary was
invariably hanging.   The most obvious method of
laying out capital was by the purchase of land or houses,
but in spite of the laws against usury, other methods
of investing money could be found.   The system,
described above, of investing the money of orphans was
sometimes resorted to by private capitalists, taking, in
the same way, half the profits of the venture ; but such
a transaction nevertheless was strictly a loan, and not
by any means a joint stock operation in the modern
sense, the merchant being fully responsible for the return

of the capital. That such partnerships were not reprobated by authority, at any rate in a commercial community such as London, may be gathered from the fact that agreements of the kind were sometimes openly registered at Guildhall. The proceeding appears, however, to have been somewhat furtive, as in an instance in 1310, when a merchant, having borrowed £40 for two years on the terms mentioned above, came again to Guildhall at the end of the period and paid back the capital in presence of the Mayor. No mention was made of the profits, but the borrower, as though by an afterthought, undertook to pay the sum of 49s. 6½d. which the lender owed to the corporation, if the latter failed to do so. It was sometimes possible to obtain interest on money by a roundabout method, as in 1284, when a man who owed £5 for rent agreed to become the landlord's servant for one year in addition to paying the arrears. The landlord thereupon sent him four casks of wine valued at £9 to sell on his behalf.

Throughout the middle ages usury, or the loan of money at interest, was considered immoral, and the laws against it were stringent. To administer them a court was held from time to time consisting of the Mayor, with two aldermen and four commoners, who by reputation must be incapable of themselves being tainted with this crime, and any man accused before this court was immediately arrested and confined to prison until his case was heard. He was not permitted to employ help in his defence, and, if convicted, was kept in prison until he had made full restitution to his victim, and had paid in addition, by way of a fine, a sum equivalent to that he had expected to make out of the bargain. Intermediaries in such bargains received for the first offence imprisonment for a year, and if convicted a second time

" they shall forswear the said city for ever, and shall be
" led through the city, with their heads uncovered,
" unshod and without girdle, upon horses without
" saddles ; and shall be so escorted from the middle
" of the place unto without one of the Gates of the said
" City : that so all others may be warned through
" them, and be the more abashed to commit such or
" other like knaveries ". It may be inquired what
exactly usury was, and we shall find that any interest
received for a loan was so regarded. The foregoing
quotation is from an ordinance of 1364, which, however,
fails to give a clear explanation of the nature of the
offence, but a decree of 1390 is more explicit and defines
it thus : " If any person shall lend or put into the
" hands of any person gold or silver, to receive gain
" thereby, or a promise for certain without risk (refer-
" ring to business risk), such person shall have the
" punishment for usurers in the said Ordinance con-
" tained ". That loans, if made, were expected to be
entirely free of interest is indicated by a case in 1376,
in which a man borrowed a sum of £10, and at the end
of the term tendered the nett amount to the lender.
The latter, on demanding £12, was prosecuted for
usury and fined the sum he had expected to make, namely,
£2, while the intermediaries, of whom there were two,
were imprisoned. In spite of these severe laws, in
claims for overdue debts the creditor was allowed
interest at the rate of 4s. 0. in the pound per annum,
but under the name of " damages ".

Another institution which we regard as absolutely
essential to business, and with which our ancestors were
totally unacquainted, is that of insurance, but the first
dawn of the idea seems to be implicit in the arrangement
by which, if a portion of a ship's cargo had to be jetti-

soned in order to save the remainder, the whole loss
was not allowed to fall upon the owner of the goods
thrown overboard, but had to be shared by the other
owners and also by the crew. For this purpose the
whole cargo was valued, the only things exempted being
the ship with its rigging, the ring on the captain's finger,
his neck-chain, belt, and silver cup, if he had one, and
the victuals of the sailors with the utensils to cook them
in. Even the money in the pockets of the crew and
passengers, and presumably the clothes they wore,
were included in the valuation, and the owner of the
vessel had to forego the freightage on the goods jettisoned.

The attitude of the citizens towards monetary problems
is nowhere better studied than in their methods of
public finance, by which, instead of paying debts directly
to a creditor, they would, on various occasions, pay
sums to third parties—creditors of the creditor—and
only after a period of years, when the accounts were
hopelessly involved, endeavour to reach a final settlement. For this reason the accounts of the famous fine
of 20,000 marks imposed on the city by Henry III in
1266 form a compendious budget. The city, although
submitting to the fine, betrayed no unseemly haste to
pay, but over a period of about thirty-five years remitted
sums of money to creditors of the King and his successor,
and eventually, in 1302, struck a bargain with Edward I
to pay him £1,000 to end the matter, though it is
noticeable that even this sum was not all paid by 1305.
One instance of a payment out of the 20,000 marks,
occurring in 1267, may be given. The Countess of
Flanders, during a dispute with Henry III, had seized
goods belonging to English merchants, and in retaliation
Henry confiscated 1,030 marks from merchants of
Ghent to distribute among his dispossessed subjects.

When peace was at length concluded he ordered the city to re-imburse the merchants of Ghent out of the sum they still owed him. However, by 1275 they appear to have paid only 730 marks of this, and then only because ten London citizens had been detained by the people of Ghent as security. This habit of procrastination in the payment of debts is frequently seen in the case of the sheriffs of London, whose accounts at the Exchequer often remained unsettled many years after their period of office had expired. Many of them suffered imprisonment before they would pay. The anxiety of the citizens, the whole body of whom were liable for the sheriff's debts, may be seen in 1311, when, a sheriff dying during his term of office, all his property was promptly taken into the city's hands until his accounts were settled. But if the King found it difficult to collect money owing to him by the citizens, the latter in their turn experienced at least equal trouble in re-imbursing themselves for money lent to the King, notwithstanding that they were supposed to stop it out of money due at the Exchequer for the " ferm " of London. In 1317 a loan of £1,000 was made to Edward II on these terms for the prosecution of the war in Scotland, and raised in small sums lent by various citizens. The Mayor started to repay these contributors piecemeal as money came in, but the process was so slow that in 1320 he called a meeting of creditors, at which it was proposed, in order to lessen the burdens of the city, that each of them should agree to forego half the amount he had subscribed. Not only was this agreed to, but it was also decreed that all those who had already been repaid, and all those who had not contributed, should be requested to pay a reasonable sum. It was perhaps the experience thus gained in the early part of the century which induced the citizens later on to stipulate that such loans should be repaid out of the customs on the security of the crown jewels. The previously mentioned method of paying debts is perhaps better illustrated by an instance in 1299, when the King owed £1,049. 13s. 11d. to certain Gascon merchants in London, who, in their turn, owed money to the citizens. The citizens on their part owed money to the King on the " ferm " of London, and so, instead of everybody collecting their debts directly, the King ordered the city to pay the citizen creditors of the Gascons up to the amount they owed on the " ferm." Presumably the citizen creditors handed acquittances to the Gascons, the Gascons to the King, and the King to the city.

The same methods may be noticed in the city's domestic finance. It is recorded in the early part of the century that four tax collectors of Tower ward, at the direction of the Mayor, had disbursed various sums of money on behalf of the commonalty, which they were supposed to deduct from the total amount they had collected. They appear to have become confused by such mixed dealings, and the authorities must have been in no better case, for in 1311 the Mayor and aldermen agreed to cry quits with them and to consider the matter ended. The length of time over which these transactions were spread may be gauged by the fact that one payment made by the tax collectors was in respect of cloth for liveries to be worn at the coronation of Edward II, an event which occurred in 1306. The method by which a King's tax was levied in the city— a tenth, a twelfth, or a fifteenth as the case might be— may be studied in the arrangements made in 1319 for raising the twelfth granted on the goods of the citizens. The assessors, or chief taxors, were appointed by the

King, and in the first place they summoned before them the wealthiest inhabitants of the city and required them to declare on oath the goods and assets they possessed, within their houses and without, at home and abroad, except income arising from foreign lands or tenements. They then called before them six or more men of substantial position from each ward, who had never before acted as taxors, to serve as collectors. These men were put upon oath to inquire fully what each citizen possessed and to inscribe the information thus acquired upon rolls under their seals, which they were to deliver to the chief taxors. These latter then carefully scrutinised the rolls to consider whether anything had been omitted either by accident or favour. The assessment of the sub-taxors was made by the chief taxors in conjunction with other citizens. The only property allowed to go tax free was a gown for the citizen and one for his wife, one bed for both, a ring and a bracelet of gold or silver, a girdle of silk for daily use, and one silver drinking-cup. Armed with these particulars, the chief taxors proceeded to levy the tax with all due dispatch. The amount collected on this occasion was £949. 11s. 6¼d. It will be observed that such taxes, unlike our modern income tax, were in reality a capital levy on the movable goods of the citizens, land and tenements only being excepted. The frequency of these imposts leaves one amazed that commerce could be carried on under such conditions, and it is not surprising to find that in 1322, when a further sixth on all movable goods was granted to the King by Parliament, the city begged him for some abatement of his demands, especially when it is remembered that in addition to supplying money the citizens at this time were continually raising troops at their own expense for the King's wars. The system of raising money by means of a poll tax was not resorted to until 1377, when 4d. per head was levied on everyone over fourteen years of age. The result proving unsatisfactory, a graduated poll tax was levied in 1379, the Mayor paying £4, each alderman £2, and so on down to the lowest ranks, among whom every person above the age of sixteen paid 4d. The result, recorded ward by ward, is an indication rather of their populousness than their wealth. Thus Farringdon ward, Within and Without, the largest in extent in the city, heads the list with £81. 11s. 5d., Cripplegate Within and Without comes next with £44. 18s. 6d., Chepe third with £40. 10s. 10d., and Lime Street, or " Farthingward ", last with £3. 1s. 10d., the total for all wards reaching £629. 18s. 8d.

A curious case, which throws light on the financial methods of the time, occurred in 1356, when the King accused three Londoners, who had been farmers of the customs, and therefore must have been men of some wealth, of pledging his crown to a foreign merchant for £4,000. The King does not state how they became possessed of it, but there can be little doubt that he had deposited it with them as security for a loan, and they, not having received the money, pledged it in their turn with the foreign merchant. Apparently this was regarded as a breach of the rules, and the King first heard of it when the foreigner, probably fearing for his own safety, voluntarily returned the crown to the King without demanding anything in return. In order to reimburse him the King ordered the Mayor to seize the property of the three citizens and hand it over to the foreign merchant. One more instance of city finance may be given, affording an extraordinary example of tergiversation on the part of the rulers of London.

A certain Sir Hugh de Hengham, who had been at one time Clerk of the " Jews' Exchequer ", had bequeathed the sum of 50 marks to one Juliana and her son Robert. As Robert was a minor, the executors brought his share of this sum (25 marks) to the Mayor, to be placed, as the custom was, in the hands of some merchant to trade with for the boy's benefit. When the boy shortly afterwards died, the Mayor, instead of paying the 25 marks to his mother, passed it on to the King's Treasurer " for the business of the city ", otherwise, towards paying the city's debts to the King. Afterwards, when Juliana claimed the money as her own it might be supposed that the Mayor would reimburse her out of the city's revenues. But no : there were certain citizens who, unable at the moment to pay their taxes, had handed in pledges to the Guildhall to be redeemed when they had more money. These were valued, and to the value of 25 marks handed over to the lady. They consisted of such a varied assortment of articles as washing-basins, blankets, brass plates, an andiron, knives, kettles, cups, saddle-bows, a pair of shears, and old clothes.

CHAPTER V

TRADE FIGHTS

THE fights between the trades in the 14th century, it is to be feared, are but one more indication, if such were needed, of the innate pugnacity of the citizens. This trait is strongly manifested in their personal relations, and no less so when they functioned in their corporate capacity ; and considering the difficulties to which they were constantly subject in their efforts to preserve their franchises and protect their trading rights against intruders, must be regarded as a notable triumph of passion over the law of self-preservation. When their bellicosity attained full swing the city must have presented a curious sight. We do not in these days expect to be confronted whilst upon our lawful occasions in the city with the sight of the hatters and the umbrella makers indulging in a scrimmage with swords and bucklers up and down Cheapside, or the fishmongers advancing with axes and quarterstaffs from Billingsgate to make an onslaught on the butchers of Smithfield. Yet this is the sort of thing which occurred on many occasions during the 14th century. The origin of these quarrels is often obscure, but on consideration appears to be the inevitable outcome of the system by which each trade was organised into a close corporation, with the consequence that wherever two or more trades overlapped, as must necessarily occur at times, acute jealousy would result. Unfortunately in many cases the records, while affording vivid details of the actual fighting, omit to go sufficiently deeply into the cause of the trouble. An instance of the overlapping of two trades may be observed in the long drawn out dispute between the Girdlers and the Saddlers, both of whom were makers of girdles, over the question of the metals with which they might be garnished. The articles of the Girdlers, confirmed by Letters Patent from the King as early as 1327, contained a clause forbidding the use of lead, pewter, or tin for this purpose. The Saddlers, taking exception to this rule, petitioned the King against it, with the result that sometimes a writ would be received for its abolition and sometimes for its enforcement. In 1356 the King left it to the decision of Parliament, and ordered four saddlers to attend to state their views. Another potent cause of troubles between the crafts is explained in the articles of the Spurriers, formulated in 1345 : " Many of the " said trade are wandering about all day, without working " at all at their trade ; and then, when they have become " drunk and frantic, they take to their work, to the " annoyance of the sick and of all their neighbourhood, " as well as by reason of the broils that arise between " them and the strange folks (i.e. non-freemen) who are " dwelling among them. And then they blow up their " fires so vigorously that their forges begin all at once " to blaze ; to the great peril of themselves and of all " the neighbourhood around. And then, too, all the " neighbours are much in dread of the sparks, which " so vigorously issue forth in all directions from the " mouths of the chimneys of their forges." [1] Happily in most cases the craftsmen exhibited sufficient common

[1] Riley's *Memorials*, pp. 226–7.

sense to submit their differences to the arbitrament of
the Mayor, a course pursued in disputes between the
Fullers and the Cappers, the Shoemakers and the Cobblers, and in 1356 between the two branches of the
Masons—the Hewers and the Light Masons or Setters
—who quarrelled as to the particular work of the trade
each branch should carry on. In this case the Mayor
ruled that any mason, providing he were competent,
should be allowed to undertake any work connected with
the craft, but in the case of a large contract it should
be his duty to find four or six ancient men of the trade
who would be willing to guarantee his competence, or,
in the alternative, to complete the work themselves.
The quarrel between the Cordwainers and the Cobblers
was due to the efforts of the former to prevent the latter
from dealing in any way in new leather, even to the
extent of forbidding them to patch old shoes with new
material. At one time the Cobblers complained to the
King that the wardens of the Cordwainers so disturbed
them that they were unable to make a living. At last,
however, in 1395, the Mayor got the parties to agree
that the Cobblers should be allowed to use new leather
for repairs and for no other purpose.

In quarrels between individuals the Mayor would
compel them to accept arbitration. An instance of this
may be observed in 1355, when two men had quarrelled
so seriously that one of them had been deprived of the
freedom, and the Mayor, calling them before him,
compelled each to appoint two representatives, who,
with himself as umpire, settled the dispute in thirteen
days. Between large bodies of men, however, this
process was more difficult, and the curious manner in
which the members of a trade or of allied trades would
make common cause may be seen from a writ of the

King to the Mayor in 1320, in which it is stated that
Bakers, Taverners, and Millers had been going about
the city at night assaulting wayfarers with swords and
bucklers, and other weapons. Curiously enough, so
far as the records show, a few trades only were concerned
in these outbreaks, and we can only speculate as to why
it was that butchers, barbers, or blacksmiths should
consistently display the kindlier human feelings, while
saddlers, goldsmiths, and fishmongers were subject to
periodical gusts of homicidal rage, leading to battle,
murder, and sudden death up and down the city. The
Fishmongers, for their part, were always foremost in
the fray, and even down to recent times Billingsgate
has been proverbial for the fierce retort to slight provo-
cation, a condition indicating an essentially bellicose
mentality. However, this is a question rather for the
psychologist than the historian.

Stow makes brief mention of a fight between Goldsmiths and Tailors as early as 1268, in which many men
were slain ; but it is learned from an old city chronicle
that the two trades mentioned were supported on one
side or the other by the Parmenters, or dealers in
broadcloth, and the Tawyers, or workers of fine leather ;
and between them a body of 500 men was able to fill
the city with noise and bloodshed for three nights in
succession before they could be suppressed. Thirty
of them were arrested by the sheriffs and imprisoned
in Newgate and afterwards put on trial before one of
the King's Justices. The jury does not appear to have
convicted any of them of actual murder or maiming,
but pronounced thirteen of them, including a parmenter
at whose house they had assembled, guilty of complicity,
and these were hanged as an example to all. The
origin of a quarrel between Goldsmiths and Saddlers

in 1325 appears to be unknown. On the night of Sunday, 10th November, shortly after curfew, twelve goldsmiths were parading West Chepe waiting to catch any saddlers who might chance along in order to beat them. When they met a solitary saddler opposite the Great Cross " the beating " was performed by three of them with a sword, an axe, and a staff. One struck him on the head with the sword, inflicting a wound 7 inches long and 3 inches deep, the second proceeded to chop off his leg with the axe, and as he lay on the ground the third belaboured him with the staff. Notwithstanding these wounds he lingered until the following Thursday, receiving his ecclesiastical rights, but no medical attention, and meanwhile five of the gang were captured and conveyed to Newgate, the others making their escape. In the following year an affray occurred near Aldersgate between two rival parties of law apprentices, and the only casualty reported on this occasion is that of a skinner, apparently a mere onlooker, who suffered death at the hands of a gentleman who stood at a neighbouring window and amused himself during the commotion by shooting an arrow indiscriminately among the crowd.

We are favoured with full details of one of these disputes arising in 1327 between the Saddlers on the one side, and the Joiners, Painters, and Loriners on the other. The three last mentioned were trades subsidiary to that of the Saddlers, performing parts of the work which went to make the completed saddle and harness ; the Loriners, who were divided into Coppersmiths and Ironsmiths, making the small metal fittings. The trouble seems to have had its origin in an attempt by the Saddlers to compel the others to work exclusively for them, and not to accept orders from outside the

saddlery trade. When considerable feeling had been
aroused by the dispute, culminating in a fight between
two individuals, six well-disposed persons from either
side endeavoured to make peace, and appointed a
" love-day " to be held at St. Paul's on 19th May,
hoping that both sides would feel inclined, in the
atmosphere of the church, to become friends once again.
The Saddlers afterwards accused the others of turning
the " love-day " into a day of hostilities by arriving at
St. Paul's armed with swords and other weapons and
incontinently attacking them. We are not told whether
they remained up all night to fight, but certain it is they
were fighting all next day, 20th May, up and down
West Chepe, in the " strete of Crepelgate ", and other
places. Many were killed and several more mortally
wounded, and they did not cease until the Mayor and
aldermen turned out in person to separate them. When
they appeared at Guildhall on the following Friday to
explain their conduct, the Joiners, Painters, and Loriners
accused the Saddlers of owing them £297. 9s. 4d. for
work done, and said that when any one of them attempted
to collect that part of the sum owing to himself he was
met with insults and blows. They further complained
that the Saddlers bought old saddles from the palfreymen
of the nobles, and polished them up for resale as new
saddles, thus not only deceiving the public, but depriving
the three trades of their legitimate profit. To the first
count the Saddlers made the rather lame excuse that
if they owed so much the others could sue them in the
courts, but to the second charge they pleaded guilty and
promised not to offend again. The Mayor, at his
wit's end to know how to settle the dispute, ordered six
of his aldermen to hold a meeting of all the parties
concerned at St. Martin-le-Grand on the following

Sunday, when, however, such a multitude of people put in an appearance and raised such a hubbub that the aldermen, unable to make themselves heard, dismissed the meeting. Afterwards a committee of twelve men, six from either side, was appointed, who, after several adjournments, arrived at a settlement, the Saddlers agreeing to treat the others fairly in future, under a penalty of 20 tuns of wine, 10 to be paid to the Joiners, Painters, and Loriners, and 10 to the city authorities.

A dispute with a more tragic ending occurred in 1340 between the Skinners and the Fishmongers, culminating on 1st August of that year in fights in various parts of the city. At one which took place in Walbrook a fishmonger named Ralph Turk was killed with a poleaxe, and in another, near London Bridge, the Mayor, who, with his aldermen, had personally gone into the streets to quell the tumult, was attacked with a drawn sword by a fishmonger named Thomas Haunsard, who seized him by the throat and would have struck him on the neck had he not been overpowered. In the same affray a porter so badly wounded a serjeant of the city that for a time his life was despaired of. These two rioters were afterwards tried and condemned at Guildhall, and beheaded in Chepe. The jury summoned to the inquest on Ralph Turk seemed so undecided that the sheriffs took the unusual course of summoning two separate juries to sit on succeeding days, composed of " the best, richest, and wisest men of the mistery " of each of the trades. Later on the King sent a letter to the Mayor and citizens commending their prompt and decisive action, and ending curiously enough with threats of what he would have done to the city had it been otherwise. The matter did not end here, however, for the bad feeling is found continuing between the two trades for some years afterwards. In 1343 a meeting of all the principal members of both trades was convened at Guildhall by the Mayor with the object of settling terms of peace between them, and as late as March 1346 a writ was received from the King ordering the Mayor to put down any disturbances which might have arisen in consequence of his predecessor's action six years previously.

The end of the century witnessed the grand climax of the quarrels between the trades, and, divided into two groups—the victualling and non-victualling trades —they kept the city in a turmoil for years, identified themselves with one or the other political party striving for predominance in the kingdom, and did not stop short at promoting fines, confiscations, imprisonment, and even executions among their opponents. The dispute which agitated the London misteries during the period under review centred largely around the question as to what restrictions ought to be imposed upon grocers, butchers, and fishmongers from outside the city who brought their goods in to sell in competition with citizen members of those trades. The many obligations imposed upon those who obtained the freedom of the city, some of which have been explained in a previous chapter, seemed to the victualling trades of London to furnish sufficient reason why they should be placed in a privileged position, and why outsiders who competed with them without incurring these duties and expenses should have this advantage neutralised by countervailing restrictions. Those trades, on the other hand, such as goldsmiths, drapers, saddlers, etc., who were not concerned with selling food, but only with buying it, contended that a cheap and continuous supply from outside was the first necessity of the city, and accused their opponents of

1. BAKER
2. BOOTMAKER
3. WEAVER
4. BUTCHER

From Turner's "Domestic Architecture"

requiring restrictions on non-freemen merely for the sake of raising prices and lining their own pockets.

Already in 1365 what were probably the first rumblings of the storm were heard when a murderous attack was made upon a fishmonger in Bridge Street by seven men armed with " swords, knives, staves, and divers other " arms ". The assailants were said to have been instigated by four leaders of the free fishmongers, one of whom became Mayor in 1386, and it was only when four surgeons certified that the victim was in no danger of death that two of them were admitted to bail. The King himself sent a writ to the Mayor and sheriffs to take sureties from a number of fishmongers not to molest the man in future, but it may be seen how much there was to choose between the parties by a further writ from the King ordering sureties to be taken from the injured man and two others for their good behaviour towards another fishmonger. The touchiness of the citizens at this time and the watchful eye with which the King viewed the course of events is indicated in the prosecution of a fuller of Cornhill for spreading reports of a conspiracy against the chief men of the city. The King suggested that if the reports proved unfounded they should make an example by punishing the man in the manner appropriate to a liar. He was sentenced accordingly to stand on the pillory with a whetstone suspended from his neck by a chain.

The contemplation of the condition of the city at this period leads us to reflect how little the underlying motives which actuate humanity have changed ; it is only the methods we adopt to outwit our antagonists which have undergone modification in accordance with the milder sentiments of the modern age. These ancient quarrels may well be likened to certain aspects of the fiscal problem in our own times, where we see some commercial interests, after voting for and advocating free trade in order to make sure of obtaining cheap food from abroad, issue advertisements in which they adjure their fellow countrymen to buy British-made goods for patriotic reasons, thus, in effect, asking for protection for themselves while denying it to everyone else. The resemblance here suggested seems justified by the speech in defence of the fishmongers by Nicholas Extone, himself a member of the trade, delivered in the Parliament of 1382. He stated that non-freemen fishmongers were able to come to the city with fish and there cut it up and sell it piecemeal, and if this were to be permitted it seemed to him useful and profitable for the city that strangers should be allowed to sell any other merchandise piecemeal by retail. His opponents—drapers, mercers, goldsmiths, etc.—comment on this that it sounded contrary to the liberties of the city and a manifest injury to all the citizens. The latter trades it is true would not tolerate any interference by outsiders so far as their own business was concerned. This may be seen in the articles of the Haberdashers, formulated in 1371, where they give as reason for their objection to non-freemen that the latter compete with them, but bear no charge within the city.

There were other matters agitating the minds of the citizens at this time, which were dragged into the inter-trade quarrels, and were coloured by their attitude towards the controversy over free trade in victuals. These included the question as to whether the citizens should be compelled to choose one trade and adhere to it, or whether they might change their trade at will ; whether foreign merchants should be allowed to live and trade in the city as freely as citizens themselves ;

and whether the Common Council should be elected by the wards or by the misteries. It is necessary to explain the history of this body at some length, for to it is directly due most of the troubles which assailed the city during the next few years. By reason of the new constitution of the council the most powerful trades were enabled to place their own representatives in the mayoral seat, and thus the curb of authority which would otherwise have been placed upon their rivalries was enlisted in support of one party or the other. The Common Council was a gradual growth from early times, originating in the system by which the Mayor and aldermen, when important questions affecting the citizens in general were under discussion, called to their counsel the more prominent men of the city. To attend such summonses was one of the duties of citizenship, but being at first somewhat informal, it resulted that many men sent for failed to attend. In course of time it was arranged that the most prominent citizens should be definitely selected to attend on all such occasions instead of being called haphazard at the discretion or whim of the Mayor and aldermen. It was a matter of course that each alderman should bring the men from his own ward, and equally a matter of course that they should be selected at the meeting of the Wardmote over which he presided, and thus it came about by natural process that the Common Council of the city, as it came to be called, should be elected by the wards. But in 1351 a sudden change occurred. All this time the various trades or misteries had been growing in power and importance, and in that year it was resolved by the Mayor and aldermen, each of whom was himself a member of some mistery, that the election should rest with those bodies. Many citizens, and not only those, probably few, who were disfranchised thereby, viewed with grave concern this departure from custom, dependent as it was upon the growing political influence of organisations formed for industrial or trading purposes pure and simple.   In the same way to-day we see many working men who, although perfectly loyal to their Trade Union so far as it performs the function of settling questions arising in its particular industry, nevertheless strongly resent its usurpation of political functions by selecting parliamentary candidates and expecting its members to contribute to the support of one party in the state.

The system of electing the Common Council by the trades thus caused immediate dissension in the city, so much so that it was continued only in the following year, 1352, after which it was abandoned in favour of the former method, and no more is heard of it until 1376.   During the intervening years, however, it seems likely that the agitation was still going on and the two factions preparing themselves for the inevitable conflict, for in 1371 we find the King ordering the Mayor, sheriffs, recorder, aldermen, and four men from each of the misteries to appear before him at Guilford.   Two days before the appointed time they sent the recorder and William Walworth to Guilford to beg the King to receive a few selected men instead of the full number, as the civic authorities feared for the government of the city and the preservation of the peace.   The King, however, would not accede to this, and so the full number were sent with the exception of a few of the aldermen. The King thereupon compelled them all to swear to maintain the peace of the city to the utmost of their power, and ordered them to exact a similar oath from all the commonalty.   This was on a Thursday, and on the following Monday the King caused twelve citizens to be arrested and sent to the Tower, among whose names may be recognised some who afterwards became prominent as leaders of the non-victualling trades. At the same time an effort was made to prevent citizens wearing arms in the streets, and strangers visiting the city were put under the same obligation. Hostelers, as the keepers of inns or lodging houses were called, were compelled to warn their guests of this, and the latter were ordered to leave their arms and armour in charge of the host during their stay. In 1372 a stranger in the city, walking abroad wearing a knife, had it seized by the authorities, whereupon the Mayor called upon the hosteler where he lodged to come to the Guildhall to redeem it, but he, failing to do so and treating the Mayor's summons with contempt, was arrested and committed to prison.

In 1376 a fillip was given to the ambitions of the misteries by the revelations of corruption and " graft " in the city made in the " Good Parliament ". Richard Lyons, the farmer of the three taverns where sweet wines were allowed to be sold, and two others were prosecuted, and on account of the evidence given at their trial a proposal was made in this Parliament to abolish the mayoralty and put in its place an official of the King, a proposal which might have been carried but for the vigorously expressed opposition of the re-doubtable John Philpot. It was doubtless the danger of losing their franchises which caused the commotion among the citizens in obedience to which the Mayor called a great council at the Guildhall. The chief complaint appears to have been that the Mayor and aldermen did not sufficiently take the people into their confidence when issuing ordinances or making grants of public

property.   As it may be observed from formal accounts
of proceedings recorded in the Letter-Books, that for
many years past the rulers of the city had constantly
called in the principal citizens to their counsels, and as
the subsequent resolutions of this meeting of 1376 were
come to by the members of forty-one misteries, it is
reasonable to suppose that the complaints of this year,
said to have been made by the " Commonalty ", were
in reality engineered by these trades in their determination to obtain the chief power.   This is borne out by
the sequel, for the result of their deliberations was the
reform of the Common Council by electing it from the
misteries instead of from the inhabitants of the wards.
Their first act was the deposition from their aldermanries
of the three men impeached in Parliament, and the
election of their successors.   They founded their next
decision on that clause in the city charters which permitted them to remedy any defects in their customs
when found necessary without reference to any superior
authority, thus giving the new dispensation the appearance of strict legality.   It was then resolved that once
every year the surveyors of each sufficient mistery should
call their members together to elect from two to six
representatives, according to the importance of the craft,
and have the men so chosen ready to present to the
new Mayor on his assumption of office as the Common
Council for the year.   These also should be the only
citizens to take part in the election of Mayor and
sheriffs.   On 9th August forty-seven misteries re-assem-
bled at Guildhall and presented the names of those they
had chosen to form the new council, and an opportunity
is thus afforded of observing the relative importance
of the trades.   We find that nine out of the forty-seven
returned six members each—the Grocers, Mercers,

Drapers, Fishmongers, Goldsmiths, Vintners, Tailors, Skinners, and Smiths—all the others electing two, three, or four. The new council then proceeded to take the following oath : " You sware that you will " readily come when summoned for a Common Council " of the city unless you have lawful and reasonable " excuse, and good and lawful counsel shall you give " according to your understanding and knowledge, and " for no favour shall you maintain an individual benefit " against the common weal of the city, preserving for " each mistery its reasonable customs. And when you " shall so come, you shall not depart without reasonable " cause or leave the Mayor, or before the Mayor and " his fellows have departed ". At the same time they were exempted during their term from serving on inquests or juries, or as collectors or assessors of tallage. These events occurred during the mayoralty of John Wade, a grocer, but not a strong partisan.

In October 1376 Adam Stable, a mercer, was elected, but in March 1377 deposed by the dying Edward III at the instigation of John of Gaunt, and Nicholas Brembre, a grocer and the champion of the victualling trades, elected in his stead. During Stable's mayoralty, in response to a petition from the citizens, the King agreed to forbid retail trading by non-freemen and to place restrictions on their wholesale trading, subject to confirmation by Parliament. This burning question suffered considerable vicissitudes at this period, the restrictions upon outsiders being confirmed by the Parliament of 1377, repealed again in October 1378, re-enacted by Charter in 1383, but lost once more by Statute in 1388. On their confirmation in 1377 Brembre caused them to be publicly proclaimed in the city. He followed this in 1378 by sending a precept

to the Grocers, Mercers, Drapers, Fishmongers, Goldsmiths, Skinners, Ironmongers, and Vintners, ordering
them to make search for merchants, non-freemen and
aliens, bringing merchandise connected with their
misteries into the city, and to return their names to
the Guildhall. These trades accordingly appointed
" searchers " who swore to see that no stranger should
sell by retail, that all foreigners should dispose of their
merchandise within forty days, and that such non-
freemen should lodge and board only with free hostelers,
and should not sell goods to one another. The free
Weavers of London probably thought this a favourable
opportunity to get rid of the foreign Weavers from
Flanders and Brabant, with whom they had lived side
by side for years, and who possessed a recognised standing
in the industry ever since they had been introduced by
Edward III early in his reign. The Common Council
had appointed a committee to hear grievances presented
by the misteries, and to these they brought their complaint, saying that foreign Weavers were for the most
part exiled from their own country as notorious malefactors, and were unwilling to place themselves under
the rule of the free Weavers, requesting that such should
no longer be allowed to meddle with their trade. In
this case, however, in view of the many years during
which the foreigners had enjoyed their privileges, the
committee cautiously resolved to wait until one of the
foreigners should be convicted of some default or deceit
before placing them under the rule of the free Weavers.

Brembre's new policy was not inaugurated without
opposition from members of the non-victualling party
and troubles among the trades they represented. As
early as May 1377 it had been found necessary to remove
five members from the Common Council—a draper,

two mercers, a goldsmith, and a tailor. The charge
brought against them was that they had betrayed the
secrets of the council and had been remiss in their
duties. On a Sunday in March 1378, while the Bishop
of Carlisle was preaching in St. Paul's churchyard, his
sermon was rudely interrupted by a rush of wounded
men fleeing from Chepe, where a desperate fight was
proceeding between the Goldsmiths and Pepperers, or
Grocers, and no little alarm was caused among the
congregation until the Mayor and aldermen arrived to
restore order. Unfortunately this affair led to the
unusual spectacle of friction between the Mayor and
one of the sheriffs, Nicholas Twyford, a prominent
goldsmith. A servant of the sheriff, accused of being
one of the chief movers of the strife, was arrested by
order of the Mayor, which so angered the sheriff that,
making very rude remarks to the city's chief magistrate,
he was arrested in his turn. To decide such a serious
matter a meeting of the Common Council was called,
who were for ejecting the sheriff from his office, but
happily it ended with apologies and sureties given by
the offender. In August of the same year the house
of a fishmonger in the " street within Ludgate ", probably Bowyer Row, now Ludgate Hill, was forcibly
entered by eight men, among whom may be recognised
a tailor, a skinner, and a sheather, and he and his family
turned out into the street and refused re-admission,
until the Mayor appeared on the scene and caused the
invaders to be arrested.

About the same time an affair with more serious
effects, so far as the rulers of the city were concerned,
was an attack made on the servants of Thomas of
Woodstock, an uncle of the King, by a party led by
one John Maynard, a wax-chandler. The uncles of

Richard II were patrons of the non-victualling party by
reason of their mutually Wycliffite tendencies. For this
affair Brembre was impeached in the Parliament held
at Gloucester in October 1378, when he stoutly defended
his conduct, but at last, for the sake of peace, agreed to
pay the Earl an indemnity of 100 marks. The Common
Council were so pleased with his conduct on this occasion,
as related to them by the city members on their return,
that they resolved to indemnify him for all his expenses
connected with the affair. But over this affray the
citizens were subjected to loss of another kind, for,
owing to the disturbed state of the city, many great
lords departed and others stayed away, causing much
loss of trade to victuallers and hostelers. In the
emergency thus created the authorities could see nothing
else for it than a resort to bribery. As at the time
there was no money in the Chamber (the city's treasury)
they called for subscriptions, which were to be regarded
not as gifts, but as loans, and were to be repaid out of
the profits of the Chamber and the receipts from
deodands. The subscriptions amounted to little more
than £350, and among the names of the contributors is
found an early mention of Richard Whittington. A
proper account of the expenditure of this money was
made by the Chamberlain, but unfortunately it has not
come down to us. A list of the recipients would have
been most instructive, but all the information we are
vouchsafed is that, combined with diligence and work
on the part of certain good folk of the city, it was instru-
mental in making good accord between the lords and
the city. Probably to this period belongs the incident
mentioned by Stow, when John of Gaunt, coming to
Tower Royal, now a turning off Cannon Street, to eat
his oysters, was surrounded by a hostile mob of Londoners,

and rose from the table so hastily as to hurt both his legs against the form. Without waiting to drink the proffered cup of wine he made his exit by a back gate, and reaching his boat on the Thames, never stopped rowing until he arrived safely at the manor of Kennington.[1]

During the next three years, under the administration of wise and impartial Mayors, although themselves members of the victualling trades, we hear little of troubles between the misteries. The first of these was the famous John Philpot, without doubt the most public-spirited and patriotic man of his time. He was elected in October 1378 and straightway commenced the process of reform and conciliation. He made the bakers of the city swear, among other things, to refrain from mixing bad meal with good, and to see that their servants worked well at kneading the dough ! He ordered the aldermen to inquire into the misdeeds of bakers, brewers, hostelers, masons, carpenters, tilers, and other labourers. In November 1378 he arrested and imprisoned a clerk for using abusive words of John of Gaunt, and in the same month appointed a man to superintend the making of bread, and fixed the prices of various commodities. He formed a committee with himself at its head to consider carrying the Conduit as far as the cross-roads at the top of Cornhill, repairing the walls, ditches, and gates, providing places where the city rakers could deposit rubbish and filth, and raising money to pay off the city's debts. For these purposes the committee resolved to summon the principal men of the wards and endeavour to persuade them to make free gifts

[1] Walsingham, in his account of what is obviously the same incident, says that John of Gaunt was at St. Paul's defending Wycliff against the Bishop of London. The only chronicler, so far as I know, who lends any colour to Stow's version is Adam of Usk, who says that John of Gaunt fled from his table, without specifying where the table was. Whether it was possible to be accommodated with a table in Old St. Paul's I do not know.

according to their means, and to cause an assessment to be made of the wealth of those who refused. They also agreed to inquire if some better means could be found for raising money than a tax on victuals sold in the city. The Mayor also caused an inquisition to be held to discover persons who had obstructed the course of law by maintenance and champerty in the Court of Guildhall since the death of Edward III, at which time a general pardon to such had been granted. The names of over sixty people were returned as being guilty of this offence, among whom may be recognised some who afterwards appear as supporters of John Northampton, the leader of the non-victualling party. Among all these distractions he still found time to fit out a fleet to scour the seas surrounding the South of England to free them from pirates. By John Philpot's untimely death in 1384 the citizens lost their best friend and a truly great man, by whose work and influence many of the troubles of subsequent years might have been avoided. He lies buried in Christ Church, Newgate Street, but a perpetual monument to his memory exists in the name of Philpot Lane, where his residence was situated.

The next year, that of John Hadlee's mayoralty, seems to have been fairly peaceful and uneventful, but in that of his successor, William Walworth, fresh troubles came upon the city, which proved that the quarrels and bickerings of the trades, though latterly little apparent, were all the time smouldering beneath the surface. It is noticeable that both Hadlee and Walworth entertained doubts of the propriety of the new method of election to the Common Council, for the former in his year caused it to be elected from the misteries and wards jointly, while the latter, in April

1381, on occasion of deciding upon a new seal for the city, ignored the council altogether, and called instead a meeting of aldermen, ex-aldermen, and the prominent men from each ward to decide the matter. In June 1381 the invasion of Wat Tyler came upon the city like a thunderbolt. The details of this affair, belonging as they do to the general history of the reign, need not be entered into here, except in so far as they affect the subject of the present chapter. The city must have suffered a dreadful forty-eight hours, with executions, burnings, and evictions, and when it was over the discovery was made that the rebels had been admitted and even welcomed by three aldermen, all members of the victualling group, traitors alike to the city and their party. Their motive is buried in obscurity, but may perhaps be inferred from two facts—one that the rebels during their occupation of the city made a special point of searching out and killing foreigners, who, as we have seen, were particularly obnoxious to that party which stood for the maintenance of the trading privileges of the citizens ; and the other that Tyler's followers made an attempt to burn a mysterious book called *Jubile*, kept at the Guildhall, the existence of which is unlikely to have been known to them unless they had been informed of it by people within the city. The method they adopted of distinguishing foreigners, and more particularly Flemings, is too good to be missed. We have it on the authority of an old chronicle that they stopped likely looking pedestrians and ordered them to pronounce " Bread and Cheese ", and those who mispronounced it " Brode and Case " were thereby assumed to be aliens.[1] Altogether nearly 200 people were accused of complicity, but to their honour be it

[1] Kingsford's *Chronicles*, p. 15.

said there is no suggestion of sedition at this time against any prominent member of the non-victualling interest. Perhaps it was the popular dissatisfaction caused by the conduct of the three aldermen which was responsible for the dramatic change which brought Northampton to power in October 1381, after the victualling group had been in office for four years and seemed firmly seated in the saddle.

The tendency of Northampton's policy is exhibited in the method he adopted of exacting an oath of fealty to the King and to the city liberties from the people. In June 1381, immediately after the rebellion, such an oath being required, was, at the order of Walworth, exacted by each alderman from the inhabitants of his ward, but when Northampton in March 1382 required the same, he summoned the citizens to Guildhall mistery by mistery to take the oath. Immediately upon his assumption of office he proceeded to reverse some of the judgments of his predecessors and to issue ordinances for the government of the city in accordance with the ideas of his party. He caused the sentence of expulsion against the five members of the Common Council, passed in 1377, to be annulled. He regulated the sale of herrings and oil, and decreed that women of loose character should wear rayed hoods and use no fur. He ordered bakers to produce a farthing loaf and brewers to produce a farthingsworth of ale in measures stamped with the letter F to indicate their value, for, as he stated, he deemed ale equally necessary for the poor as bread. For these purposes he caused to be coined at the Tower £80 worth of farthings, which he distributed among bakers and brewers so that they should have no excuse for refusing change for a halfpenny. Furthermore, because parsons of the city churches had in the past refused such small contributions as a farthing, he ordained that henceforth no one attending a vigil for the dead or similar ceremony should give any larger coin for a mass, and if the parson could not, or would not, give change for a halfpenny, the worshipper should leave without giving anything. This Mayor was also not without a sense of humour. It was he who, as narrated in a previous chapter, solemnly sentenced an alderman to entertain him (the Mayor) and his fellow aldermen to dinner as a penalty for appearing improperly dressed on a Whit-Monday. He made stringent regulations as to the sale of foodstuffs, directed mainly against the fishmongers. He forbade them to enter into partnership with any non-freemen in the ownership of fishing vessels or nets, although they were at liberty to become entire owners of these. They were forbidden to keep any salted or cured fish in stock without offering it freely for sale. As justification for these regulations he appealed to ancient charters and ordinances in which the substance of them would be found. He obtained confirmation of them in the Parliament of 1382, but at the urgent request of Brembre, when he regained power, they were repealed in 1383. The latter, nevertheless, issued a proclamation that outside fishmongers were still to be allowed to sell their fish freely in the city. Northampton now, supported apparently by the Common Council, accused the free fishmongers of evading the ordinances by diverting fish from London to the country, and preventing strangers selling fish in London except through themselves. The bailiff of Southwark, himself a fishmonger, was accused of detaining the fish belonging to strangers so that it arrived too late for the market, and he was dismissed from his office. In future all fish coming to London from that direction was not to be unloaded in Southwark, but to be taken straight through to Cornhill, the Stocks Market, and Chepe. It appears that the free fishmongers had been sufficiently powerful to prevent outside fishmongers from standing in the Stocks Market, but at this time the former were ordered to permit them to do so " as of old accustomed ". The non-freemen were ordered not to sell any fish to the free fishmongers, but only direct to the public. The free fishmongers were next ordered to surrender their charters at Guildhall on the plea that, in 1377–8, when all the other misteries had done so, they had escaped. It must be said that no such surrender is previously recorded in the Letter-Book. A raid was then made upon them in the matter of the size of their baskets, large numbers of which were seized and burnt for being of short measure, and the fish they contained confiscated. In the Letter-Book a great parade is made of all the prominent men who inspected these measures and approved of the action taken. A fishmonger, Nicholas Extone, who was also an alderman, ventured to criticise the Mayor, and then absented himself from the meetings at Guildhall, and for this he was discharged from his office, a measure with which he sarcastically expressed himself in full agreement. Another alderman who supported the cause of the free fishmongers went to the Stocks Market and roundly abused and cursed the non-freemen, shouting that he would rather a freeman should make twenty shillings out of him than one of them twenty pence. For this offence he was degraded from all his dignities. Another ebullition of temper was displayed by a free fishmonger who bought herrings in Billingsgate for twenty-two a penny, and, going to the Stocks Market, mingled with the crowd of non-freemen and proceeded to cry them at the high price of six a penny. This effort to discredit his adversaries was rewarded with an hour's detention on the pillory on Cornhill with the herrings suspended from his neck. Pursuing the same policy, a large quantity of fish belonging to a free fishmonger was seized and condemned as bad by a jury of five cooks, a fishmonger, and several other men described as " good and " experienced men of the city ". Reginald atte Chaumbre, the owner of the fish, was sentenced to stand on the pillory for one hour on six consecutive market days, but as he held some office under the King the sentence was respited until the latter's wishes should be known.

In October 1382 John Northampton was re-elected for another year under curious and unusual circumstances. A week before the election the King addressed a letter of Privy Seal to the sheriffs, aldermen, and commoners of the city pointing out that his re-election would be agreeable to him, as he had heard well of him, at the same time disclaiming any intention of interfering with the free election by the citizens. On 13th October, the day of the election, another letter was received from the same source addressed to Northampton, begging him to accept office if he should be re-elected. This was publicly read before the proceedings started, and seems to have decided the matter ; Northampton was returned and accepted office " on account of his " reverence for the King ". A nice piece of jobbery this, in which may be seen the hand of John of Gaunt, the patron of the Mayor, who thus saved him from defeat at the hands of the exasperated victuallers.

In his second year of office he continued to persecute the fishmongers, and endeavoured to stifle all criticism of his policy. He imprisoned one of the hated trade

for speaking contemptuously of him, although within
the four walls of a private house ; and the details of the
case furnish an excellent example of the methods both
of vituperation and praise employed by partisans of the
period. The fishmonger opened the conversation by
remarking to his friends that the Mayor had falsely and
maliciously deprived the members of his trade of their
livelihood, and extolled the conduct of Nicholas Extone
by saying that they were all bound to place their hands
under his feet for his championship of their cause.
Another of the party replied that he would not be in
Extone's place for a house full of gold, whereupon the
fishmonger rejoined that for half that sum he would
call the Mayor a false scoundrel and a harlot, and would
be pleased to fight him at Horslydown. Extone himself soon got into trouble through his agitation on their
behalf. After advocating their cause in the Parliament
of 1382, as mentioned above, a meeting of the Knights
of the Shires was held in the refectory of Westminster
Abbey, whereat he sarcastically observed that had the
Mayor been able to catch him the night before he would
have led him through Chepe like a robber and a cutpurse. On this speech being reported to Northampton
he called a meeting of the aldermen to consider what
action could be taken, and we get an early, if not the
earliest, reference to parliamentary immunity, for some
of the aldermen held that Extone could be called to
account, while others denied it. Northampton, however,
triumphed by threatening to appeal to the King, and it
ended with Extone entering into a surety of 1,000 marks
for his future good behaviour. At about the same time
evidence is afforded of the Mayor's leanings towards the
Wycliffites by the King's answer to a petition from
Northampton and the aldermen, affirming that the

ordinary laws against usury were sufficient without the interference of Holy Church.

In the Parliament of this year a law was passed, probably by Northampton's influence, forbidding victuallers to hold any judicial post in the city, and taking advantage of this Statute, the Mayor shortly afterwards re-issued an old ordinance to the effect that no official of the city, from the Mayor down to the officers of Newgate, should be a baker, brewer, carter, or retailer of victuals. He also caused the sheriffs, with their clerks, serjeants, and other officials, to swear to maintain to their utmost power the laws recently passed against fishmongers and brokers.

Northampton's following were much aggrieved at the return of Brembre as Mayor in October 1383, and accusations of having used force were freely bandied between the parties. Later on, in the Parliament of 1386, the guilds of the non-victualling class accused Brembre of having obtained his election by this means, while at Northampton's trial his enemies declared that on the occasion in question he had posted a guard at the gate of the Guildhall to prevent any of his opponents entering. The latter accusation is hardly likely to be true in view of Brembre's return unless a fight had occurred, of which there is no record. The new trend of affairs is seen in the following month, when Parliament once again forbade non-freemen to sell by retail in the city, the old restrictions on foreign merchants were reimposed, and the liberties of the city reaffirmed. Brembre was not slow to make proclamation of all these ordinances in detail. Northampton, for his part, did not take his defeat lying down, but conceived the idea of overthrowing his supplanter by force, and held many secret meetings in the city to concert measures with

this end in view. When his conduct came to the knowledge of the King he was bound over in the sum of
£5,000 to keep the peace. That trouble was expected
at the end of 1383 is observable from the orders issued
by Brembre enjoining each alderman to set an armed
watch at Christmas to prevent riots, at the same time
forbidding congregations, conventicles, and assemblies
without his express leave, or anyone except himself and
his officers to walk the streets after nine o'clock at night.
He also ordered all men who possessed arms to provide
themselves with a red slop or smock as a distinguishing
mark, and to be prepared to give him warning should
any cry be raised in the ward in which they lived. In
February Northampton, neglecting to take warning from
his first failure, collected a band of rioters and led them
through Chepe ; and the Mayor, who happened to
be dining in the neighbourhood, rallied a few followers
and pursued him as far as the house of the White Friars
near the Temple, where he was arrested and conveyed
to Brembre's house in the parish of St. Michael, Pater-
nosterchurch. Two days later the King gave orders
to send him with two others to Corfe Castle, and a
fourth, a saddler, to Berkhampstead, and because it was
contrary to the franchises of the city that those arrested
within the walls should be sent outside for trial, he
granted Letters Patent announcing that this action
should not prejudice the liberties. However, two of
the prisoners, one of whom was Northampton's brother,
had not been delivered up by June, for in that month
a writ was received again ordering them to be sent to
Corfe, " as their continued presence in London was
" likely to cause a disturbance, as it had done on a
" former occasion ". In the meantime, on 11th February,
a riot broke out in the city headed by one John

Constantyn, a cordwainer, who was seized, summarily tried, and beheaded in the street, a proceeding for which the King afterwards gave formal sanction.

In August 1384 Northampton was tried before the King at Reading, and the Mayor, aldermen, and some of the principal citizens were ordered to attend. At the same time the Common Council passed a resolution that it were better for the peace of the city that he should not be permitted to return. Northampton was sentenced to be hanged, but this was commuted to imprisonment for life and the confiscation of all his property. It was probably because this assumption of judicial power by the King was considered not altogether legal that Northampton was afterwards retried at the Tower, together with two mercers, Richard Norbury and John More, who were accused of exciting sedition and threatening the governors of the city. This new trial was held on 12th September, 1384, when all three were accused of making conventicles, assemblies, and covins, principally in the parish of St. Mary at Bow, whereby many shops had to be closed in Chepe, Budge Row, and Fleet Street, their aim being the death of the Mayor and certain of the aldermen. It is probable that the prisoners received secret instructions to plead guilty, for, although they were sentenced to be hanged at Tyburn, the King's Chancellor immediately produced a writ of Privy Seal suspending judgment, and eventually they were sent to imprisonment for ten years in various castles, and were ordered, at the termination of this period, not to approach within 100 miles of London. Afterwards John of Gaunt endeavoured to obtain some amelioration of Northampton's sentence by persuading the King to allow him to come within 40 miles of the city. The King promised to grant a charter to this effect, but in March 1386 Brembre, who was still Mayor, called a meeting of the Common Council, at which it was declared that such a concession would engender discord and debate in the city, " which God forbid ". This led to some heated correspondence between John of Gaunt and the Mayor, the former declaring that Brembre need have no fear as Northampton, on obtaining his pardon, was about to follow him to Spain. However, it was not until December 1390 that all judgments passed against Northampton were revoked by the King on the petition of Parliament ; and in the following year yet another trial was held at St. Martin-le-Grand, where the previous judgments at Reading and the Tower were reversed and he was declared innocent. His forfeited estates were thereupon restored, and finally in 1395 he, with Norbury and More, were reinstated in the freedom of the city.

After his election in October 1383 Bembre soon proceeded to reform the Common Council, and appointed a committee to consider its constitution. It was stated that matters brought before the council had often been carried by clamour rather than by reason, and sometimes by people who were not qualified to sit. At the end of January 1384 he called a meeting at Guildhall to consider the committee's report, whereat it was resolved that the council should no longer be elected by the misteries, but that the aldermen, within fifteen days of their election in March each year, should assemble their wards and elect two, four, or six representatives, who should be presented to the Mayor and sworn. Recognising the evils resulting from the previous system, they arranged that the Common Council should not in future contain more than eight members belonging to the same mistery, and if more than that number of any one trade were returned, the Mayor, with the help of six aldermen, should select from among them the eight he considered most suitable, and send the remainder back to their wards for others to be elected in their place. The total membership was to be ninety-six, and they were all to be eligible for re-election in the following year. His return to power, however, did not mean that the free fishmongers were to have things all their own way, but, seeing that at the Stocks Market they paid over £60 a year towards London Bridge, while the non-freemen paid nothing, he appointed a committee to consider whether it were possible to compel the latter to pay something too. At the same time he retained those enactments of Northampton's to the effect that non-freemen should not sell fish to free fishmongers for resale, and that the two classes should not be allowed to form partnerships.

Brembre entered on his second year of office in October 1384, and his re-election was as remarkable as that of Northampton in 1382. The King, who on this occasion favoured his return, sent three representatives to the city to ensure its accomplishment according to his wishes, while Brembre, for his part, took precautions of his own. In order to disarm the Mayor's opponents the King on 2nd October sent his writ forbidding anyone to bear arms in the city, and a formal proclamation to that effect was issued on 12th October, the eve of the election. Over 300 citizens were summoned to attend at the Guildhall, and are said to have been specially selected for their loyalty to Brembre, who took the further precaution of having a band of armed men close at hand for emergencies. The Letter-Book contains a purely formal entry of his election, with, of course, no hint of disturbance or of anything unusual taking place, but it is learned from other sources that Nicholas Twyford, a goldsmith, stood against him, and that some of his supporters gained admission to the hall and caused a disturbance, but were quickly ejected by Brembre's armed forces.

During the following year nothing is heard of any quarrelling between the trades. Many orders for safeguarding the city were issued, and for having armed guards in the wards at Christmas and Midsummer, but these seem to be merely in the usual course or on account of a threatened French invasion. In October 1385 Brembre was re-elected for yet a third year, apparently without any trouble or disturbance, and this term was as uneventful as the last so far as the misteries were concerned. In December the Common Council decreed that the new method of electing their body should last for ever, as it had been found convenient and advantageous. The citizens appear to have been mainly pre-occupied with the scare attendant on the threatened invasion, and the authorities were almost in a state of panic. On one occasion they ordered all the inhabitants to get in a stock of provisions to last for three months when not a single foreign soldier had so much as landed.

At the end of his third term Brembre was at the height of his popularity, so much so that the Common Council passed a resolution that all money disbursed by him for the benefit of the city should be repaid out of the first money coming into the Chamber, and that this order should stand without repeal or contradiction no matter what might happen in the future. Nicholas Extone, the fishmonger, and his chief supporter was now elected in his place, and the victualling party seemed to be more firmly in power than ever. A notable but somewhat mysterious event of this period is the burning

of the book called *Jubile*. This was agreed to at such
a great assembly of the prominent citizens that the
upper room of the Guildhall, the usual meeting-place of
the Common Council, was not large enough to accom-
modate them, so that they had to adjourn to the hall
below. *Jubile* was a compilation of rules for the
governance of the city, described on this occasion as
" being repugnant to the ancient customs of the city ",
but in a petition addressed to Parliament by the Cordwainers and other city guilds, as having " comprised
" all the good articles appertaining to the good govern-
" ment of the city "—a distinction which suggests
that it was most probably compiled by Northampton's
party. On the other hand, it may be the volume in
which " it appeared that certain articles required fuller
" explanation " referred to in 1378, long before Northampton was elected to the mayoralty, to consider and
amend which a committee was appointed, who, at the
end of their labours, reported that they unanimously
agreed to the articles as written in the book.

But notwithstanding the triumph of the victualling
party and the discomfiture of their opponents, the latter
were quietly awaiting their opportunity to destroy
Brembre, whom they regarded as their arch enemy.
This opportunity they found at length in Brembre's
friendship with the King, which led to his undoing, and
soon after the commencement of Extone's second term
of office the blow fell. Towards the end of 1387 power
passed from the King to the " Lords Apellant ", as they
were called, who, backed by an armed force sufficient
to overcome all opposition, were determined to destroy
all those who had aided and abetted Richard in his evil
and extravagant courses. Among others they arrested
Brembre and compelled the King to agree to his trial

on a charge of High Treason before the Parliament which was to assemble early in 1388.   In the meantime the King endeavoured to get the city to consent to military intervention on his behalf, and it was at this critical moment in Brembre's fortunes that the courage of his supporters failed them and he was left to his fate.   Richard summoned Extone and the aldermen to a conference at Windsor, but when they were asked in plain words if they would rise and help him, they replied that they were traders and no fighters, and the Mayor, feeling the embarrassment of his position, begged, but unavailingly, to be relieved of his office.   The rulers of the city had evidently resolved to play for safety by showing favour to neither party, for when the " Lords Apellant ", making in their turn a bid for the city's support by coming to the Guildhall and offering to make peace between the guilds, the reply of the Mayor and aldermen was to put upon their trial certain people accused of aiding and abetting Northampton some years previously.   When Parliament met in February 1388—the " Merciless Parliament " as it was called, or by its friends the " Parliament that wrought " Wonders "—Brembre was put upon his trial on a charge of extortion brought against him by members of several city guilds of the non-victualling type, and in order to secure his conviction, no matter, however trifling, was omitted to be raked up against him.   He was accused of setting up a pair of stocks in every ward of the city, and with causing to be made a " Common Axe " for the purpose of beheading his opponents, 8,000 of whom he was said to have indited ; also with having extracted from the people an oath of allegiance to the King without the latter's consent, and with issuing a proclamation forbidding anyone to speak ill of the King and Queen, although the last, at any rate, originated with Richard himself. He received no mercy from his persecutors, and in spite of his claim as a knight to be allowed to prove his innocence by mortal combat, was condemned and forthwith hanged at Tyburn, or, according to Stow, beheaded with the same axe which he had prepared for others. An effort was also made to involve Extone in the fate of his leader, but failed, and the King sent Letters-Patent to the citizens forbidding anyone to defame him in future. In May 1388 Parliament once again passed the Act granting complete freedom of trade in victuals in the city to foreigners and denizens alike, and this was proclaimed in June, and in the same month they compelled the Mayor, aldermen, and leading citizens to swear to uphold all statutes passed by the " Merciless Parliament ".

Owing most probably to the revulsion of feeling among the citizens by reason of these events, the fortunes of the victualling party were now on the wane, and in October 1388 Nicholas Twyford, the goldsmith, was elected Mayor, after a Letter of Privy Seal had been received ordering the citizens to secure the peaceable election of a trusty and loyal Mayor, and warning the sheriffs that they would be held responsible for any danger that might arise from a disturbance of the peace. The Parliament of September–October 1388 now resolved to take the guilds, not only of London, but of the whole country, in hand with a view to curbing their more violent activities. The first evidence of this is seen in an order dated 1st November, 1388, addressed to the Mayor and sheriffs to make proclamation to Masters, Wardens, and Surveyors of misteries and crafts in the city to bring into Chancery by 2nd February following any

charters or Letters Patent in their possession granted
by the King or his progenitors, and to await judgment
on the same by the King and his Council. From this
time forward we seem to observe a gradual diminution
of the friction between the trades, although Twyford,
reaffirming some of Northampton's regulations, ordered
the aldermen to see that bakers produced a farthing
loaf as well as a halfpenny one, and that brewers sold
their beer by legal measure, and not by the " hanap ",
or drinking-cup. He also looked after the sale of
victuals even in small matters, forbidding " pastelers ",
or piebakers, to make pasties with giblets obtained from
the houses of the lords, or to make beef pasties to
represent venison. He toyed with the constitution of
the Common Council, but the time had passed when
it would have been possible to revert to the old bad
method of its election by the misteries, and he contented
himself with a new arrangement, which appears never
to have been carried into effect, that it should be elected
from the wards indeed, but by the Mayor in the presence of twelve aldermen, and not by the inhabitants.
He was succeeded in October 1389 by William Venour,
a grocer, not without strong opposition from Adam
Bamme, a goldsmith, supported by members of some
of the other non-victualling trades. Venour was unable
to override the law which permitted strangers to
trade freely within the city, but he did what he could
to discourage their activities. He made a rule that
when bargains were concluded between strangers half
the brokerage should be paid into the Guildhall towards
defraying the expenses of the Mayor, aldermen, and
recorder on those occasions—the Mayor's procession
to Westminster and the religious procession on Whit-
Monday—when they were all clothed alike, and for

this purpose the terms of such bargains were to be disclosed to the Mayor and aldermen when required. Also for the same purpose strangers were to pay to the Mayor one-half of the " scavage ", the fee exacted for the display of their goods when entering the city. In the following October Adam Bamme became Mayor, and, in an endeavour to obliterate the old rancours, he gave orders that no one in the city should speak or express opinions about Brembre or Northampton, nor show by any sign which they favoured, but to be silent upon everything connected with the late controversy, under penalty of imprisonment in Newgate for a year and a day. This may be considered the end of the trade fights of the 14th century, except for a curious echo of the old disputes to be observed as late as 1399, when the King, a few months before losing his throne, in a last effort to obtain the support of the city, launched a proclamation giving back to the fishmongers all their old exclusive rights. It seems to be merely an indication that Richard, in the midst of the troubles which were crowding upon him, had lost all sense of proportion, and, having no effect upon the development of the political situation of the time, was rendered void as soon as Henry IV mounted the throne.

CHAPTER VI

WORK AND WAGES

BEFORE the advent of the factory system and the industrial revolution the craftsman was an independent workman, a freeman of the city, a member of a guild, and produced his manufactures in his own home ; the retailer knew nothing of the multiple shop system, or the great emporium, but had one shop and lived over it. The only man whose position was at all comparable to that of his modern prototype was the wholesaler, the merchant who bought goods in bulk from the foreigners who brought them to London and distributed them among the retailers. Even he did not aspire to palatial showrooms, but like many such to-day, hired a cellar or shed to serve as a warehouse, living elsewhere himself—in a " hostel ", or inn, a single room in a tenement house, or in a mansion on Cornhill or elsewhere, according to his degree of prosperity. Nevertheless there were still employers and workmen. The craftsman who found orders coming in fast, or the shopkeeper doing a brisk business, would alike require assistants, and could not always find a sufficient number of new apprentices to serve his purpose. He would therefore engage certain servants, " Journeymen ", " Yeomen ", or " Vadlets ", as they were called. These men would sometimes be free of the craft and sometimes not. In the former case they could not aspire to the position of " Liverymen " of the guild, that is, they

could have no voice in its government. An apprentice
who had served his term but could not afford to start in
business, one who had started but failed to succeed, or
a workman migrating from the country districts with
little or no capital but a knowledge of some particular
craft or mistery, would be eligible to join the ranks of
the "Vadlets", but in the case of a new-comer an employer would be unable to engage him until he had been
examined by the surveyors of the craft as to his capability
and good character. The ruling of the workmen was the
special province of these surveyors, to whom they had
to be obedient on all occasions, and to whom they looked
for protection in cases of unfair treatment on the part of
their employers.

Regulations concerning the employment of workmen
are found in most of the articles of the crafts. Overtime
was objected to as much then as now, but for a different
reason ; it was held that work performed by candlelight
must of necessity be inferior work. Sunday was a
compulsory holiday for the workman, although for the
convenience of the poor the craftsmen themselves were
permitted to open their shops, but not to come out into
the street to sell as they did on week-days. In many
trades they had the Saturday afternoon holiday, while
the eve of a feast was a general holiday for workmen,
and in the latter case they received no pay for their
enforced idleness. A reflection on their habits is found
in the order that they are not to work when drunk.
Drunkenness was a prevalent habit of the poor, and if
we may judge from the remarks of Higden was specially
characteristic of the English from Saxon times. Many
deaths due to this cause are recorded in the Coroners'
Rolls. Loyalty to his employer was considered the first
duty of a workman. He could be punished for teaching

his master's business to a stranger, and if he left his
employment before completing any agreement he might
have made with his employer, or in his debt in any way,
he could be brought back and imprisoned. This may be
seen in operation in 1353 when the King ordered the
Mayor to arrest any workmen found within the city who
had fled from their work of repairing the Palace of
Westminster, and when one of them was caught in 1356
he was imprisoned in Newgate. It was a punishable
offence for an employer to entice away another's workman, or for a workman to leave his employment merely
on account of dissatisfaction with the officially established
rate of pay. A modern habit of the workman may be
seen as far back as the 14th century in the order forbidding
them to parade the streets with collecting-boxes during
hard times, and they were equally prohibited from forming any confederacy for the purpose of obtaining better
conditions from their employers. Any workman with a
grievance, unable to obtain satisfaction from the surveyors
of the mistery, could bring his complaint to the Mayor,
and special regulations were made against employers
who withheld the wages of their men.

Notwithstanding, however, the hard and fast regulations which bound the workman to his work, it is possible at times to find instances of independent contracts
between employer and employed. A very curious one
is found in 1286, when two men engaged the services
of another for three years at a stipend of 1 mark a
year and his entire keep. Unfortunately the trade of
these people is not stated, but the agreement provides that
the employers shall pay to the man a sum of £11. 13s. 0.
by way of capital to start with, and he shall make goods
for them and receive goods from them. Presumably
these were for sale, for at the end of the three years he

is to account to them for the original capital, the goods made and received, together with any profit which may have accrued.

In the clauses dealing with workmen contained in the articles of the crafts the duties of the employers are sometimes not forgotten. In some cases, as, for example, the Pouchmakers, the Braelers, and the Glassmakers, it was obligatory upon the trade as a whole to support any respectable workman during illness, and in others, notably the Cordwainers, there was a charitable fund for the maintenance of indigent employees during disablement or old age. The Whittawyers, or workers of fine white leather, arranged to keep a candle perpetually burning before the image of the Virgin in the church of Allhallows, London Wall, and for this purpose to keep a box into which the members of the trade should put whatever money they could spare. Out of the funds so subscribed they paid sevenpence a week to members of the craft incapacitated by infirmity or old age, and a similar sum to widows of those who died in poverty. Presumably this charity would be available in the case of their assistants, who would be more likely to be in need of it than their employers.

A description of the independent character and status of a workman in the 15th century is given in a contemporary poem thus :—

> " Lystyn, and ye schall here ;
> " Of a wright I wyll you telle,
> " That some tyme in thys land gan dwelle,
> " And lyved by hys myster.
> " Whether that he were yn or owte,
> " Of erthely man hadde he no dowte (fear),
> " To werke hows, harowe, nor plowgh,
> " Or other werkes, what so they were,
> " Thous wrought he hem farre and nere,
> " And dyd tham wele I-nough."

But although the poem does not pretend to be staged in
London, it probably embodies more fiction than fact,
judging by all the evidence we have, and Stow's description is more likely to be the correct one, where he says
in a well-known passage : " The private riches of London
" resteth chiefly in the hands of the merchants and
" retailers, for artificers have not much to spare, and
"labourers have need that it were given unto them ".
However, to understand their position in 14th-century
London it is necessary to inquire what wages they
received, and what they had to spend to obtain the
necessaries of life.   It will be found, of course, that money
possessed a very different value then as compared with
the present day.   In official proclamations issuing from
the Guildhall it is found that masons, plasterers, carpenters, and sawyers received 6d. a day for one half of the
year and 5d. a day for the other half ;   tilers, 5½d. and
4½d. ; labourers, 3½d. and 3d.   Piecework was generally
condemned because it was found that men scamped their
work in order to produce a quantity, but it appears to
have been permitted among the tailors, who are found
receiving from 1s. 2d. to 1s. 6d. for making a man's
gown, 10d. for a coat and hood, 4d. for changing a pair
of sleeves, and 2s. 6d. for a lady's gown ; and among
the curriers of fur, who, by their articles formulated in
1300, were to receive from 5s. 0. to 10s. 0. for dressing
a thousand of furs, according to its kind and description.
With the Cutlers and the Fullers it was the custom for
the wardens of the trade to examine each man individually
and to fix his wages, and any master cutler or fuller
employing him was not allowed to pay him beyond the
the sum so fixed.   The same wardens, however, could
order the man a rise in wages as he became more proficient,
but if at his first examination he was found inefficient

he was not allowed to work at the trade until he had passed through a period of apprenticeship. In many of the crafts the workman received food and drink as part of his wages. Thus we find the Shearmen receiving 3d. a day for part of the year and 4d. a day for the remainder, plus their food and drink. From a case which arose in 1396 it appears that the proper pay for a journeyman saddler was 5 marks a year, which works out at about 1s. 3½d. a week, and his board ; though it was admitted that many men, by agitation, had been receiving twice as much. Any employer paying more than the standard wage was liable to a fine of 40s. o., and any workman accepting more to forty days' imprisonment. And yet, as might be expected, they did ask and receive more when opportunity arose. In 1359 a builder repairing a house in Cornhill paid his men 7d. a day besides a halfpenny for beer, and one carpenter, who may be supposed to have been more expert than the rest, as much as 8½d. a day. Again, in 1350, three men who were laying a water-pipe from the main conduit to the royal stables at Charing Cross received 8d. a day and twopennyworth of beer between them, though on a similar job in the same year only 6d. a day was paid, plus a penny for beer. Even the fees of city officials were on a proportionately modest scale, though in their case, possessing the privilege of full citizenship, they were able to combine some other business with their civic duties. In 1335 the Serjeant of the Chamber of the Guildhall was paid 40s. o. a year ; in 1319 the Common Serjeant, or Common Crier, received £5 a year ; while the Town Clerk used to be paid £5 a year, which was increased in 1335 to £10, together with certain emoluments.

The Black Death of 1348 and the following plagues

of 1361 and 1369 had so decimated the population of
the country that artisans and labourers were thereby
encouraged to demand higher wages. The Black Death
first appeared in the country in August 1348, and is
said to have reached London by the following November.
In 1351 Parliament passed the Statute of Labourers to
enforce the same rates of wages as were customary before
the plague, but Edward III, without waiting for the
passage of the Act, issued Orders in Council to the same
effect as early as June 1349. At the same time he ordered
the collectors of King's taxes to seize all wages paid in
excess of the old rates and devote the proceeds to public
services, or in other words to his Treasury—not an
easy task for the collectors. In obedience to this order
the Mayor in 1350 issued regulations fixing the wages
of each kind of artisan and labourer and the prices of a
great number of commodities, even to the fee of a halfpenny for taking off a horseshoe, and appointed officials
in every ward to see his orders obeyed. The state of
subjection in which the poor were held at this time may
be realised from an Act of Parliament of 1388 which
forbade any child who had been kept at the plough until
the age of twelve to be taught any trade or craft. Between
the years 1357 and 1359 an opportunity is afforded of
watching the Statute of Labourers in operation. In the
former year the Mayor, sheriffs, and three commoners
were appointed by the King to be commissioners for
enforcing the Statute, and ordered to make a report of
their proceedings thereon. They reported at the end of
two years that seventy-four workmen, comprising tilers,
daubers, carpenters, masons, paviours, and lathers, had
been fined sums ranging from 1s. 0d. to 3s. 4d. for infringements of the Act. The futility of the law, however,
is indicated by a proclamation issued as late as 1362,

in which its terms are restated, the wages of tilers, carpenters, etc., fixed at from 3d. to 6d. a day, and a statement added to the effect that the citizens had suffered damages and grievances by the high wages demanded. At the same time, in justice to the workmen, the Mayor did not omit to announce that Saturday, notwithstanding the half-holiday, and providing that the man had performed a full week's work, should be paid for as a whole day. At this period some trades, notably the Fullers and Dyers in 1353, appointed certain of their members specially to see that no workman took more for his labour than before the pestilence, and it is probably for this reason that the return made by the commissioners comprises almost entirely members of the building trades. Taking into consideration all the trades, one with the other, it is safe to estimate the average wage of an artisan of the period at 5d. a day where no food was provided, and 3d. a day in the case of unskilled labourers.

A consideration of the cost of living at the same period will reveal that the workman might in good times be able to obtain most of the necessaries of life, but certainly none of its luxuries. The principal item in his food bill would be, of course, bread, and so it is that we always find the greatest concern displayed by the rulers of the city to ensure that this article of diet was sold at its purest and cheapest. Every year, at Michaelmas, when the harvest having been gathered the price of corn might be expected to remain stable for the ensuing year, a grand assay of bread was made at the Guildhall to ascertain and fix the proper weight of the halfpenny loaf. A halfpenny was the standard price of a loaf of bread ; it was the weight that varied. A quantity of wheat was purchased and sent to be milled. The cost of milling, together with a sum sufficient to cover the expense of baking, were added to the original price of the wheat, and as many loaves made therefrom as there were halfpennies in the total cost. The resultant loaf was weighed whilst hot, and that weight was proclaimed as the standard for the ensuing year. A reasonably low price for wheat was 5s. o. the quarter, which produced a halfpenny loaf of about five-sixths the size of our modern half-quartern. Simnel bread, made from the finest white flour, was only about half that size. Unfortunately for the poor, the price of wheat was subject to violent fluctuations, owing to the uncertainty of the harvest, often reaching as high as 10s. o. the quarter, when the loaf would be only half the usual size. In 1311 the bakers complained that the assay made in that year had been badly baked, and consequently if they had to sell their bread by it they would be unable to make a profit. The Mayor thereupon made an unusual concession, agreeing to a fresh assay providing the bakers would pay for the corn. An instance of the solicitude of the authorities in this matter is afforded in 1379, when, as the result of inquiries, it was found that the scarcity of bread in that year was due to a shortage of water for turning the mills which ground the corn, and it was therefore ordained that everyone who used as much as two bushels of wheat in his house a week should set up a handmill for the purpose of grinding it. Any baker detected in selling bread short in weight or otherwise overcharging was very severely dealt with by being drawn through the streets tied to a hurdle or confined in the pillory. A hurdle for this purpose was first provided in 1282.

The authorities were no less solicitous in regulating the sale of the corn from which the bread was made, and of all other commodities more particularly constituting the food of the poor. Nowadays numbers of people make a good living out of the necessaries of life by a process of keeping them in stock at times, and at other times throwing them upon the market. This is esteemed a virtue, and often leads to the conferment of a knighthood, or even a peerage ; but in the 14th century they used to give them the pillory. Speaking generally, the principle adopted by the city rulers for cheapening the primary articles of consumption was, as far as possible, the elimination of the middle man. In 1344, during a time of scarcity caused by continual warfare, they forbade all wholesale dealing in corn, compelling the holders of it to sell by retail direct to the public. In 1347 they gave a dealer forty days' imprisonment for raising the price of corn to the extent of twopence a bushel in Grascherche Market, and threatened that the next offender should have the punishment of the pillory. Sure enough, later in the same year a dealer in Newgate Market raised the price by threepence halfpenny a bushel, and duly suffered the promised retribution. This incident, it may be pointed out, demonstrates that the pillory was considered a worse punishment than prison. In 1356 and 1357 fresh regulations were made with a view to keeping down the price. Corn which had been landed at Billingsgate or Queenhithe was forbidden to be sold to a dealer before it had been offered freely for sale to the general public for three days, so that private citizens could buy enough for their households. In order to prevent speculation in this prime commodity it was not allowed to be sold by sample, but only in bulk in open market ; no dealer after making his purchase could leave the corn in the hands of the vendor for resale contingent on a rise in price ; and no one was allowed to meet it on its way to market to buy it. Dealers, however, were permitted to go into the country to purchase growing

corn, or corn in barns. This latter privilege was with-
drawn in 1370 by order of the King—a short-sighted
policy, which was scarcely likely to have the effect of
reducing prices in London, as in the absence of buyers
from the metropolis corn in the country would probably
be diverted to other parts. In 1375 a quantity of corn
was confiscated for being purchased by a dealer direct
from Kent, where it was grown, and in 1390 a similar
course was pursued in the case of corn found hidden
in the private house of a cordwainer in the parish
of Allhallows, Gracechurch Street.   In February 1391,
there having been a great scarcity for two years past, tne
Mayor borrowed £400 of the money belonging to city
orphans lying in the Chamber of Guildhall to purchase
corn for the people, guaranteeing to repay it by the
following Michaelmas.

No objection was raised against farmers from the
surrounding country bringing their produce into London
and hawking it round the streets, but dealers were not
allowed to do the same.   Butter and cheese were brought
in in this way, and in 1377 a complaint was made by the
Cheesemongers that dealers residing in the outlying
districts were buying these articles from the farmers and
selling them in London as the produce of their own
farms.   At that time butter was sold in liquid or semi-
liquid form, at the rate of three-halfpence a pint, and a
cheese called " talgar " was brought from as far away as
Wales.   Fish, as has been explained in a former chapter,
was one of the staple foods, and throughout the century
its sale was strictly regulated.   Although for the purpose
of keeping down the price it was usual to compel its sale
to be conducted in open market, fishmongers had special
permission to carry it round those streets where workmen
dwelt.   Fish caught in the Thames was largely consumed

by the poor, and in 1391 there is even mention of minnows sold for food. Among these regulations fuel was not forgotten. Charcoal was the usual domestic form of this article ; seacoal, as mined coal was called at the period, was well known, but used mainly for manufacturing purposes. Charcoal was brought to London by horseload from the surrounding country, and a large proportion of it came from Croydon. The law of the city was that every sack should contain eight bushels, and the vendors were frequently arrested and punished for supplying short measure. We read in 1377 of two men bringing three horseloads of charcoal from Croydon which was seized and measured before the Mayor, when each sack was found to be at least a bushel short. The men pleaded that they were only servants, but because they admitted having assisted their master in filling the sacks they were put in the stocks on Cornhill, and the horses were kept in custody in order to compel their employer to come to London to answer for his conduct. The price of a quarter of charcoal of eight bushels varied between 9d. and 1s. 0. at various times during the century.

A few specimen prices from the domestic budget, as gathered from entries scattered throughout the Letter-Books, will afford some idea of the cost of articles of general use. We hear of a loin of beef 5d., a leg of pork 3d., a loin of pork 4d., a ham 1s. 0., a shoulder of mutton 2½d., a whole sheep 2s. 0., a lamb 8d., a rabbit 4d., a hen 4d., a capon 6d., 4 larks 1d., a goose 6d., eggs ten a penny, herrings, white or red, roast or boiled, six to ten a penny, oysters and mussels 4d. a bushel, oats 8d. a bushel, faggots of wood a halfpenny each, candles 2d. a pound ; candles, round or square, could be hired for funerals on payment of a penny a

pound plus the cost of wastage ; shoes of common
bazen, or sheep's leather, 5d. a pair, but the finest qualities
could reach as high as 3s. 6d. a pair ; children's boots
of white cloth, 2d. a pair ; gloves 1d. a pair and upwards ;
linen 4d. an ell, linen thread 1s. 0. a pound ; a wooden
comb 1d. ; a cloth gown 4s. 0. to 5s. 0. ; a tunic and
hood 1s. 4d. ; a surcoat 2s. 0. ; a gown of russet or
coarse burel cloth as worn by the poor 9d.   Cloth of
Candlewyck Street was worth 1s. 8d. a yard, but really
fine cloth, such as that made at Brussels, would fetch
as much as 7s. 6d. a yard.   The latter sort was worn only
by the highest in the land, and in 1337 two pieces of it
were considered a suitable present for the city to make to
the Archbishop of Canterbury when he had been instru-
mental in obtaining a certain confirmation of their liberties.

The cost of board and lodging, of course, varied
considerably according to the position in life of the party.
There is a record in 1311 of a lady supplied with board
and lodging for 50s. 0. a year, and in 1319 an orphan of
good position so supplied for 6d. a week plus 6s. 8d.
yearly.   In the case of workmen it often occurred that
they lived on the premises where they were employed.
Thus we hear of a fishmonger living in his home in
Crooked Lane, near London Bridge, with his wife,
children, and several employees.   In other cases workmen
are found living in one or two rooms of a tenement house
of three or four storeys, and paying about 3s. 0. or 4s. 0.
a year for rent, the yearly value of the entire house
being somewhere in the neighbourhood of 30s. 0.   Stow
tells us that his father paid 6s. 6d. a year for his house
and garden in Throgmorton Street, and in 1511 the
Mayor of London lived in a house rented at no more than
26s. 8d. a year.   In 1308 a house was built with hall,
larder, solar, and cellar, complete to the locks, for

£9. 5s. 4d. in cash, 50 marten skins, fur for a woman's
hood value 5s. o., and a fur for the builder's own robe ;
while in 1313 one was built at St. Mary-at-Hill for £36.

A calculation of the income and expenditure of a
working man with a wife and two or three children, based
on the above figures, appears to leave a deficit even on
the necessaries of life.   In such conditions it is good
to remember that the rich men of London were always
famous for their charity, as may be seen to-day by the
large number of almshouses and hospitals in and around
London which were founded by their piety.   It was a
not uncommon occurrence for such men to leave a sum
of money by will with which to pay the King's taxes of
a street or of a whole ward, and their zeal was unceasing
in promoting the education of the young, the care of
the poor, and the maintenance of the sick and infirm.
St. Bartholomew's, St. Mary Spital, without Bishopsgate,
St. Mary Overy in Southwark, and St. Thomas's
Hospital were all homes for poor people, and the blind
and the lame were housed at Pappy Church, between
Aldgate and Bevis Marks, where they were provided with
14d. a week, together with a barber, a laundress, and
a servant to wait on them.   St. Bartholomew's was also
a lying-in hospital for women with illegitimate children,
as was St. Thomas's.   In the latter hospital Sir Richard
Whittington endowed eight beds for this purpose, with
the proviso that secrecy should be observed in each case,
so that the woman's chance of ultimate marriage should
not be prejudiced.   Bedlam without Bishopsgate was the
home for the insane, and St. James's Hospital at Charing
Cross, on the site of the present St. James's Palace, and
also the Lock in Southwark, for lepers.   It was customary
for wealthy men to bequeath land and tenements in
various parts of the city for the upkeep of these founda-

tions. Much money was given for the assistance of poor prisoners confined in Ludgate, Newgate, and the Compters of the sheriffs, for it was not the duty of the authorities to feed such ; and another favourite form of charity, of which many instances are found, was the endowment of poor maids' marriages. Often charitable donations assumed special forms, as in the number of bequests for giving away meat or bread to the poor, or as in the case of John Bernes, Mayor in 1370-2, who left his property in the city to be sold, and the proceeds to be kept in a chest under four keys to be held by the Grocers, Mercers, Drapers, and the city Chamberlain, the contents to be devoted to loans to needy persons. "Barnes's Chest", as it came to be known, is believed to be still in the Guildhall, but cannot be identified with certainty. In 1386 the Mayor and aldermen borrowed £300 from this chest at a time of threatened invasion from France, under bond to repay it. It was, however, still unpaid three years later, at which time they resolved to commence doing so out of rents belonging to the city. Doles of money were often given to the poor at Leadenhall and at the house of the Friars Preachers, which stood at the spot now known as Blackfriars. An idea of the great number of destitute persons in London at this time may be gathered from the account of a terrible tragedy which occurred at the gates of the Blackfriars in 1322, when at daybreak on a July morning such an enormous crowd collected to participate in a distribution of alms that fifty-two, or according to some authorities fifty-five, men, women, and children were crushed to death.

Charity in the middle ages always went hand in hand with religion, and as a consequence its recipients were expected to display a degree of gratitude at least equivalent to the giver's piety. An amusing instance of this comes from the 16th century. One Cutberd Beechar, a draper, who was buried in the church of St. Mildred in the Poultry in 1540 left a sum of money to purchase weekly thirteen penny loaves for a shilling, thus obtaining the benefit of the "baker's dozen", to be distributed every Sunday among thirteen poor persons of the parish. Each recipient, in return for his penny loaf, was thereupon to go before the High Altar, kneel before the Blessed Sacrament, and repeat three Paternosters, three Ave Marias, and one Credo, and to pray to God to have mercy upon the soul of the donor, and upon all the souls that he himself would have prayed for, and upon all Christian souls.[1]

[1] Milbourn's *History of St. Mildreds*, p. 13.

CHAPTER VII

THE BIRTH OF TRADE UNIONISM

IT is notorious that the formation of Trade Unions among agricultural workers is so difficult as to be wellnigh impossible, for the simple reason that the members of that calling are so widely scattered ; but where traders and manufacturers settle in communities such as cities and towns, and large numbers of men assume the status of employees, attempts to form such unions become not only possible, but inevitable. Not only were such conditions fully present in 14th-century London, but the further circumstance that each trade tended to form a little community of its own, living and working in one localised spot, rendered it impossible to prevent the workmen, following the example of their employers with their trade guilds, from joining together for the purpose of mutual action to improve their condition. Thus it may well be said that the 14th century witnessed in London, in spite of set-backs and disappointments, the birth of that system of Trade Unionism which is to-day an all-powerful factor in our social organisation. The surveyors of the misteries, as employers and the representatives of employers, backed by the full weight of the governing authorities, used every effort to nip in the bud these early efforts, and promptly subjected their originators to fine and imprisonment. Many special enactments dealing with this phase of the social struggle are found in the articles of the misteries, many complaints of such activities on the part of the workmen have been recorded, and in a few instances the Letter-Books contain detailed accounts of the forming of unions and the fomenting of strikes.

In the articles of the Fullers, formulated in 1363, it is laid down that any workman attempting to form a union should suffer imprisonment for one year. The expression used is : " Combining to obtain more than " their proper wage, to the hurt of the people ", such proper wage being that fixed by the rulers of the craft, themselves employers. Again, in the articles of the Shearmen, under date 1350, we find a description of the method adopted by the workmen, and the manner in which the authorities proposed to deal with it, in these words : " Also—whereas heretofore if there was any " dispute between a master in the said trade and his " man, such man has been wont to go to all the men " within the city of the same trade ; and then, by covin " and conspiracy between them made, they would " order that no one among them should work, or serve " his own master, until the said master and his servant, " or man, had come to an agreement ; by reason whereof " the masters in the said trade have been in great trouble, " and the people left unserved;—it is ordained, that from " henceforth, if there be any dispute moved between any " master and his man in the said trade, such dispute " shall be settled by the Wardens of the trade. And " if the man who shall have offended, or shall have " badly behaved himself towards his master, will not " submit to be tried before the said Wardens, then such " man shall be arrested by a serjeant of the Chamber, " at the suit of the said Wardens, and brought before " the Mayor and aldermen ; and before them let him be

" punished, at their discretion ".[1]   In 1362 a similar complaint, couched in almost the same words, was made by the Alien Weavers, and in reply a similar order was made by the Mayor.

A more detailed description of one such attempt to form a union is furnished in 1396, when the wardens of the Saddlers complained to the Mayor at Guildhall that the journeymen of their trade had formed an illegal " covin ", as they called it, to coerce the employers, and that once a year they were wont " to array themselves " all in a new and like suit ", and then and at other times to hold meetings at Stratford, or even within the city itself.   Six men were named as ringleaders, and accordingly were ordered to appear at Guildhall to answer the charge.   Apparently they had a bad scare, and thought the best course they could take would be to cover their actions with a religious glamour, and accordingly pleaded that they had been accustomed, time out of mind, to assemble at Stratford on 15th August each year, that day being a feast of the Virgin Mary, and to march to the church of St. Vedast in Foster Lane, to hear a mass in honour of the Blessed Virgin.   There were, indeed, many guilds existing in London for religious and social purposes, and some of the trade guilds themselves had their religious side, involving an annual procession in honour of their patron saint ; but the city authorities did not see fit to extend any such privilege to the work-men of a trade separately from their employers, for fear that a combination of the kind would be used for purposes of agitation.   This was, in fact, the claim of the master Saddlers, for they replied that the custom in question had only been observed for the last thirteen years, and that the journeymen were merely using religion as a cloak

[1] *Memorials*, p. 247.

under which to carry on an agitation for increased wages ;
with the result that whereas a journeyman saddler could
formerly have been engaged for 40s. o. or 5 marks a year
and his board, such men were now demanding 10 or
12 marks, and sometimes as much as £10. This
was not the only trouble caused to the trade by this
" covin ", for it was said that often the leaders would
cause all their followers to be summoned by a beadle
to leave their work for the purpose of attending vigils
for dead members, a penalty being levied on any man
refusing to obey. This is curiously reminiscent of the
modern Trade Union habit of levying money on members
for purposes not strictly connected with union objects.
At first the Mayor endeavoured to temporise, and ordered
the men's leaders to hold a consultation with six or eight
of the employers, and to come back at a later date
with the result of their deliberations ; but he added that
in any case he should refuse to permit any more meetings at Stratford. Afterwards, no agreement apparently
being arrived at, the men came into court and formally
petitioned to be allowed to hold their meetings as usual.
This was refused, and they were ordered, under heavy
penalties, to render obedience in future to the wardens
of the trade ; but the Mayor promised that if in any
case of grievance they could obtain no satisfaction, they
could come before him and receive speedy justice.

A curious case of the same kind arose in 1387
among the journeymen Cordwainers, who endeavoured
to obtain the highest ecclesiastical sanction for their
designs. It appears that a brother of the order of Friars
Preachers, William Bartone by name, had undertaken
to obtain for their fraternity the confirmation of the
Pope himself, by virtue of which he promised that no
one would dare to interfere with them, under pain of

excommunication, "and of still more grievous sentence "afterwards". The friar's motive may be understood by the fact that a collection had been made among all the members of the trade and the proceeds given to him, but of his ability to carry out his promise some doubt may be felt. Indeed, considerable suspicion attaches to him in view of the flourishing trade in forged Papal Bulls which is known to have been carried on at this time. However that may be, the men proceeded to hold a mass meeting at the church of Blackfriars, and there being found one dissentient among them, they beat him so severely that he barely escaped with his life. This brought about the arrest of three of the ringleaders, who were sent to Newgate pending the decision of the Mayor as to what should be done with them. The sequel, unfortunately, has not come down to us, and so we miss the interesting remarks which the Mayor most probably made to the friar.

In 1415 it was the turn of the Tailors, whose wardens complained to the Mayor that the "yomen taillours," instead of lodging separately like law abiding citizens, chose to live all together in several houses in the ward of Garlickhithe, from whence they used to issue in a body and raise tumults, and seize and beat citizens, notably one of the wardens of their own trade, named Thomas Trepenelle. They had also attacked the officers and serjeants of the city for the purpose of releasing brawlers who had been arrested, and, as in the case of the Saddlers, had dressed all alike and held meetings both within and without the city. The Mayor took a very serious view of the matter, and severely blamed the wardens for allowing such a state of things to continue. He then summoned before him three of the ringleaders and pointed out that such conduct "did manifestly redound to a

" breach of the peace of our Lord the King and commo-
" tion among the people ". He strictly forbade them in
future to wear a livery or to hold meetings, and ordered
them to leave the houses in question by a certain date,
threatening them with fine and imprisonment unless
they obeyed. The " yomen taillours ", however, did not
yet give up hope, for they are found two years later
coming before the Mayor, and petitioning to be allowed
to assemble once a year on the feast of St. John the Baptist
in the church of St. John of Jerusalem near Smithfield,
to make offering for the souls of deceased brethren and
sisters of their fraternity. The final reply of the Mayor
was to the effect that they should not hold such conventicles except in the presence of the Masters of the mistery,
under penalty of fine and imprisonment.

Trade Unionism has had a hard struggle to survive,
and little progress was achieved during hundreds of years ;
indeed, it is only in comparatively recent times that it
has succeeded in living down the antagonism which
pursued it from the start, and obtaining recognition
from the law. In this connection it may not be without
interest to observe a similar case to those cited above,
occurring as recently as 1822, and the penalty imposed
upon the leaders. At that time the journeymen Weavers
of Coventry formed the " Weaver's Fund or Aggregate
" Committee " for the purpose of regulating wages.
As in ancient times, however, they resorted to violence,
for any member accepting wages less than the Committee
had fixed was placed upon an ass, facing the tail, and in
this attitude drawn through the streets exposed to public
ridicule. When, as inevitably happened, the union was
suppressed, the leaders were fined £20 each, had to give
security for their good behaviour for five years, and were
imprisoned for terms varying from six to nine months.

CHAPTER VIII

SWINDLERS AND SWINDLING

IN the days of our grandfathers it was customary for people in a certain station of life, on account of the lack of kitchen space in the small houses of the period, to take their week-end joint to a baker's shop for the purpose of having it cooked. This simple custom may not at first sight appear to lend itself to the requirements of farce, but in a pantomime at the old Saddler's Wells theatre it once gave occasion for one of the clown's merry jokes. In the baker's shop which usually forms a not unimportant part of the knockabout scene he busied himself in handing out the cooked joints to the customers, one of whom indignantly protested that he had brought in a joint of beef consisting of three bones and had received back one with only two bones. To the implied accusation the clown replied—" shrunk " in the cooking, Sir ". This might well have been made the excuse for a curiously similar swindle found in the records of 14th-century London. It appears to have been the custom among the poor of the city to prepare the dough for their bread in their own homes and to take it to a baker's shop to have it baked into loaves. The baker had a " moldingborde " upon which he placed the dough, cut it up, shaped the loaves, and passed them on to the oven. In the year 1327 one John Brid, whilst engaged at his moldingborde, conceived a brilliant idea for making an extra profit out of these transactions. He cut a circular hole in the board, replaced the cut-out piece of wood to serve as a plug, and concealed a member of his family beneath. When the dough was placed upon the moldingborde the person hidden below removed the plug, and, while the loaves were being shaped by the baker, abstracted some of the dough through the hole into a receptacle provided for the purpose. At a signal from the baker he replaced the plug in its original position, and the loaves, minus some of their substance, passed on to the oven. Thus the customers standing by could not see their property disappear, for apparently the same quantity reached the oven as they had brought in. Still, even though customers may make no complaint, they have a habit of thinking things over when they get outside the shop, and after a while this man's clients, viewing the unaccountable smallness of their loaves, began to " smell a rat." At length some of them betook themselves to Guildhall and breathed their suspicions into the sympathetic ear of the Mayor, whose constant anxiety it was to check all malpractices in the city trades. The Mayor dispatched a serjeant of the city to the shop while business was in full swing, and he, seizing the board and pushing it aside, revealed the whole swindle. The next step was to visit all the bakers' shops and examine their premises, with the result that nine of them were found with similar holes in their moldingbordes. On the following day they were all tried before the Mayor at Guildhall and sentenced to the pillory, and those under whose boards dough had actually been found had portions of it hung round their necks.

As the desire to get the better of one's fellows is a deeply implanted trait of human nature, it follows that in every age there have been those who have pursued

this object by foul means as well as by fair ; it is only
the method that changes according to the circumstances
and the opportunities of the times. So it is that swindles
under many headings are found in the records of Old
London, some bearing a remarkable resemblance to
modern misdeeds, whilst others display the quaintness
of ancient ideas and manners. It is probable that more
openings for fraud will present themselves in the course
of trade than in any other department of life, and although
the dubious honour of pre-eminence on the shady side
of business seems to have been about equally shared
between the bakers and the taverners, there are instances
of many other traders who did not neglect their opportunities in this respect. The thickening of the bottoms
of measures was a favourite dodge on the part of taverners,
brewers, and corn-merchants. In 1364 an ale-wife was
found selling her ale in quart pots in the bottoms of which
she had placed an inch and a half of pitch with a covering
of rosemary to hide it. What her customers thought of
rosemary in their ale is unknown. It was the pecca-
dilloes of these tradespeople which gave opportunity to
other rogues to victimise them in their turn. Thus in
1375 a man who had been a servant of one of the Mayor's
serjeants and was consequently well known to the ale-
wives as a public official, went round to their houses
asserting that he had been sent to confiscate any ale he
might find there, and, producing his tablets, pretended
to write down their names and addresses. What more
natural than that he should be offered money by these
poor women to let them alone ? After collecting a
shilling from one, sixpence from another, and sundry
gifts from several more, he was captured and put in the
pillory. Similarly in 1310 a rogue meeting two baker-
esses with their cart bringing bread from Stratford to

1. THE FIREPLACE AND ITS USES
2. THE ALE-WIFE'S END

From Wright's "Domestic Customs and Sentiments"

London, pretended to be a serjeant of the sheriffs, put them and their cart under arrest, and accepted a bribe of tenpence to let them go.   The wholesale trades were also not exempt from the nefarious practices of their time, and some of their members delighted in swindling the innocent stranger from the provinces.   In 1394 a merchant from Gloucestershire ordered from a dealer a quantity of powdered ginger, worm-seed, and frankincense, the whole transaction amounting to the sum of £129. 13s. 4d.   For the first he was sent a concoction of rape-seed, roots of radish, and similar substances ; for the second, tansy-seed ; and for the last, resin.   In the early part of the century the defrauding of country people bringing their produce into London had become so notorious that a public warning was issued to the butchers and the bladers, or corn-dealers.   The method employed was to obtain delivery of the goods and at once proceed to spoil them, by wetting the corn or by slaughtering the animals, and then invite the countryman either to take them back or to accept a much lower price than had been agreed upon.   The farmer would be unable to find a use for the damp corn, although the buyer could use it for malting ; nor meat, which he could drive in whilst alive, had he any means of removing when dead or of selling while it remained fresh.

In medieval London business was carried on in leisurely fashion, and its rules of procedure were not as strict as they are to-day.   When purchasing a cloak or a bar of soap it was permissible during a shortage of ready money to tender in payment specimens of the family plate without arousing the suspicions of the worthy shopkeeper.   Consequently what is known as " ringing " the changes " was as well known and as frequently practised as it is to-day, but with variations to suit the

customs of the time.   In 1418 an expert prestidigitateur
visited various shops, ordered goods, and offered in
payment a number of silver spoons and some jewellery
which he placed in a glove, but in handing it across the
counter dexterously exchanged it for a similar glove
containing tin spoons, beans, and stones.   In this way he
obtained at various times 12 pounds of pepper, some
boots, and a coverlet.   Another of the same kidney
bought two satin cloaks for £5.   On the excuse of taking
one away to show to a friend he paid then and there one
gold farthing, or quarter noble, and offered as a deposit
fifteen similar coins which he placed in a purse, and the
purse in a casket of the kind then used as handbags.
He locked the casket and handed it to the tradesman,
but before doing so deftly exchanged the fifteen coins
for fifteen counters.   When arrested he had in his
possession a great number of these imitation coins, and
as a punishment he was placed in the pillory, with the
counters, pierced and threaded on a string, hung round
his neck.

Other frauds upon tradesmen for the purpose of
obtaining goods were of the kind in which the thief
" pitches a tale ", an accomplishment in which the
rogues of Old London were quite as proficient as their
modern representatives.   In one such case in 1396 a
man representing himself to be a serving-man entered a
mercer's shop and ordered cloth of gold, velvet, and satin
to the value of £55, ostensibly for his employer, requesting
the mercer to allow his assistant to accompany him to
his master's hostelry, when he could leave the goods and
receive payment.   The serving-man's purpose being to
get possession of the goods, he led the mercer's assistant
from place to place on one excuse or another, until,
with that spice of humour which seems inseparable from

ancient doings, they reached a hostelry with the ominous name of " Le Walssheman sur le Hoope ". Here, by a simple ruse, the thief succeeded in shaking off his follower and decamping with the goods. At the suggestion of the pretended serving-man they proceeded to an upper bedroom, where they deposited the parcel while they went down to the hall to await the return of the master, the rogue locking the bedroom door and pocketing the key. Arrived below, the latter left his victim, promising to return in a few moments, returned upstairs, secured the goods, and decamped by another door. It was only after waiting for five hours that the patient shop assistant realised that he had been " done ".

Cases of forgery were also rife in London at this time, and by reason of the lack of popular education even in the metropolis were usually performed by the intermediary of a " scrivener ", or public writer of deeds, the latter not necessarily being a party to the fraud. In 1377 a man forged a bond purporting to be an acknowledgment of debt by a single woman for £1,200. After her marriage the forger claimed the money, and before his crime was discovered actually caused her husband to be imprisoned for three weeks in the sheriff's compter in Milk Street for debt. He had to pay his victim £10 as compensation, besides being condemned to the pillory. The system by which Papal Bulls and letters of dispensation signed by high dignitaries of the church were scattered broadcast and eagerly snatched up and paid for by sinners, naturally gave encouragement to forgers, who carried on a thriving trade in these desirable documents. On one occasion a scrivener, described in the records as a " notary public ", was found in possession of a chest containing large num-bers of imitation seals of the Pope, Archbishops, Bishops, Abbots, and Priors, with forged letters of dispensation to attach them to, and playing upon the superstitious fears of the people, had, with his two assistants, sold them all over the city, by which means he had amassed a large sum of money. Even men whom one would have expected to display better sense were not without a weakness for acquiring such scraps of paper, for in 1351 we find the Mayor himself paying money to a certain Master Nicholas de Hethe on his promise to obtain Papal Bulls for the city. However, on his failing to produce them within a reasonable time, he was committed to prison, but was ultimately released by the King's intervention.

Another kind of swindle introduces a character peculiar to the middle ages. This is the " Appealer ", a man who, in prison awaiting a probable hanging for felony, thinks to prolong his own life by accusing all sorts of people of all manner of crimes. In some records he is referred to as the " King's Appealer ", by whose means the King collected large sums by way of fines from the accused people, which he bestowed in charity upon the poor ; and we even hear of such a one being paid a retaining fee of three halfpence a day to carry on the nefarious work. What more natural than that a blackguard of this description should endeavour to augment his income by demanding money from innocent citizens by a threat of prosecution ? So in 1388 an appealer confined in Newgate, in collusion with another prisoner, sent a demand to a brewer of the city for 6s. 8d., or alternatively he would accuse him of harbouring thieves, which, as the record states, " might easily have lost him his life " and property ". The brewer, however, declined to be intimidated by this 14th-century form of blackmail, and repairing at once to Newgate, demanded, in the presence of the coroner, an explanation from the appealer. In the result it was the confederate that was sentenced

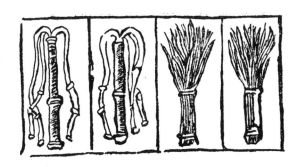

WHIPS AND PILLORY
Harman's "Caveat for Common Cursitors" (E.E.T.S.)

to the pillory, but nothing seems to have been done to the professional criminal. The same appealer attempted to blackmail a goldsmith, the price of his silence on this occasion being a " pilche ", or fur tippet, a gown, and 5s. od. in silver, and the victim parted with the pilche before he plucked up sufficient courage to prosecute.

The army of officials of the King, the Archbishop of Canterbury, the Bishop of London, and the civic authorities who paraded the city streets for one purpose or another, gave further opportunity for intimidation and extortion by the rogues of the period. Thus we see a pretended summoner of the Archbishop of Canterbury, with his white wand of office, calling upon the Prioress of St. Mary, Clerkenwell, to announce a visitation of her house by two of the King's clerks, in hope of receiving a gratuity for his information. In the same way another swindler, representing himself to be a King's messenger, called upon the Countesses of Norfolk and Bedford with pretended invitations to dinner from the King, and from the latter lady extracted a gratuity of 40 pence. This he was compelled to return to her, and after undergoing the pillory and imprisonment, was warned never again to enter the city upon pain of losing his ears. The anxiety of the people to placate officials of the King in order to keep out of their clutches is revealed in another case where a man went round to various brewers, and pretending to be the King's ale-taker, marked several of their barrels with the device of an arrow-head to indicate that he seized them for the use of the royal household. The brewers, as might be expected, preferred to give the man a gratuity in order that he should leave them in peace, rather than to take their chance of obtaining payment for the commandeered ale. Purveyors of the King, as these men were called, also carried a white wand in

token of their office.   Officers of the Marshalsea, the
court of the Marshal of England, carried a staff with
horn at either end, called a tipstaff, and performed the
duties of seizing houses for the accommodation of members of the court, and of arresting any offenders against
the King or members of his household within a radius of
twelve miles around the court, wherever it might be
temporarily situated.   A pretended official of this kind,
parading the city with his tipstaff, attempted to arrest
a London brewer, but himself being arrested instead,
was put in the pillory still holding the staff in his hand.

The love of gambling, that ineradicable trait of human
nature, was as prevalent in the 14th century as it is in
the 20th, and gave birth to a host of sharpers on the
lookout for victims to fleece.   Dice were the favourite
means of indulging this passion, and, under the name of
" hazard ", were played in all the taverns.   Another dice
game was played on a board, and called " tables ".   It
is always spoken of in the plural, probably because there
were two sections to the board, or possibly because both
sides could be played upon.   It resembled the modern
backgammon, and one variety of it was " chequers ",
shortened to " quek ", or " queek ".   The tragic side
of the gambling habit is displayed in various cases in
the coroner's court, in one of which we get a picture of
two men in a brewhouse playing a game of hazard which
led to a fatal quarrel ; and in another of a game of tables
played in a tavern, at the end of which the loser fatally
stabbed the winner on his way home.   The method of
the sharks may be understood by the prosecution of a
tailor living in Friday Street, who was accused of in-
veigling people to his house for the purpose of robbing
them by false play.   He used to send out a confederate
with the appropriate name of Outlaw to tout for clients,

1. MEDIÆVAL GAMBLERS
2. ORNAMENTAL DICE
3. A PARTY AT TABLES

From Wright's "Domestic Customs and Sentiments"

who accosted people in the streets and suggested that he knew of a place where they could make money by gambling, with himself as partner. But when they went to the house and played with the owner the dice were loaded and the chequer board had all the black squares depressed below the white ones, a matter difficult to detect except upon a close inspection. Two men who were taken there to play under these conditions lost 39s. 2d. before it occurred to them to examine the board, after which they refused to play again ; whereupon the tailor and his confederate stripped one of them of his cloak. When complaints against them increased they were tried at Guildhall by a jury of their neighbours in Friday Street, sentenced to the pillory, and compelled to disgorge much of their ill-gotten gains to their many victims. In 1382 two more gaming-houses are mentioned, one in Lombard Street and one in the Ropery, where the same nefarious practices were pursued. Young people were enticed into these places and robbed, sometimes of their parents' money, and of course country people visiting London were frequently among their victims. We even hear of two Scotchmen from Dumfries who were caught and defrauded of 40s. 0. and a knife valued at 4s. 0.

The credulity and the lack of clear thinking which characterised the mass of the people in the middle ages is nowhere more displayed than in the facility with which charlatans of one sort and another plied their trade. Even then there were men who legitimately pursued the study of medicine so far as it was known, yet in cases of accident or illness a priest was much more frequently sent for than a doctor, as a perusal of the Coroner's Rolls of the city will reveal. This state of things furnished a splendid opportunity to quacks and sorcerers. In 1382 one such pretended physician was consulted by a man whose wife had been taken ill, undertook to cure her, and obtained a preliminary payment of a shilling. His method of cure was to tear a leaf of parchment from an old book, wrap it securely in cloth of gold, and suspend it from the patient's neck. This process failing to produce the desired effect, the husband, doubtless with thoughts of his shilling rankling in his mind, became suspicious and caused the doctor to be arrested. The latter, when called up at Guildhall, attempted to bluff the court by claiming that an incantation, most efficacious in cases of fever, was written upon the parchment. Asked to recite the words he repeated them in Latin, which may be freely translated : " Soul of Christ, sanctify " me ; Body of Christ, save me ; Blood of Christ, " drench me ; as thou art good Christ, wash me ". Bluff is only useful until it is called, and a sceptical Mayor ordered the bundle to be opened, when no such writing appearing on the parchment, the husband lost even the poor satisfaction of a Latin inscription for his shilling. Curiously enough, the confidence in magic was not confined to the ruder classes, but the vagabonds who professed it were sometimes able to delude even the highest in the land. An instance of this occurred in 1390 when a converted Jew (unconverted Jews were not allowed to live in England at that time), professed to be able to detect thieves by magic, and was actually consulted by the Council of the Duke of York when his grace had been robbed of two silver dishes. He accused a servant of the Duke, who was arrested, imprisoned, beaten, and on the point of being made to swear that he would never come within ten leagues of the Duke's house again, when the fraud was discovered. In the same way he falsely accused two men when Lady Le Despencer

lost a scarlet cloak. However, the Mayor and aldermen
of London were under no illusions as to the value of this
kind of evidence, for when the Jew appeared at Guildhall
they ordered him to the pillory in Cornhill, and afterwards
compelled him to take oath to leave the city for ever.
Another case of pretended magic was of a more sinister
type. A woman, suspected of stealing a veil, the property
of another woman with whom she had been very familiar,
persuaded a cobbler to practise a form of deceit calculated to divert suspicion from herself. She imparted
to the cobbler some intimate matters concerning the
owner of the veil, armed with which he proceeded to her
house and offered to find the thief, repeating the private
information he had received to prove his powers of
divination. The lady, unaware of the cobbler's acquaintance with the object of her suspicions, was greatly
impressed and prepared to believe anything she might
be told. Thereupon the cobbler, improving upon his
instructions, assured her that it was as true as anything
he had just related that she would be drowned within a
month, which threw the poor lady into such a fever of
apprehension that she nearly expired of melancholy.
We are not told how or by what means she came to a
realisation of the fact that she had been tricked, but at
any rate she afterwards prosecuted the cobbler, who was
confined for an hour in the pillory. In other cases we
are permitted a glimpse of the methods employed by
these plausible rogues to delude their victims. One man
who professed to discover thieves by magic made thirty-
two balls of white clay and over them muttered his
incantations, while another performed similar rites over
a loaf of bread into the top of which he had inserted a
round wooden peg, and into the sides four knives at right
angles to imitate the appearance of a cross.

Another case which illustrates the profound super-
stition which beguiled the minds of the poor and ignorant,
and may well cause the modern reader to marvel, concerns
a man from whom, as a pastor and teacher, a different
line of conduct might have been expected.   It should be
observed that from early Christian times it was a popular
belief among Roman Catholics that the corpse of a very
holy man would emit a delightful aroma as of spice.
Evidence of this belief is met with again and again in
early accounts of the translation of saints.   In the year
1440 a priest who by his preaching had become very
popular in London was burnt for heresy on Tower Hill,
and crowds of the common people, regarding him as
a martyr unjustly executed, came to the spot where he
had suffered carrying waxen images in his honour, and
bending on their knees, devoutly kissed the ground.
At the same time they contributed small sums by way of
alms to the neighbouring church of Allhallows Barking.
The vicar of that church, his worst feelings of cupidity
aroused by this new and unexpected source of income,
and in order to increase its flow while opportunity served,
secretly mixed a quantity of ashes and spice overnight
and strewed it upon the sacred spot in readiness for the
next day's crowd of visitors.   By means of this " sweet
" odour of sanctity " the holiness of the deceased became
only too famous, and reaching the ears of authority, the
vicar soon found himself in prison minus his benefice.

The records of Old London reveal a great procession
of ingenious swindlers battening upon the respectable
citizens, some having their representatives still with us,
others with methods appropriate to their own times,
but long since relegated to the limbo of forgotten villainy.
Among them may be seen dealers in imitation jewellery,
haunting taverns in search of dupes who might purchase

plated articles as solid gold, quacks of many kinds, sorcerers, fraudulent beggars, professional false witnesses pacing the precincts of the court with a wisp of straw in their shoe (" men of straw "), men whose business it was to get on juries in order to give false verdicts, bogus pilgrims with a sprig of palm or a scallop shell in their hat, claiming to have made the journey to Rome, Jerusalem, or Compostella.   One such, walking the streets barefooted and with long hair, confessed that although he had never visited any of these places, he had made a living for six years on the strength of a reputation for having done so.   Beggars, many of them frauds of the most blatant type, wandered the streets carrying a staff known as a " potent ", with a crossbar to lean upon, craving alms of the charitable.   One of these makes us realise how near the 14th century is to our own by claiming to have been wounded in the assault on Ypres in 1383 ; while two others, pretending to be dumb, and able by some trick to conceal their tongues, opened wide their mouths at intervals and gave vent to dismal roars to excite the pity of passers-by.   A deplorable feature of the time is the child beggars who picked up a living in the streets.   On one occasion we hear of a child of seven and at another time of a child of twelve, both described as paupers and mendicants, and it must be borne in mind that they are only mentioned on account of fatal accidents happening to them, necessitating a coroner's inquest.

To bring a swindler to book was regarded as a display of public spirit and an exhibition of good citizenship, and thus on many occasions the record states that the aggrieved individual " prosecutes for the commonalty ". In most cases of fraud, extortion, or intimidation, the punishment inflicted was the pillory, and our ancestors exhibited a lively wit in the method of its application.

They often conducted a delinquent thither mounted on a horse, sometimes facing the tail, a fool's cap on his head, and with basins suspended around him, or at other times preceded by a band playing on trumpets and pipes. When standing in the place of castigation, the spurious article which he had been guilty of foisting upon the public would be burnt beneath him, or the means which he had employed for his swindle, such as false coins, loaded dice, etc., would be hung round his neck. The most curious addition, however, to the punishment of the pillory was the suspension of a whetstone from the culprit's neck, used on occasions when the fraud was perpetrated by means of a direct lie. It seems to have been used only in such cases, the official report of the sentence usually adding : " with a whetstone suspended " from his neck, that being the sign of a liar ". The origin of this device is buried in obscurity, but possibly had its beginning in a joke against shopkeepers, inasmuch as nearly every tradesman keeps a whetstone, ostensibly to sharpen his knives, but just as likely for the purpose of sharpening his tongue or his wits to evolve fresh lies for his customers.

CHAPTER IX

TRAGEDIES

I
T is perhaps hardly necessary to point out that the peculiar value of such records as the Coroner's Rolls and the Letter-Books, as contrasted with the Old Chronicles, lies in the fact that their compilers were not consciously writing for posterity, or even for the delectation of contemporaries, but were merely recording, as a matter of business and without any ulterior motive, the ordinary happenings of the city as they occurred from day to day. Such records suffer from the defects of their virtues, consisting as they do of formal statements of events, without those explanations and descriptions which, superfluous to people living at the time, would have been invaluable to us. In consequence, entries have to be pieced together, reading between the lines resorted to, and supplementary information sought from other sources. On the other hand, such information as is found in the Chronicles, though less reliable and often unimportant, is frequently accompanied by a wealth of detail which causes the events to live as though they were the news of yesterday. The Coroner's Rolls of the 14th century, although at first sight they may not appear to promise very delectable reading, will nevertheless be found instructive and even entertaining, and they constitute perhaps the most valuable documents we possess for the social history of ancient London ; for although

to a large extent they record the seamy side of life, in them we are brought into contact with the people themselves, where it is possible to observe their more intimate manners and customs, to hear their racy language, in which they did not boggle at calling a spade a spade, and to enjoy the nicknames which, after the manner of their kind in all ages, they frequently bestowed upon each other. So we find a woman called " Houdydoudy," a man called " Renaboute ", others called " Frelove ", " Mate ", " Fulberd ", " Litelrobyn ", and the curious nickname " Maucovenaunt ". A certain John was known as " Lyttle Jakke ", yet was not so small but he could wield a poleaxe with such effect as to kill a fishmonger at a blow. We learn that the original diminutive of Richard was " Dicoun," half-way to our modern " Dick ", and yet the reason for it remains unexplained. It must be remembered that many of our modern surnames had their origin in nicknames, and in the early part of the 14th century we find many such already established as family names. Thus there is a William Agodeshalf, Katharine Robynhood, William Melksop, Roger Pigsflesh, John Neverathom, Geoffrey Godbeherinne, Henry Pudding, and William Etebred. One cannot forbear mention of two interesting names, though not derived from nicknames, found in the records of the period ; one with literary memories—Oliver le Goldsmith—and the other with which events of recent years has made us familiar—Peter le Peyntour.

One of the first things to strike the reader of the Coroner's Rolls is the pugnacity of the citizens. Small causes of quarrel which in our times might possibly lead to a bout of fisticuffs, but would more probably evoke no more than expostulation or abuse, resulted then in the rapid drawing of a knife and a mortal blow. In 1300 we have a picture of two servants quarrelling over the where-abouts of a strong-box belonging to their master, when one called the other a liar, and the aggrieved one promptly seized a piece of wood and brained his fellow. There are many cases of stabbing for some slight abuse, but more chivalry is indicated in the case of a man who mortally wounded another because he saw him strike a woman with his fist. There is a case in 1301 of two men playing " chequers " in an ale-house when there entered two other men accompanied by a woman who in her passage stepped over the board. After a few angry words one of the players seized one of the new-comers, stripped him to the waist, and in doing so, finding that he had a con-cealed knife, took possession of it. The man who had been stripped then ran upstairs out of the way, while the man in possession of the dagger chased his fellow out of the house as far as Paternoster Row, where he stabbed him to death. A still more foolish but equally sordid quarrel in the same year, originating in nothing more serious than the badinage of a drunken woman, reached the same tragic end. Several workmen were digging the foundations of a house at the corner of Silver Street, a turning leading out of Wood Street, when a woman the worse for drink called them " tredekeiles ", a term of abuse of the period, and in retaliation one of them seized her and bumped her on the ground. The woman's mistress thereupon came out of a neighbouring house and called the workmen ribalds and other opprobrious names. A stranger passing by reprimanded the too vociferous lady for her language, and turning upon him she called him a thief, in reply to which he called her something a great deal worse. Threatening that before night the matter should be " squared ", as she expressed it, she called to avenge her several male friends, one of

whom was a chaplain. These knights-errant then purchased a bundle of wood for a farthing, and each selecting
a stick proceeded to the tavern where they thought the
stranger was staying. In the doorway of the hostel stood
a man of whom they inquired if he were the man they
sought, and without waiting for a reply, commenced to
beat him with their sticks ; whereupon he drew a dagger
and stabbed the too bellicose chaplain to the heart.
The treatment meted out by the authorities to viragoes
such as the one mentioned above may be observed in the
case of a woman living in Tower ward in 1375, who was
prosecuted at Guildhall as a common scold. The record
states : " And for that all the neighbours, dwelling in
" that vicinity, by her malicious words and abuse were
" so greatly molested and annoyed ; she sowing envy
" among them, discord, and ill-will, and repeatedly
" defaming, molesting, and backbiting many of them,
" sparing neither rich nor poor ". For this conduct
she was tried by a jury, convicted, and sentenced to stand
in the " thewe ", a form of the pillory specially designed
for women.

Often when a commotion occurred many citizens
appear to have completely lost their heads, so causing
tragedies which, with a little coolness, might easily have
been avoided. This trait in their character may be seen
in an affray in 1326, leading to a thorough mix-up and
the death of the young son of a knight. Three servants
of Sir John Felton had been asked, not by their master,
to deliver a horse to a man living in Bread Street, and
walking the horse along that thoroughfare met the owner,
who requested them to give it up. For reasons unexplained, they refused, and an altercation arising, one
of them threatened the owner of the horse with a knife.
Another man then arriving on the scene, apparently

having no concern with the matter in hand, violently
assaulted with his fists the man who held the knife.
Thereupon from a neighbouring house emerged young
John Felton, son of the knight above mentioned, sword
in hand and with a determination to attack somebody,
although the only interest he and his father's servants
possessed in the horse was to deliver it at its destination.
Instead, however, of attacking any of the disputants, he
proceeded to strike with his sword a man standing in
a neighbouring doorway, who appears to have been no
party to the quarrel, knocking him down.   Then came
upon the scene two more men, also apparently with no
concern in the matter, who, together with the man who
had used his fists, attacked John Felton with staves,
smashing his head in.   As an exhibition of indiscriminate
fighting for no better reason than that somebody started
it, this would be hard to beat.   Another murder which
seems equally uncalled for occurred in 1276.   A half-
drunken man was making a great noise in endeavouring
to gain admittance to a house when the people living next
door requested him to go away.   On his refusal to do
so they attacked him with swords and drove him into
a neighbouring tavern where he hid between two barrels.
As the pursuers entered the tavern one of the customers
innocently inquired : " Who are these people " ? whereupon one of them ran him through twice with his sword,
killing him upon the spot.   A curious street scene,
where similarly irresponsible conduct was displayed,
is presented in 1326, when, on a June evening at curfew
two goldsmiths were walking from Chepe to Aldersgate
carrying swords and bucklers in their hands.   What was
their object in being arrayed in such martial guise is not
divulged ; it was certainly contrary to the laws of the
city.   A cobbler, standing at the door of his shop, con-

cluding from their appearance that they must be " mis-
" doers and disturbers of the peace ", promptly set an
example of disturbing the peace by seizing a staff and
knocking one of them down. The fallen man rose up,
slashed at the cobbler's arm with his sword, and ran away,
when without further ado his fellow goldsmith split
the cobbler's head with his weapon and fled in his turn.

Such gusts of passion, and even the commission of
more sordid crimes, were not confined to the lower orders
of society, but were often to be attributed to men of education and social standing, who might have been expected
to set an example of good behaviour to others. But in
the 14th century the whole population appears to have
entertained a disregard of the sanctity of human life
which may well fill with amazement the people of a more
cultivated age. Thus in 1337 the wife of a knight,
having quarrelled with a chaplain, engaged her brother,
two of her servants, and two other men, one of whom
was also a chaplain, to waylay and kill him. Accordingly
they waited for him in Chepe, and, meeting him at the
corner of Bread Street, the chaplain engaged him in
pleasant conversation as they strolled westward, and at
Foster Lane the others set upon and stabbed him to
death. Another lady of the period, sister to the Dean of
St. Martin-le-Grand, supplied knives to some prisoners
in Newgate with which they murdered the gate-keeper
in order to effect their escape. So far as the upper
classes were concerned, the clergy appear to have been
more often guilty of private crime than the laity, or at
any rate they find more frequent mention in the Rolls.
Matthew Paris gives us a picture of two canons of Holy
Trinity, Aldgate, quarrelling about " goats' wool ",
which signifies quarrelling about nothing, when one of
them drew a dagger and mortally wounded his fellow.

He then mutilated himself in several places to give his crime the appearance of self-defence. In 1324 we hear of a knight and a rector on their way to visit the Bishop of Bath and Wells arriving at the gate of the Carmelite Friars, where they drew their swords and fought until the rector inflicted a mortal wound upon his antagonist. Again in 1326 is found a case where a chaplain, visiting his mistress and finding another lover in the room with her, stabbed his rival to death. The pride of the gentry and the dangers of the traffic are exemplified in 1321, when an esquire of the Earl of Arundel, riding through Thames Street on his way to the Tower, nearly knocked over a woman carrying a child. Upon a passer-by telling him to ride more carefully the esquire cut him down with his sword.

The night life of the city is depicted in many of these cases. Efforts were made at various times to keep the people within doors after curfew, and night-walkers were liable to be arrested by the watch and confined in the Tun on Cornhill ; the result being that while respectable citizens stayed at home, malefactors roamed the streets. We get an account in 1322 of three men lying in wait at midnight for an enemy at the corner of Soper Lane in Chepe. On his approach they attacked him with knives and drove him as far as the Cripplegate end of Wood Street, where, as he tripped over a heap of refuse, they dealt him five mortal wounds. Another night-time incident illustrates the fact that people found away from their homes at unreasonable hours were assumed at once to be abroad for no good purpose. In 1301 three workmen, out for the evening, arrived at their master's house too late to be let in, and for want of a better place went to sleep in a shed. The watch, discovering them, proceeded to beat them so severely that one was killed.

Roysterers in the streets at midnight, disturbing the
rest of the neighbours, were not uncommon, as may be
seen in 1322 when a band of fourteen youths came singing
and shouting along Bread Street, and a shopkeeper
coming to his door begged them to go away quietly.
They in frolicsome humour dared him to come out, and
nothing loth, he rushed out with a staff and smashed
the head of one of them.   In 1311 it is obvious that
complaints must have reached the ears of the King
concerning the turbulent condition of the streets at
night, for we find him sending his writ to the Mayor
to arrest all nocturnal disturbers of the peace.   The
result was a grand round up of all known bad characters,
who were committed to prison on the general charge of
being night-walkers who assaulted peaceful citizens,
without any specific instances being alleged.   One man
was accused of keeping open house at night for the
reception and entertainment of evildoers, and another of
keeping a fencing-school to which he enticed the sons
of respectable citizens and induced them to spend their
money foolishly.   As nothing much came of these prosecutions, most of the accused being released on bringing
their friends to stand surety for them, and one unable to
do so allowed to depart on his own recognisances, it is
legitimate to assume that the culprits consisted for the
most part of young men out for a spree rather than actual
rogues and vagabonds.   Indeed, not a single case is
found of bands of robbers roaming the streets ; the
nearest spot to the city where anything of the kind
happened was Charing Cross, and we only hear of it
because a wounded man succeeded in reaching the city,
where he died.   The danger of travel and of cultivating
strange company by the way are illustrated by the case
of a London cordwainer who, making the journey to

Rochester, was robbed and murdered at Blackheath by
a chance acquaintance. The same affair shows that the
poor, even in those days, were not without that milk of
human kindness which still impels them to assist their
fellows in distress, for we read that a carter, passing the
spot shortly after the tragedy, took the wounded man
on his cart to Greenwich " for charity's sake " ; and
for the same reason a number of boatmen brought him
back to London and restored him to his friends.

Of sordid and brutal murders there are quite a number,
including attacks on women. An instance is found where
a woman, interposing between two quarrelsome men,
receives a kick on the abdomen ; another killed by a
cobbler with a blow from his fist ; and again in 1337
a man waiting outside a church in Milk Street to beat
a woman, and mistaking an approaching female for the
object of his vengeance, stabs her in the leg. In another
case a man made a brutal assault upon a married woman,
beating her with his staff. Her husband coming up,
endeavoured to pacify his wife's assailant with fair words,
but in his turn was violently assaulted and pursued for
some distance, when, turning in desperation, he stabbed
his antagonist. Unfortunately, we do not hear what
happened to the husband after he, as the record says,
" surrendered himself to prison " ; but in the middle
ages those who killed in self-defence did not usually
escape scot free, but were kept in prison during the
King's pleasure or until they had made fine. Of murders
of women there are two which for sheer depravity it is
hard to choose between ; one of them cold and calculated
and the other the result of the most disgusting passion.
In the first case a man and his wife invited a woman
to spend the night at their house, and smashed in her
head with a staff merely to gain possession of the clothes

she wore. In the other a man and his wife went to bed leaving a candle burning, which during the night first set on fire the bed and then the house. Being warned in time they both made their escape, but on reaching the street it suddenly occurred to the husband that the accident was entirely his wife's fault, and in a fit of violent rage he thrust her back into the flames where she was burned to death.

In every form of law-breaking, whether murder, accidental killing, robbery, or even debt, the culprit usually fled to sanctuary in the nearest church, where the neighbours were supposed to keep watch in order to prevent his escape, a duty, so far as London was concerned, more honoured in the breach than the observance. In one case, however, this duty was fulfilled but too well, and led to a tragedy worse than the offence from which the delinquent had fled. A thief had taken refuge in the church of St. Mary, Staining Lane, near Cripplegate, and a window of the church being broken, one of the watchers, thinking it likely the thief would escape by that way, approached to make a closer inspection. The clerk of the church, who was standing just within, thereupon prodded at him with the shaft of a lance, struck him a blow in the eye, which penetrated the brain and so killed him.

It is probable that in the records of accidents the habits of the people and the conditions under which they lived are best displayed. Many casualties were caused by falling down the outside stone stairways which were a feature of many of the houses, and usually the victims were drunk at the time. Several cases occur of people being run over in the streets, one by a cart drawn by three horses ; another by a cart carrying a cask of water, a reminder of the difficulties of the domestic supply ;

and a third, in Bishopsgate, where two empty carts were racing and the carters whipping up their horses. We hear of people drowned in the river whilst filling their water-jugs or washing their clothes, the usual method of performing laundry work in the 14th century ; of men drowned or suffocated while cleaning out wells ; of workmen falling off ladders ; and of one case where labourers digging up the bed of an old water conduit were overcome by escaping gases ; but this comes from a chronicler, the continuator of Matthew Paris, who opines that the accident was due to a miracle caused by servile work being performed at an improper hour in the evening. That the proclivities of boyhood have not changed throughout the centuries will be realised on reading of a boy climbing up to a gutter to retrieve his lost ball ; of others playing on a heap of timber when one fell and broke his leg ; and of another, a schoolboy returning over London Bridge after dinner who must needs climb out and hang by his hands from a plank on the side of the bridge, and fell in and was drowned. London Bridge, throughout its history, has been the scene of many accidents. One occurred in 1395, when Isabella, the bride of Richard II, entered London. So great was the crowd on this occasion that seven persons, including the Prior of Tiptree in Essex, were crushed to death. Other accidents occurred there by reason of the swirling waters rushing through the narrow spaces between the piers of the bridge. A famous incident of the kind happened in 1429, when the Duke of Norfolk's barge, while attempting to pass through, collided with one of the piers and overturned. The Duke and a few others leapt on to one of the piles and were rescued by people on the bridge who lowered ropes and hauled them up, but over thirty persons were drowned. In 1406 the Lieutenant of the Tower was drowned at London Bridge, probably in the same way, as he came from Westminster on his barge.

Some of the cases recorded in the Coroner's Rolls shed a flood of light on the conditions of life of the poor. We are reminded by a case in 1326 that nightshirts had not come into fashion, and people used to enter their beds in the same state as that in which they were born. A man lodging in a house in the High Street of Vintry ward arose at midnight naked from his bed and approaching a window 30 feet from the ground for a purpose which is unprintable, but which to-day would be considered highly indecent, fell out on to the pavement and was killed. Indeed, a lack of privacy in attending to the most intimate physical necessities is characteristic of the period, and is mentioned in the most casual manner and without condemnation in chronicles and records ; so a sheriff of London in 1418, a few days after assuming office, went down to the shore of the Thames, fell backwards into the water, and was drowned.[1] The material of which the beds were made is likewise indicated by the numerous cases of fire caused by the candle igniting the straw. For the most part the remainder of the household appointments were on a similarly primitive scale. Rushes were used as floor covering, and yet we read of carpets valued at 10d. and 1s. 4d. respectively possessed by a citizen not of the highest class, and in other cases of sheets, blankets, and coverlets for the bed, and feathers for stuffing a couch. More sumptuous bed furniture, such as feather beds and ornamental coverlets, was not unknown among the wealthy, and were sufficiently prized and cared for to be handed down from father to son. Thus in 1331 a feather bed worth 3s. 0. and two

[1] Kingsford's *Chronicles of London*, p. 72.

blankets and two sheets worth 5s. o. are mentioned in an inventory of effects inherited by an infant from his deceased father. The coverlet of the bed had a still greater value, one such in 1328, furred with minever, being valued at 8 marks. An accident which occurred in 1277, when a man who climbed into the belfry of St. Stephen's, Walbrook, after a pigeon's nest, fell and received fatal injuries, is a reminder that the pigeons which haunt the churches and public buildings of the city have visited us from very early times. But in many other respects the conditions of city life are shown to have been widely different from those prevailing to-day. What an enormous difference is indicated by the record of a fishmonger in 1337, living in Crooked Lane, near London Bridge, who, after dinner, took his wife and children out into the fields to play. This merely involved a short walk through Aldgate or Bishopsgate. Again, the great expansion which London has undergone in modern times may be realised from the account of a murder in 1278. In harvest time of that year a man was reaping his corn in the fields adjoining the village of Stratford, on ground where is now one of the most populous suburbs and a great railway junction, when he was murdered by the chaplain of the Prioress of Stratford because he had resented the theft of his crops. Another harvest scene, this time at Stepney, indicates how circumscribed was the area of the city in 1325, when we find the Dean of St. Paul's sending seven of his servants, including his cook and his palfreyman, to guard his crops during the night.

We are enabled to visualise the curiously different aspects of the medieval city, surrounded on all sides except the river front by its walls and ditches, by an entry in the Rolls of 1336, when a boy is reported to have been drowned in Houndsditch whilst bathing, and his body washed up at Aldgate two days later. What is now a paved street and a busy shopping centre was then a running watercourse, not only where Houndsditch is now situated, but for the entire circuit of the walls ; and many accidents were caused by men watering their horses in the stream. The name of Houndsditch was applied to its entire course, not restricted to the short thoroughfare which extends from Bishopsgate to Aldgate. Thus we often hear of " Houndsditch " between Ludgate and Newgate, where the Old Bailey now runs, and in 1372 there is record of the lease of a house near " Houndsditch " outside Aldersgate. The street now known as the Old Bailey is first referred to as the " bailly near " Newgate and Fleet Street " in the year 1391. The city ditches inevitably became the dumping-ground for all manner of rubbish, and owing to the slow movement of the water continually became choked and stagnant, and were thus a constant source of annoyance to the citizens. Schemes were started periodically for cleansing them. This was performed in 1321, and took five days to complete, starting on a Wednesday and ending on a Monday. The method pursued was the division of the city wards into five groups, each group supplying labourers daily in rotation. In 1375 the executors of a deceased citizen gave £100 for the purpose of cleaning the ditches, on condition that the chaplains of the chapel of St. Mary at Guildhall should pray for his soul and that of his wife ; and afterwards the city Chamberlain rendered account showing that the money had been expended for this purpose. Again in 1379 the Mayor, John Philpot, ordered that every householder should either work himself or provide a labourer for cleaning the ditches for one day in every five weeks until the work was completed, each ward sending men day after day in rotation.

A striking point in connection with most of the crimes and mishaps recorded above is the absolute lack of medical attention, whereby many lives might have been saved ; and not only so, but a seeming lack of any appreciation that such assistance was even desirable. The usual method of dealing with an injured person was to convey him to the nearest house, make him as comfortable as possible, send for a priest to shrive him, and leave the rest to fate. The most curious fact in connection with this point is that although there is only one recorded case in the Coroner's Rolls where the victim was taken to a doctor for treatment, there are three instances of wounded men brought to London from the provinces for this purpose. Although medical assistance was so rarely invoked, there were many surgeons living in the city who compounded medicines as well as applying external cures, and were just as subject to the supervision of the Mayor as the members of other callings. Thus in 1369 three men were sworn before the Mayor and aldermen as Master Surgeons of the city, undertaking well and faithfully to serve the people, to demand only such fees as were reasonable, to present to the Mayor the defaults of any others undertaking cures, to be ready at all times when called upon to attend the maimed and wounded, to give notice of any such to the authorities, and to state whether they were in peril of death or not. Although the surgeons belonged to the mistery of Barber Surgeons, it is doubtful if all barbers practised surgery ; in fact, that they did not do so is tacitly admitted in an inquisition taken before the Mayor in 1415 as to the scandal of barbers, inexperienced in the art of surgery, venturing to undertake cures of complaints which were beyond their understanding. Moreover, during the latter part of the 14th century, the Masters of the Barbers and of the Surgeons seem usually to have been appointed separately. Many wounds are recorded in the Coroner's Rolls where no attempt was made to summon medical assistance, and yet by their trivial nature it seems fairly obvious that had even such simple remedies as were at that time available been applied the life might have been saved. A boy died of a broken leg ; a drunken woman fell and broke her arm, lingering over two months before she died ; a man struck on the head, side, and hand with a doorbar survived for nearly a month ; it took as long for another man to die who had a finger cut off ; a girl three and a half years of age was scalded and lingered from Tuesday to Friday ; two men were romping together when one accidentally inflicted a wound an inch deep in his fellow's abdomen, and they continued living together in the same house, hoping that no evil result would ensue, but after three weeks the injured man sickened and died ; and many other instances could be given. At the inquest, moreover, the witnesses were never asked whether a doctor had been sent for, but they were always questioned as to whether the deceased had received his ecclesiastical rights.

The King's Butler was, by virtue of his office, the coroner of the city, but invariably appointed a deputy to perform the actual duties. At least two Mayors were elected to the mayoral seat while they held the position of King's Butler, and were therefore Mayor and Coroner at the same time ; and one was so elected while acting as deputy coroner, and contrived to perform the duties of both offices concurrently during his term. All deaths in the city from wounds or misadventure, quaintly described in the Rolls as "died of a death other than "his (or her) rightful death", had to be immediately reported to the acting coroner. That official then proceeded to the spot where the body was lying and summoned a jury of the inhabitants, not only of the ward where the fatality had occurred, but as a rule from the two or three nearest wards in addition. The reason for this is not clear, but the result was that the number of jurymen varied enormously, the lowest recorded during the century being twelve and the highest fifty. These men were then left to make what inquiries and investigations they pleased, and afterwards came before the coroner and gave their verdict. Seldom were they at a loss, for a verdict of "persons unknown" is a rarity; but at least in one instance it can be seen from a later entry in the Rolls that a different person to the one indicated by the jury afterwards confessed to a murder.

In each instance the weapon with which the crime was committed is carefully recorded, and in the aggregate they form quite a compendium of the offensive arms of the period. Many quaint names occur among them, and in a number of cases it would be difficult to decide the precise variety of weapon intended. Among daggers and swords we find Irishnyf; misericorde; anelace, a short knife or stiletto; fauchon; trancheon; panade, or poniard; twytel; baselard; and trenchour, or carving knife. Among longer weapons: belte, a kind of axe; poleax, halberd, and sparth, which were practically identical; gysarme, having a two-edged blade in line with the shaft; and bideu, bidawe, or bidowe, probably with a blade resembling a sickle. Among less dangerous wooden weapons: shide or talwhschide; balstaf; pyked-staffe; fagotstaff, a pole for carrying faggots of wood ·

durbarre ; wombedstaf, or bedstaff, used for keeping the bedclothes in order, and the value of which we find to be one penny ; and potent, or beggar's staff. We arrive on more modern ground on finding that one man was killed with a " shovele ".

CHAPTER X

ADMINISTERING THE LAW

THE administration of the law in London in the middle ages has a peciliar interest for all those who love the history of their ancient city because it displays, perhaps more than anything else, the mentality of our ancestors ; and in it we can discern, not only the assiduous care which they took to make their city peaceful and law-abiding, but also their efforts to prevent any outside interference with their liberties. They tolerated as little intermeddling by the King's Judges as possible, and obtained by successive charters from Edward the Confessor onward, that the maintenance of law and order should be in their own hands, except for the Iter at the Tower of London, when the itinerant Justices came there at long intervals, sometimes as long as twenty years ; the courts of gaol delivery at Newgate, though here the Mayor was admitted as one of the judges ; and the King's Court held at St. Martin-le-Grand, the purpose of which seems chiefly to have been to inquire into any matter arising in the city which affected the rights of the King or his heirs. The citizens were very particular as to what cases they would permit to be tried by the King's Justices at St. Martin's, in case anything might be done which would constitute an infringement of their privileges. Writs of error were tried there and proceedings instituted against the

Mayor and aldermen in their corporate capacity. Thus in 1303 the King caused the sheriffs to be attached to answer for allowing a debtor to abscond, and in 1285 the corporation as a whole was sued by the Bishop of London and the Dean and Chapter of St. Paul's for erecting houses near the churchyard wall which became a nuisance to the clerics by reason of the rainwater which dropped from the roofs on to their wall, and because the tenants threw dirt out of their doors and windows into the churchyard. On the other hand, when in 1325 the King sent a commission to St. Martin-le-Grand to try a case of assault committed by some citizens in Fleet Street, the Mayor would not permit it, but, showing his charters, refused to produce the defendants, and the Justices were unable to proceed with the case.

The Iter at the Tower, like the other Iters held periodically throughout the country, was mainly devoted to the purpose of raising money for the King by a process of fining everybody whom it was possible to fine. The King's Justices inquired into all the deaths, other than natural ones, that had occurred in the city since their previous visit, and fined as they went, sheriffs, aldermen, officials, and witnesses for any mistake, large or small, which they made in presenting the cases, or in the procedure they had adopted at the time of the occurrence, perhaps years previously. In addition they tried any cases of felony which might be awaiting trial, and the method which they followed forms a striking contrast to similar trials at the present day. Indeed, from the days of the ordeals by fire and water onwards there is a topsy-turvyness observable in early legal procedure, or rather in the conceptions on which it was based, which lends it a whimsicality all its own. Trial by combat was unknown in England in Saxon times, was introduced at the Conquest, but abolished as far as London was concerned in the reign of Henry I ; in fact, people of English birth appear to have been always at liberty to refuse it. In the earliest times to which 'our laws go back, trial by jury in criminal cases was the general rule, and the method adopted at the Iter of the Tower in the reign of Henry III is only a development of the early practice. The theory upon which trial by jury was originally founded was diametrically opposed to the conception which is its basis to-day. Whereas we hold that the ends of justice will best be met and the guilt or innocence of a defendant established if the case is considered by a number of men possessing neither interest in, nor previous knowledge of, the matter to be tried, our ancestors considered that the persons most likely to be in a position to form a correct judgment were those who had lived side by side with the parties for years and knew them intimately, and perhaps from childhood. It was for this reason that the jury was formed from the neighbours and not from strangers selected at random. There seems to be some argument in favour of both theories, but it is obvious that with the early method prejudice is certain to be imported into many cases, and even personal animus. In fact, glimmerings of doubt as to the wisdom of their method appear to have assailed our ancestors at times, based most probably on complaints of favour and partiality, for we find them in the 14th century appointing " triors " to make a preliminary examination of the jurymen with a view to determining whether any personal motives might actuate them in addition to the intimate knowledge which they were expected to possess. The underlying principle, then, was not that the prosecution should prove the prisoner guilty, but rather that the latter whould be able to persuade a number of men not personally connected with the case at issue to swear to a belief in his innocence. This process was called, on the part of the accused, " waging his law ", and if all the jurors, or, as they were called, " compurgatours ", swore their belief in his innocence, he was acquitted; but if even one of them would not do so, he was said to be " cast ", or convicted, and the appropriate punishment was duly administered. The curious notions held in the 14th century regarding fair play towards an accused person may be seen from a prosecution of 1319, when two bullock carcases had been condemned at the Stocks Market by the " surveyors " of meat. When, at the Guildhall, the butcher, denying the putrid condition of the meat, demanded a jury, strangely enough the two " surveyors " who had already condemned the meat were included among their number. No wonder the butcher was sentenced to the pillory with the carcases burnt beneath him. In other cases a curious appropriateness is to be observed in the formation of the jury, as in 1378, when, a quantity of leather having been seized as being badly tanned, a jury consisting of saddlers, pouchmakers, girdlers, leather bottle-makers, tanners, curriers, and cordwainers was called to decide the matter.

At Iters held at the Tower the prisoner accused of felony was first brought into court and the accusation read over to him, and he was then asked how he would plead. If he pleaded " guilty " he was punished according to the offence, but if he pleaded " not guilty " he was compelled to " wage his law ", or, as it was sometimes expressed, " put himself upon the country ". Thus it was only a man who pleaded " not guilty " who

could be tried, for if he pleaded " guilty " there was
no occasion to try him, and by a curious piece of legal
sophistry he could not be tried if he refused to plead
at all. But in the latter case a much worse fate awaited
him, for, by an equally curious sophistry, he was sent
to prison to perform what was euphemistically termed
" penance " for a crime of which he had never been
convicted. The unfortunate prisoner took no active
part in performing the " penance " in question, but
was merely the passive victim of his gaolers' attention,
or lack of attention. They confined him in a bare cell,
devoid of even a truss of straw to lie upon, and gave
him on one day half enough barley bread to support
life with nothing to drink, and on the following day a
small draught of water and nothing to eat, and so
continued on alternate days until the victim either
collapsed and died, or else capitulated and agreed to
plead.[1] It is scarcely to be wondered at that the Coroner's
Rolls for the 14th century, scanty as they are, record
several instances of prisoners in Newgate dying of this
form of " penance ".

There were three ways of " waging law ", the " Great
" Law ", the " Middle Law ", and the " Third Law ",
according to the nature of the offence. The " Great
Law " was only applied in cases of homicide, burglary,
and wounding, when the defendant was accused by
alleged eye-witnesses, and this was the only law of the
three which carried with it the penalty of loss of life
and limb. In this case the reputable men of the city,
but occupying no official position, such as that of
sheriff or chamberlain, had to select thirty-six jurors
or compurgatours, of good character and freemen of
the city, eighteen of them to be called from that part of

[1] *Eyre of Kent*, Selden Society, vol i, p. 125.

the city lying east of Walbrook, and the other eighteen from the west of Walbrook. These men were brought into court in the absence of the accused, and examined by the sheriffs to ascertain if they were related in any way to the prisoner. Any so related were rejected and others called to fill their places. Next a list of their names was handed to the accused, who had the right to object to any of them for good cause shown, as, for instance, that one of them might be a personal enemy, or might be related to the person he was accused of injuring. When the compurgatours were finally selected, they left the court in company of the accused, after he had found sureties for his future attendance, who were afterwards liable to heavy monetary penalties if they failed to produce him on the stipulated date. A certain time was then allowed before the case came on again for final decision. The city claimed that not less than forty days should be allowed, but in effect the period varied from a fortnight to a month, or sometimes longer, at the discretion of the judge. In the meantime it was the business of the accused to persuade all these thirty-six men of his innocence. On the day of the trial they all entered the court, when the procedure was as follows. The accused took a solemn oath with his hands on the Bible or some holy relics that he was innocent of the crime imputed to him, and then came forward six of the compurgatours and similarly swore to their belief in his innocence. He then swore a second oath to the same effect, followed by six more compurgatours swearing, and so on until the whole thirty-six had sworn. If this were gone through successfully he was acquitted and allowed to go free, but if even one of them refused to swear he was convicted, and usually sentenced to be hanged. It should be added that if the accused were not a freeman of the city forty-two compurgatours were required instead of thirty-six.

The "Middle Law" was used in cases where the evidence was indirect, and the proceedings were the same as for the "Great Law", except that only eighteen compurgatours were required, nine from each side of Walbrook. The penalty on conviction by the "Middle Law" was, however, very different; for the culprit had to pay the "were", the Saxon "wergeld", equivalent to the value of a man, amounting at this time, as before the Conquest, to a hundred shillings for a freeman of the city not of noble birth. Sometimes in addition a portion of the felon's goods were confiscated. The "Third Law" was used in the case of crimes committed during the feasts of Christmas, Easter, and Whitsun, or Pentecost as it was called. In this case the number of compurgatours was only six, and here, as in all other city courts, whether the Mayor's Court, the Sheriff's Court, or the Coroner's Court, the jury was chosen from the ward in which the accused resided, or in which the felony had been committed. The "Great Law" and the "Middle Law" as practised at the 13th century Iter at the Tower constitute apparently the only departure from this otherwise invariable rule. The proceedings under the "Third Law" were simpler and easier for the accused, and the punishment lighter, possibly because felonies committed during times of festivity were regarded as more venial than those committed at other times. There is yet another class of trial where the prisoner is prosecuted by the Crown on suspicion of having committed an offence, there being no independent accuser, such as the sheriff, or a private individual with a grievance. In this case the number of compurgatours was only six, as in the "Third Law",

but the penalty was loss of life and limb as in the " Great
Law ". The English law has always been in a state
of progressive development, and it must not be supposed
that the above formalities were observed everywhere and
at all times, even during the middle ages ; in fact,
throughout the 14th century in ordinary cases tried at
the Guildhall the number of jurors was almost invariably
twelve.

In spite of the severity of the laws in the middle
ages, when hanging was the regular punishment even
for offences which would to-day be considered quite
minor ones, or perhaps because of this severity, evasion
of the penalty was not at all impossible, at any rate on
the part of a man of determination ; and so we find
many felons not slow to take advantage of the opportunities afforded them. The most obvious thing to do
was to take sanctuary in the nearest church immediately
after the commission of the crime, a manœuvre not so
very difficult when one considers that in the small area
of the city there were more than a hundred churches.
Here the fugitive could remain under the protection of
the Church for forty days, during which period his safety
was inviolable, and any attempt to remove him by force
led to serious trouble for the perpetrator. Thus in
1334 the Mayor himself was cited to appear before the
Archbishop of Canterbury at St. Paul's for dragging
a man out of sanctuary and compelled publicly to
restore him. The right of sanctuary was the prerogative
of the Church, based on its fundamental attribute of
mercy to sinners, and as it could grant the right so it
could refuse it, and did so if the victim of crime were
a member of its own community. In 1321 a woman
murdered a clerk of the church of Allhallows, London
Wall, and remained within the same church trusting

to receive protection from the consequences of her act. Such an impudent proceeding was, however, repudiated by the Bishop of London, who declared that the Church would not save her, and after five days she was dragged out and taken to Newgate, where she was hanged three days later. During his forty days' seclusion the fugitive was fed by the officials of the church, and could at any time send for the coroner and announce his intention of abjuring the realm. If he so decided he was deprived of all his possessions—money, arms, and clothing—except his shirt and breeches, and sometimes a jacket. He was assigned a particular port at which to embark, the road he was to take, the time he was to occupy on the journey, and the places where he was to stop each night. He then had to swear to keep to the direct road, not to remain at any place for more than a night, and not to return during the King's lifetime. He had to carry a cross to indicate that he was under the protection of the Church. There is a curious case in 1340 of a man taking sanctuary in St. Paul's after committing a murder in Chepe, to perpetrate which he appears to have been sent specially from Northampton by his employer, a knight. When the coroner went to the Cathedral to interview the felon he abjured the realm on confession of a murder committed in Cambridgeshire eight years previously, no mention being made of the more recent crime, although the coroner was well aware of the facts. If the fugitive at the end of his forty days' grace had neither capitulated nor abjured the realm, his surrender was hastened by the withdrawal of his food supplies.

The most famous, or perhaps it would be more correct to say the most infamous, sanctuary in London was the precinct of the church of St. Martin-le-Grand, a large

enclosed area surrounding the church and built over
with houses for the accommodation of the fugitives,
or sanctuary men, as they were called. It was situated
partly on the site lately occupied by the General Post
Office, but stretched beyond that to Newgate Street,
with the present street of St. Martin-le-Grand, then
known as St. Martin's Lane, running through its middle.
Here, by special privileges dating from the time of
William the Conqueror, robbers, cutpurses, felons of
all kinds, makers of imitation jewellery, and fugitive
debtors were able to reside for indefinite periods, often
issuing out at night to commit assaults and robberies,
or carrying on their nefarious work within the sanctuary,
with none to say them nay. Fraudulent goldsmith's
work was produced there in large quantities, in the
form of chains, brooches, rings, cups, and spoons, made
of inferior metal gilded or silvered, and intended to be
sold as the real article, until " St. Martin's beads "
became notorious. At times the Masters of the Goldsmiths' Company were enabled to go there to inspect
the shops of their members, but only by the courtesy
and with the special permission of the Dean. Indeed,
so potent was the authority of their ancient charters,
that when in Edward IV's reign a statute against makers
of fraudulent goldsmith's work was passed, the precinct
of St. Martin's was excepted from its operation. This
state of affairs arose by reason of the fact that the usual
forty days during which a fugitive was permitted to
remain in sanctuary did not, by right of their charters,
apply to St. Martin's ; and by the same charters the
church and its precinct were technically outside the
city and beyond the jurisdiction of the civic authorities.
Even men accused of High Treason were safe there
from molestation, and the King, on more than one

occasion, after a fresh inspection of their charters, fore-
bore to exercise his undoubted right of withdrawing
the privilege of sanctuary from offenders of this description. For many years during the 14th century this
condition of lawlessness was a thorn in the side of the
Mayor and aldermen, and in 1405 they petitioned
Henry IV to have the right of St. Martin's annulled,
but although he expressed his sympathy with their
desires he was unable to help them. The result was
that during the following years the citizens often took
the law into their own hands, invading the precinct
and forcibly removing some notorious malefactor ; but
on each occasion they were ultimately worsted by the
power of the Dean and Chapter and compelled to restore
their prisoners, with apologies and gifts of huge wax
tapers, gold, and jewels. It was not until about 1457
that definite rules were laid down for the conduct of
the sanctuary, but even then the Dean was under no
compulsion to deliver up any felon who continued to
pursue his evil courses, but only to keep him in confine-
ment within the precinct.

As a rule the fugitive from justice taking sanctuary
had no idea of abjuring the realm, but rather relied on
his capability to escape during the night and get clear
away. This process, at any rate in London, was facili-
tated by the laxity of the watch kept by the citizens ;
in fact, in 1298 they publicly resolved no longer to
keep any watch at all. They got into trouble for this
at the Iter held at the Tower in 1321, when they
unsuccessfully pleaded ancient custom, and it ended
with a solemn undertaking on their part to keep good
watch for the future. The escape of the felon from
sanctuary appears usually to have been the end of the
matter, unless the crime was so notorious that the

authorities felt compelled to take action, in which case they pronounced sentence of outlawry. The form of outlawry is thus described in an ancient legal treatise : " Which judgment is this, that when on account of " a felony anyone has been ordered by solemn cry to " come to the King's peace in three successive county " courts, and he does not come, then he shall be " accounted a wolf, and ' Wolfshead ! ' shall be cried " against him, for that a wolf is a beast hated of all " folk ; and from that time forward it is lawful for " anyone to slay him like a wolf. And there was a " custom to bring the heads to the chief place in the " county or the franchise, and one received 10 " marks from the county for the head of every outlaw " or wolf ".[1] In London the fugitive was called in five successive fortnightly Courts of Husting before sentence of outlawry was passed. Such a sentence, drastic as it may appear, was more sound and fury than anything else, for in days when there was no properly organised police system, and when communications were in such a primitive condition, the felon, if he could reach some distant part of the country, could usually afford to ignore it.

If the accused were a freeman of the city, even though the charge were such a serious one as that of murder, he still possessed the right to be bailed by his friends, which opened up fresh possibilities of escape. Bail was known as " mainprise " and the bailers as " main-pernours ", and if they failed to produce the accused for trial they were liable to forfeiture of goods and imprisonment. If, however, every trick failed and the prisoner was actually brought into court, he still had a shot in his locker providing he were not entirely

[1] *Mirror of Justices*, Selden Society, p. 125.

illiterate. This was " benefit of clergy ", and to obtain it there was no necessity for him to prove that he was in Holy Orders, but merely that he was a " clerk ", or, in other words, that he could read and write. A church official known as the " ordinary " was then sent for to examine him, to whom he read out a verse from the New Testament, which, from its potency in saving necks from the hangman, became known in popular parlance as the " neck-verse ". If he passed this test successfully he was handed over to the Church for punishment, when, although he might have to spend a protracted period in doing penance, or might even be branded on the hand, his life at any rate was safe.

Fitzstephen, a 12th-century writer, in his description of London, says : " Each class of suits, whether " of the deliberative, demonstrative, or judicial kind, " has its appropriate place and proper court " ; and although in the 14th century there seems to be a certain amount of overlapping, it is possible to distinguish to a large extent the different functions of the city courts. The Court of Husting, held at the western end of the Guildhall, and presided over by the Mayor and aldermen, was used for the enrolment of wills, deeds, and indentures. At that time the surest way to make an agreement operative was to get it publicly enrolled. This court also heard pleas of land and tenements, and suits of rent, or services in lieu of rent, including cases of wrongful seizure of property, and also disputes over wills. Next was the Sheriffs' Court, presided over by the sheriffs, which heard personal actions, such as pleas of debt, or trespass, battery (where no blood was shed), or seizure of goods, or claims of account between merchants ; but the Mayor, if he thought fit, could order a case to be taken out of the Sheriffs' Court and brought to his own. The Mayor's Court was the supreme court of the city, and tried cases of swindling, theft, false representation, or riot or brawling. The progressive nature of the city courts may be observed from the fact that the use of the vernacular in place of Norman French was permitted in them as early as 1356, six years before it became the general law of the land. The proceedings in the Sheriffs' Court are of particular interest. A man sued for debt was promptly arrested and imprisoned in one of the sheriffs' compters, or sometimes in the private house of the sheriff ; the reason for this being that a man so accused would take the first opportunity to remove his goods outside the city, where the court had no jurisdiction. He could, however, be mainprised by his friends the same as in other courts, and if he defaulted the mainpernours were sent to prison in his stead, forfeited the amount of the surety, and were nevertheless still under the obligation to search for and produce him. When the trial came on, if there were no authentic documents, the defendant could " make his law with the seventh hand ", or, in modern language, could obtain six men of repute, himself being the seventh, to take oath that to the best of their belief he owed nothing. If the accused were not a freeman of the city, but a stranger from outside, he could " make his law with the third hand ", but if he could not find two men to be his " oath-helpers ", he could go, in the company of a sergeant of the city, to the six churches nearest to the Guildhall, and take solemn oath in each of them that he owed the plaintiff nothing. If he were successful in all this he received the verdict.

The administration of the law in the city courts was assisted by numerous officials, the nature of whose duties was for the most part such as we might expect to find. The most interesting of them all was the Recorder, whose name and whose office owe their origin to the unique position held in the city in Norman times by the holder for the time being of Baynard's Castle on the banks of the Thames, near Blackfriars, built by one Baynard, who came over with the Conqueror. The owner of this castle was invested with an office which, under another name, dated from Saxon times—that of Bannerer of London, or leader of its armed forces. Until late in the 13th century it was his duty in time of war to come with his followers, armed and mounted, to the west door of St. Paul's, and there place himself at the head of the citizen troops ; whereupon the Mayor, sheriffs, and aldermen, with due ceremony, emerged from the Cathedral and handed him the banner of the city, together with a horse worth £20, and a further £20 in money. He possessed the right to hold a court of his own in the vicinity of Baynard's Castle, and the peculiar privilege of sitting with the Mayor and aldermen in the Court of Husting at Guildhall, where during his presence he alone pronounced or recorded by word of mouth all judgments given, and hence the origin of the name " Recorder ". These rights and duties fell into abeyance by one cause and another in the early part of the 14th century, for whereas Stow mentions that in 1320 the citizens formally acknowledged the rights of Robert Fitzwalter, the then owner of Baynard's Castle, the city Letter-Books record a meeting of the Mayor, aldermen, and commons at Guildhall in 1347, at which it was declared that the representative of that family no longer possessed any franchise in the city, or the right to intermeddle in any pleas holden at Guildhall. But some years anterior to this date an

official called a " Recorder " had been appointed to
fulfill the same functions in court as had appertained
to the Fitzwalters.   He was selected from among the
most skilful and vertuous of the law apprentices of
the whole kingdom, and had other duties added to the
original one of pronouncing the judgment of the court,
for he acted as general legal adviser to the Mayor and
aldermen, and on most occasions as the mouthpiece of
the city.   When the Mayor and his brethren attended
a Court of the King's Justices at the Tower, or St.
Martin-le-Grand, or Westminster, it was the Recorder
who recited the liberties of the city, and similarly on
ceremonial occasions, when kings or princes visited
the city, it was he who pronounced the address of welcome.
On assuming office the Recorder had to take oath to do
equal justice to all, to come readily at the warning of
the Mayor and sheriffs, to give them good and wholesome counsel, to ride with them to keep and maintain
order in the city, and to accept nothing in the way of
fees or robes from anyone except the Chamber of London.
He appears to have been summoned by Royal Writ
to the court for gaol delivery of Newgate for the first
time in 1368, and thus started that career which has
led to his becoming to-day the chief judge in city
criminal trials.

Another legal assistant of the Mayor was the Common
Serjeant, who appears to have united in his own person
the additional offices of Common Crier and Mace-
bearer.   It was his particular province to prosecute on
behalf of city orphans in any case brought to his notice
in which the guardian was guilty of ill-treatment, or
of wasting the ward's property, or forcing him or her
into marriage.   The Mayor, the sheriffs, and the
Chamberlain, all had serjeants to assist them—to summon

people to their courts and to execute the judgments given. The serjeants of the Mayor performed the additional duty of seeing that the ordinances made by the Mayor and Common Council were published and carried out. The serjeants in their turn were assisted by yeomen or vadlets, who, under their supervision, performed the actual work of making arrests and distraints. The sheriffs were also assisted by under-sheriffs, clerks, and an official known as the Keeper of the Paper. All these officials were required to take oath to do injustice to none, either for fear or favour.

The attorneys attached to the courts were not permitted to undertake cases on the model of Bardell *versus* Pickwick, where the lawyer agrees to share any damages obtained, and if none are forthcoming to forego his fees. This offence was known as " champarty ", and counsel practising it were liable to suspension. They were not encouraged to be too argumentative, at least not so much so as to change the aspect of a case before the court, or, as the oath they took expressed it, " ye chaunge no quarrell owt of his nature after your " understanding ". They were forbidden to advance any argument impeaching the jurisdiction of the court, an instance of the constant fear entertained by the authorities of any invasion of the city liberties. Contrary to the modern practice, where it would be a grave breach of decorum for counsel to express his personal conviction of the justice of his client's plea, they were expected to act only in cases where they believed themselves engaged in defending the right.

To make the system of justice complete, the ward-motes, or periodical meetings of the inhabitants of each ward, were minor courts presided over by the aldermen, and investigated infringements of the local bye-laws, inflicting small punishments, or in refractory cases reporting to the Mayor. Attached to each ward, for the purpose of carrying out the arrangements made in the wardmote for the good government of the locality, were a beadle and several constables. The number of the latter varied in each ward according to its size, and their duties were very similar to those of our modern police ; they arrested evildoers and disturbers of the peace and conveyed them to the compters of the sheriffs. The beadle was the general overseer of the peace and good order of the ward. It was his duty to report to the alderman the presence in his ward of robbers, men of evil life, hucksters of ale, brothel-keepers, and common women, with a view to having them ejected within fifteen days as the law required, and if the alderman failed in his duty in this respect the beadle would report to the Mayor. If any armed affray occurred he reported it to the sheriffs, so that they, by their serjeants, could deal with the matter according to the law of the city. Other duties which he performed were the calling of juries for the sheriffs' and coroner's courts, and reporting to the Mayor any case coming under his notice of victuals sold in private instead of in open market, and for the latter reason no brewer or baker was eligible for the office. Once every year, on Plow Monday, the first Monday after the feast of the Epiphany (6th January), a " Great Court of Wardmote " was held at the Guildhall, when all the aldermen assembled under the presidency of the Mayor and reported to him any matter which had arisen in their wards with which they themselves were incompetent to deal.

The sessions for gaol delivery of Newgate were held each year at the Guildhall, and a fresh writ from the King for the constitution of the court, naming the judges who were to sit, was received on each occasion. Among them the Mayor was always included, and the court was incompetent to sit without his presence. Here remanded cases of burglary and theft were finally disposed of, and the penalty inflicted was almost invariably death, unless the accused were able to claim benefit of clergy. Thus we find men hanged for stealing goods to the value of 6s. o., of 10s. o., of 15s. 9d., and of many similar sums ; a woman was hanged for stealing goods to the value of £5 ; and a man in 1340 similarly disposed of for stealing in the Goldsmithery in Chepe a silver-mounted drinking-cup worth 8s. o. At first when a man was accused on two separate counts he underwent two trials by two separate juries, and was sentenced to death on both counts, and so there are instances of men being consigned to the hangman twice on the same day. But in 1382 they adopted the more sensible course of trying the two counts together before the same jury. It was the rule at this period to inflict the death penalty on anyone stealing goods to the value of a shilling and upwards, but below that sum the penalty was relatively trifling. Thus in 1327 a thief who had stolen a sum less than a shilling was committed to prison from November until the following Good Friday, when he was given a flogging and set at liberty. If the thief stole some such small sum and afterwards committed another small theft which brought the total above the shilling, he was then hanged. However, most of the culprits sentenced at these sessions appear to have been habitual criminals, and in the ordinary Mayor's Court, which was a court of summary jurisdiction, the law was administered in a much milder fashion. In 1379 a man who had stolen two knives worth 20s. o. during a meeting at the Mayor's house was condemned to stand for half an hour in the pillory and then to abjure the city. Even so, it is sometimes difficult to follow the reasoning behind some of the sentences imposed. There is a case in 1374 where several butchers, including one female butcher, were prosecuted for having putrid meat in their possession, and a jury composed of cooks was called to pronounce upon its quality. They condemned it all except the meat belonging to one of the male defendants, whereupon the guilty men were stood on the pillory for half an hour while their meat was burnt beneath them, and strangely enough the innocent man was fined, and he and the woman committed to prison. When sending an offender to prison it was unusual to specify any definite period of detention, the prisoner being kept there until either he was forgiven by the Mayor, or else paid a fine or found sureties for future good behaviour. An extra infliction was sometimes added to the sentence given in the Mayor's Court, the culprit's name and the nature of the offence being inscribed on a tablet which was hung up in the Guildhall for all to see. This frequently became a subject for protest on the part of those who, having already suffered fine and imprisonment, regarded it as an outrage that the memory of their offence should be thus perpetuated. In 1354 a mercer appealed in such a case to the King's daughter, who so moved her father that he sent a special request to the Mayor for the tablet's removal, pointing out that it redounded to the " everlasting scandal and undoing of his (the " mercer's) estate ". In like manner we find in 1356 the tax-collectors of the ward of Farringdon protesting against their conviction for extortion being exhibited in the same way, but in this case they based their objection on the fact that no such course had been taken when the collectors of Bishopsgate had been similarly convicted. In cases of libel or slander it was usual to condemn the defendant to pay by way of damages several tuns of wine, or on some occasions to deposit the wine at the Guildhall as a guarantee of future good behaviour. For cases of petty theft, false weights and measures, brawling, or spreading false reports, the favourite punishment was the pillory. In 1382 a man who had defrauded poor people by selling them charms to cure their complaints was led through the middle of the city, riding on a horse without a saddle, the false charm and a whetstone hanging round his neck, and a certain piece of chamber crockery suspended before him, and another at his back. For assault there was a regular scale of charges : for drawing sword upon a man without shedding blood, a fine of half a mark, or 15 days in Newgate ; if blood were drawn, 20 shillings, or 40 days ; striking with the fist without bloodshed, 2 shillings, or 8 days ; and the same with bloodshed, 40 pence, or 12 days. However, in 1387 a man who drew his sword and attempted to attack an alderman was sentenced to have his right hand struck off, and an officer of the court, producing an axe, laid the accused's hand upon a block in order to chop it off there and then, when, in the nick of time, the injured alderman interposed and begged the Mayor to show mercy. The culprit had eventually to proceed from the Guildhall through Chepe and Fleet Street, carrying in his hand a lighted candle 3 pounds in weight, and make offering of the same in the church of St. Dunstan. A similar penalty was imposed in 1388 in the case of a man who insulted an alderman by using a filthy expression to him. If a man were convicted of perjury when taking oath on his own behalf he was sent to Newgate until the next Court of Husting, when he was brought to the Guildhall and perched upon a high stool bareheaded before all the people while his offence was publicly proclaimed ; if he offended a second time he was put in the pillory. In the city courts the way of the witness was sometimes a hard one, for if a plaintiff brought forward two witnesses to prove his claim and they differed in their testimony they were sent to the pillory, while the plaintiff lost his case and the defendant was awarded damages.

The two chief prisons within the city were Newgate and Ludgate. The former was used principally for felons and judgment debtors, and the harshness of the conditions prevailing there may be judged from the case of an inmate who had been imprisoned because he was unable to pay 3s. 6d. damages which had been awarded against him, and died of starvation. The assistance of such poor prisoners was frequently the object of charitable bequests on the part of the citizens, and the authorities were not always unmindful of them, as may be seen by an ordinance of 1377, wherein it was decreed that any cheese confiscated by reason of being sold at improper hours should be given to them. Various cases of prison-breaking at Newgate are recorded, in one of which in 1325 ten prisoners escaped through a hole they had made in the wall, and it is curious to find that some of them who took to sanctuary were permitted to abjure the realm. Stow relates an affray there in the middle of the 15th century when the prisoners revolted and kept the sheriffs and all their officers at bay for a long while from their position of vantage on the roof of the gate. Ludgate was more particularly a debtors' prison, and such was the fatherly care exercised in the treatment of the prisoners that it was run rather like an

almshouse, until it was complained that bad characters
got there who indulged in cheating and conspiracy,
and that imprisonment there had become rather the
occasion of non-payment than of payment of debt. On
this account the prison was closed in 1419 and the
inmates transferred to Newgate, but when the latter
proved so unhealthy that several of them died, Ludgate
was speedily re-opened the same year and the debtors
taken back again. This prison was under the general
jurisdiction of the sheriffs, and when new ones were
appointed each year it was customary for them to proceed there to take over the keys from their predecessors.
On such an occasion in 1409 the warder of the prison,
resenting for some reason the change of authority, with
the help of his friends resisted the sheriffs' entry by
pelting them with stones from the top of the tower so
that they were unable to enter. At various times there
were compters of the sheriffs in Milk Street, Bread
Street, Wood Street, and the Poultry, and prisoners
under remand in the Sheriffs' Court for any offence
less than felony or High Treason had the privilege of
going to one of them in preference to Ludgate or
Newgate on payment of from 4d. to a shilling a week
according to their means, or of one penny for the first
night's lodging.

And what, it may be asked, was the result of all the
care and hard work bestowed upon the administration
of the law in 14th-century London ? What of the
security of person and property, and was it possible for
a man to go about his business with reasonable safety
and comfort ? The best answer, perhaps, is to be
found in the fact that in 1386, during the troublous
times of Richard II's reign, when Parliament appointed
certain lords to inquire into and administer the public

funds, they directed them to take up their residence in the city as being the safest place in the realm. During the case related above of the man who was about to have his right hand struck off for drawing his sword upon an alderman, the scribe whose duty it was to write the details of the case in the Letter-Book was moved to include in his account the following remarks : " By counsel of the whole of the last Parliament holden " at Westminster, it was ordained that divers lords, " chosen by the same to ordain and advise for the govern- " ance and tranquillity of our said lord the King, and of " his realm, should dwell within the same city for one " year then next ensuing, for peacefully making their " ordinances there, as being the most safe and secure " place in the realm, etc. ; and also, because that there " is a greater resort, as well of lords and nobles, as of " common people to that city, than any other places in " the realm, as well on account of the Courts there of " our said Lord the King as for transacting business " there ; and therefore there is the greater need of good " governance therein, and of peace, in especial ; and " more particularly, seeing that it is the capital city and " the watch-tower of the whole realm, and that from " the government thereof other cities and places do take " example ". [1]

---

[1] *Memorials,* p. 492.

CHAPTER XI

THE LIBERTIES OF LONDON

WHEN portions of the population turn from a pastoral and agricultural existence to the more settled conditions of commerce and manufacture, and thus become domiciled in restricted areas, it is only natural that they should aspire to self-government in their communal affairs, free from the interference of overlords ; and London was only more successful in these efforts than other cities because her geographical position made her the capital of the kingdom and its richest and most populous city. It is thus that the history of the Liberties of London is a record of the constant struggle by the citizens against the encroachments of kings and others, in which form of warfare their most potent weapon was the power of the purse. When money is exacted too forcibly it quickly vanishes and further instalments are hard to find, and so impecunious kings in search of loans and gifts soon discovered that it was wisdom to placate the Londoners by extending protection to them and granting them privileges at little cost to themselves, in return for the good money of the citizens. In accordance with this policy we find sovereign after sovereign granting them charters to maintain and extend their franchises in return for a consideration in cash, but the frequency of these renewals is an indication of the difficulty of preserving their

liberties, and a tribute to the determination of the citizens
to maintain them.   The earliest charter which has been
preserved is that of William the Conqueror, and merely
declares the citizens to be law-worthy, or subject to the
full protection of the laws, a valuable concession at a
moment when England was overrun by a victorious
invading army, with leave to seize elsewhere practically
whatever it pleased.   In Norman times the citizens
were not permitted to elect their own officers, but were
ruled by a bailiff appointed by the King, and it was not
until Richard I so urgently required money for his
crusade that he appointed them a Mayor from among
their own number, and allowed them to elect two bailiffs
or sheriffs to assist him.   It is recorded that when a
friend expostulated with him regarding such a dangerous
experiment, Richard replied that he would sell the
whole city if he could find a purchaser.   Afterwards,
during John's reign, the citizens received permission
to elect their own Mayor also.   When the King required
the citizens to advance him money their first efforts
were directed to reducing his demands as much as
possible, but it may be assumed that the King took care
to anticipate such tactics by asking for a higher sum
than he expected to get.   Thus in March 1340
Edward III sent a messenger to the Guildhall summoning the Mayor, aldermen, and wealthier men of the city
to appear before him at Westminster on the following
day, and when they arrived it was to find that he required
a loan of £20,000.   On the following day they came
to the Chapter House at Westminster and offered
5,000 marks, and the King, declaring such a sum to be
quite inadequate, bade them bring him a written list of
all the wealthy men in London.   Their fright at such
an order may be gauged from the fact that on the day

appointed they met at the Guildhall immediately after sunrise, and instead of submitting the required list, despatched a messenger to the King raising their offer to £5,000, which was accepted. To raise this sum the citizens were assessed according to their wealth, and the amount was contributed by 235 of them in sums ranging from 40s. o. to £400. The names of the subscribers with the sum paid by each were entered in the Letter-Book, furnishing a permanent record of the richest citizens of the period. Just how wealthy the citizens were may be seen from the details of a loan of 3,000 marks granted to the King in 1346, when it was arranged that everybody possessing £10 or more in movable goods should contribute, and it was found that 376 citizens were in this condition of life. The loan of 1340 was not lent without good security, for several of the King's friends, including the Archbishop of Canterbury, the Dean of York, and a famous and patriotic London citizen, Sir John de Pulteney, the same who gave his name to St. Laurence Pountney Hill in Cannon Street, entered into a bond to repay the £5,000 by the following midsummer, or in default to submit to distraint upon their lands.

A trouble from which the city frequently suffered was the habit exhibited by many successive kings, on the excuse of commotions among the commonalty or of improper conduct on the part of the civic authorities, of taking the liberties into their own hands, dismissing the Mayor, placing their own officials in his stead, and collecting the city revenues for their own pockets. Henry III, a queer figure of a King, unstable of character and uncertain of temper, was probably the worst offender in this respect. He harrassed them time after time with fines and exactions, with or without excuse, and once described London as an inexhaustible well. At another time he summoned the citizens to Westminster for the purpose of offering them a humble apology, with a solemn promise not to persecute them in future. When, in revenge for the support they had given to Simon de Montfort, he usurped their liberties at the end of the Barons' War, he demanded an indemnity of 20,000 marks before he would restore them. Edward III granted a charter to the city guaranteeing them immunity from this kind of persecution for the future, and his successor, Richard II, was the last of the medieval kings to impose such a penalty. Since his time it has occurred only once—in the reign of Charles II, an act afterwards reversed and declared null and void under William and Mary.

The King's Justices were often guilty of attempts to infringe the city liberties when they held an Iter at the Tower, or when, at St. Martin-le-Grand, they attempted to try any case concerning matters that had arisen in the city. At the Iters of the Tower, in order to resist the exactions which the judges endeavoured to impose upon the citizens for supposed breaches of their prerogatives, it was necessary for them, at great trouble and expense, to prove their liberties one by one, until they obtained a charter from Edward III exempting them from the necessity of giving formal proof each time. Better still, Edward IV granted a charter by which, if any of their liberties were called in question in any court of the King, it should be sufficient proof of such liberty if the Mayor and aldermen, by the mouth of their Recorder, pronounced it to be good and true. The main objection on the part of the citizens to the King's Court at St. Martin-le-Grand centred round the question of appeals from the city courts, and at one time litigants

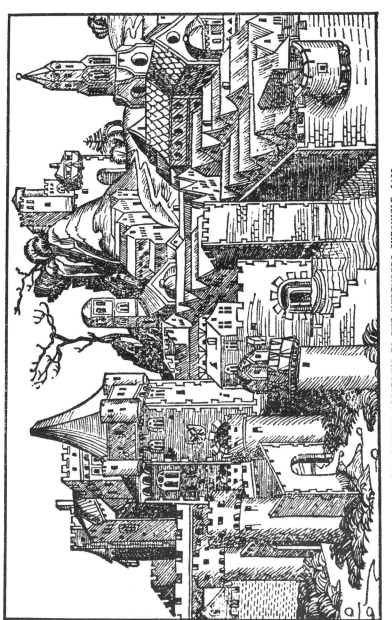

OLD LONDON ACCORDING TO THE NUREMBERG CHRONICLE, 1493

From a copy in the Guildhall Library

were warned not to institute proceedings there without the consent of the Mayor and aldermen on account of the danger entailed to their franchises. The civic authorities consistently refused to make a return of the records of cases in the city courts to the judges at St. Martin-le-Grand, and the only modification of this rule they would admit was to permit their Recorder to go there and recite such records by word of mouth. A case in point may be observed in 1357 in an action between the Prior of St. Bartholomew and several citizens regarding possession of certain tenements in the parish of Allhallows, Honey Lane. This case had first been tried in the Sheriffs' Court, and the verdict appealed against in the Court of Husting, from whence it was taken to St. Martin-le-Grand. In 1344 the judges tried time after time to collect a jury of twenty-four men from the city to try a case of assault, but on each occasion the Mayor declined to allow it, showing his charters, and at last by order of the King the case was dropped. Similar tactics were adopted on occasions when the King attempted to take actions arising in the city to his court at Westminster. In 1369 a case in which several merchants of Lucca had sued a Lombard for debt having been tried in the city, the King demanded that the record of the proceedings should be returned to him at Westminster. The Mayor replied that it was contrary to the liberties of the city that such records, other than cases of felony, should be returnable. After the receipt of a further writ the Mayor gave way so far as to allow that part of the record which concerned the King, namely the proceedings against the defendant for having withheld payment of the customs, to be returned, but the other part, the action for debt, he declined to return.

Direct refusals of the demands of the King or his emissaries were resorted to whenever the civic authorities felt themselves sufficiently strong to take such a course, and it will not be surprising to find that such outspokenness was oftenest induced by matters which touched their pockets.   In 1312, when Edward II was expecting trouble with his barons, he ordered the citizens to provision the Tower with 60 quarters of corn, 100 quarters of malt, 10 casks of wine, 40 quarters of oats, 20 quarters of salt, 10 carcases of oxen, 40 bacons, 1,000 stockfish, or cured fish, and 5 " mays " of herrings. They replied pointing out that there were no funds available for the purpose, as all the money had, by the King's own orders, been expended for the payment of his debts.   A similar flat refusal was given to the same King in 1319 when he wanted the citizens to install one of his officials as warden of the port of Queenhithe. The customs and dues raised there were at that time the property of the city, having formerly been made over to them by Richard Earl of Cornwall, to whom and his heirs they paid £50 a year for the " ferm ". The amount of money which the city were often out of pocket by the constant demands of the King may be judged from their own statement made in 1357, in which they affirm that they had lent the King for his wars in France, including the siege of Calais, £137,000, and that notwithstanding they had been taxed for the same purpose more heavily than any other part of the kingdom ; and this, too, at a time when, as a result of the Black Death, much of the property belonging to wealthy victims of the pestilence had fallen into the hands of the Church, and one-third of the city was empty.

Although the citizens were at all times ready to defend their liberties and to produce their charters in proof of the justice of their cause, they were not unmindful of the maxim that valour should be tempered by prudence, and so they often found it safer and more convenient to dodge the issue by offering excuses and making delays. With this end in view the usual excuse they offered for non-attention to the King's writ was that it had arrived too late to be acted upon. This they did in 1310, when the King's Escheator issued a writ to the Mayor to summon a jury of eighteen citizens to appear before him at St. Bride's Church in Fleet Street to decide a plea of land. It was, in fact, entirely contrary to the liberties that any outsider should call a jury of citizens except the itinerant Justices when they came to the Tower. Similar tactics were resorted to in the same year on receiving a writ from the King complaining that a previous writ ordering them to arrest a gang of pirates hiding in London had not been complied with. They replied that the writ in question had been received by a previous Mayor and sheriffs, and what they had done about it could not be ascertained. To yet a third writ upon the same subject they replied that the men had been arrested and put on trial, but nobody appearing to prosecute, they had been set at liberty. In a case in 1315 the King's persistence proved too much for them. A man and his wife who were legatees of certain tenements in the city and had failed to obtain possession of them, having appealed to the King, the latter sent no less than six writs before any satisfaction could be obtained, such obstruction on the part of the civic authorities being due to their resentment at what they regarded as unwarrantable interference with the conduct of the city courts. To the first writ they replied that the will under which the plaintiffs claimed to benefit contained certain ambiguities, and that in consequence the other heirs of the testator had raised objections to its execution. To the second writ they merely repeated their former answer, and the reply to the third is not recorded. To the fourth they replied that proper execution had been done according to the law and custom of the city, and reminded the King that causes which had been tried in the Court of Husting ought not to be removed to any other court except that held at St. Martin-le-Grand for the correction of errors arising in the city. The fifth writ was sterner in tone, described their previous answer as frivolous and insufficient, and ordered the Mayor and aldermen to appear before the King at Westminster. At a loss to concoct a further argument they fell back on the plea that the writ " had come too late ", but when a sixth arrived they could wriggle no longer and agreed to appear before the King.

When, as happened on many occasions, London felt the repercussion of the national political situation, it behoved the authorities to step warily in order to preserve their cherished liberties. Such an occasion arose towards the end of the reign of Edward II, when the opposition of the barons to the King, which ultimately hurled him, in 1326, from his throne, began to have its effect upon the Londoners, who, with lively recollections of having taken the wrong side in the Barons' War, would have preferred to remain neutral. The two sides, however, vied with each other to obtain the city's support, and the latter, unable entirely to shirk the issue, concluded that the only safe course was to dissimulate as long as they could, and the subsequent interchange of letters between the parties—King, barons, and citizens—is a model of tergiversation. The first letter came from the King asking if they would hold

the city for him, to which they replied that they were
ready to live or die with him, at the same time giving
practical demonstration of their loyalty by putting the
city in a state of defence, a precaution which they would
have been bound to take whichever side they espoused.
As a set-off to this they addressed a letter to the barons
begging them to believe no evil reports of London,
assuring them of support in any measures they might
deem necessary, and promising that they would afford
no aid to the King's friends, the Despencers, who were
the root of the trouble. The King, doubtful of their
good faith, demanded a formal assurance of support
under the Common Seal of the city, and ordered them
to arrest some of the lords who, he had heard, had
taken refuge in London. To deal with this explicit
demand required extreme caution, and after much
deliberation it was resolved to reply by two letters, one
under the Common Seal and one under the Mayor's
seal. In the first they made excuses for not giving
the required assurance, asserting that the assurance
already given was sufficient, and pointing out that a
guarantee under the Common Seal would involve the
responsibility of the whole community, so that if any
individual should display disaffection all would suffer
for his conduct, a result which they felt sure the King
did not desire. The second letter, under the Mayor's
seal, which partook more of the nature of a private
communication, offered to give the required guarantee
should the King insist upon it, assured him that the
fugitive lords had been diligently sought for, but could
not be found, and requested that the King would give
a commission to the Mayor and aldermen to punish
them at their discretion when captured. The King
granted the commission as requested, and reiterated

his insistence on the guarantee ; but the Mayor, thankful that his offer had been made more or less unofficially, informed the King that he had called another meeting at which the whole commonalty had renewed their determination to live or die with him, but were still obdurate on the question of the proposed guarantee, unanimously deciding that the assurance already given was sufficient. To assuage the King's wrath the Mayor followed with another letter offering an aid of 300 armed men, providing that such assistance should not be drawn into a precedent. The King appears to have been somewhat mollified by this offer, for we hear no more about the guarantee, and his next letter is devoted to chiding the citizens for sending so few men, and for not stating when they would arrive, how long they would serve, or who would pay their expenses ; and finally ordering them to send all their great men in a body with horse and arms. The affair ended with the city sending 500 men to serve for forty days, and the receipt of a letter of thanks from the King, in which he informed the Mayor that he had instructed the keepers of the Great Seal to issue Letters Patent to the effect that such service should not be drawn into a precedent. In the national crisis which followed the citizens did not take sides until the last moment, and fortunately for them it was the winning side.

On other occasions the citizens showed that they were well versed in the art of lubricating the wheels of business, by making judicious presents to those servants of the King who were in a position to confer favours upon them, or who, by their influence, could get them out of scrapes which might have proved unfortunate for them. Thus in 1324, when they had obtained an allowance of about £250 on the amount they owed at the Exchequer, they spent about £11 in making presents to those concerned. To one Baron of the Exchequer they sent a swan and six capons at Christmas, a carcase of beef at Easter, and at another time a silver-gilt water-dish. To another Baron they sent four shillingsworth of salt fish, and a swan and six conies worth 7s. o., and the same man did not scruple to accept £5 in cash at their hands. A third Baron accepted a beaver cap lined with scarlet cloth, besides salt fish, bread, wine, and poultry. Various clerks of the Exchequer received smaller sums ranging from 10s. o. to 50s. o., and one of them a dish, a ewer, and a pair of trenchours or metal plates. Even the doorkeepers of the same institution had 7s. 5d. distributed among them, and some other assistants gloves. Similar methods were resorted to at the Iter held at the Tower in 1321, when the sheriffs of London, having been fined £20 by the Justices over a little matter of the escape of a prisoner, they were forgiven by persuasion of several of the Justices' clerks. These friends of the city were rewarded with presents amounting to £3. 6s. 8d., the King's steward received a beaver cap lined with green velvet, and various small sums were freely sprinkled among the serjeants of the court.

In normal times the city of London possessed many privileges beyond those granted to other cities and towns. No officer of the Crown had power to enter the city to make arrest or distraint, or to call a jury. No King's Escheator could enter to seize forfeited property or to call a jury of citizens to decide upon the position or value of such property ; any such falling to the King had to be dealt with by the Mayor, who was himself the only King's Escheator in London. No one could sue a citizen outside the city except in an action involving the tenure of land lying outside the city. On the other hand, any debt owing to a citizen by an outsider had to be paid in London, or, alternatively, the debtor had to come to London to contest the suit of his creditor. If the debtor had no goods of his own in London on which distraint could be made, any goods in the city belonging to the town from which he came could be distrained upon. In the same way a citizen of London travelling through the country was exempt from the usual tolls levied on merchants for the repair of bridges, roads, or walls. Among such levies from which the citizens were exempt we find the ancient names of Brudtol, the toll for passing under bridges ; Yeresgive, a compulsory New Year's gift to the sovereign or other overlord ; and Scotale, probably an invitation compulsorily accepted to drink and pay for ale. If any town or district ventured to levy such toll, the goods they possessed in London could be distrained upon to reimburse the citizen, and as London was the principal port of the Kingdom there would usually be some goods belonging to somebody domiciled in almost any district of the country. This penalty was known as " withernam ", and as early as the 12th century we find the citizens threatening to put it in force against Bury St. Edmonds, the Abbot of that monastery, who was overlord of the town, having illegally exacted market tolls from London merchants. In 1314 40s. 0. was exacted from a merchant of Dublin because a London merchant had been mulcted in a like sum in Dublin by way of toll. In 1323 the Abbess of Barking in Essex suffered a similar penalty because one of her servants had seized goods belonging to a citizen, and to letters from the city demanding redress she had not deigned to reply. Many other cities throughout the Kingdom possessed some of the foregoing privileges, but it was of no use for the King to give out new charters to provincial towns or to increase their existing rights, for the citizens of London would simply decline to admit them. In 1319 they refused to admit the charter of Colchester, merely permitting the merchants of that town to trade in London free of one toll only—murage. In the same way Edward II had granted a charter to Cambridge exempting their merchants from liability to pay not only murage, but other tolls in London known as pavage and pickage. In 1331, when these privileges were claimed, the Mayor and aldermen, after examining the charter in question, remitted murage only. If it came to a contest in the execution of " withernam ", London, by reason of the enormous quantities of goods stored there, was certain to get the best of it.

London merchants attending any of the annual fairs held throughout the country were quit of the charge known as stallage, or payment for occupying a stall, which means that they could attend the fairs with no other expense than that of getting there. They could not be arrested or tried by the local authorities for any misdeed alleged to have been committed at the fair. For this purpose the city sent several of its more prominent citizens to form a court before which only could such prosecutions be brought. Thus we find recorded in the Letter-Books year by year the names of the citizens sent to form the court at the annual fair of St. Botolph, held at Boston in Lincolnshire. In 1260 some London citizens were arrested by the municipality of Northampton on a charge of homicide at the local fair, but the authorities in London were able to compel Northampton to give them up. No man arrested for an offence in London could be sent for trial to any other part, even though he were also accused of an offence at the place where the King proposed to try him. On many an occasion the citizens did not hesitate to refuse compliance with the direct mandate of the King in such cases, returning his written order with the intimation that such a course was opposed to the liberties of the city. A like order was received from the Justices of the famous Eyre of Kent, held at Canterbury in 1313, and was also rejected. The city also possessed the ancient rights of Ingfangthief and Outfangthief, and of confiscating for their own use the chattels of convicted felons.

Wherever the King moved it was the duty of his Marshal to find accommodation for all members of the court by the simple process of seizing whatever houses were found suitable. This right, however, was strictly limited in London, where the Mayor, sheriffs, and aldermen selected lodgings for the court, taking the King's Marshal with them in order that he might satisfy himself that the accommodation offered was suitable and sufficient. In 1325 a too officious Marshal took, without permission, a house near Billingsgate belonging to John de Caustone, one of the sheriffs, made a chalk mark upon it to indicate that it was temporarily the King's property, and installed therein the King's secretary with his retinue. When the sheriff arrived on the scene and saw what had happened he obliterated the chalk mark and ejected the intruders. For this he was prosecuted by the aggrieved official in the Court of Marshalsea at the Tower, a court which travelled with the King and held jurisdiction within the "verge", or a twelve-mile radius of his person. The Mayor and citizens, however, arrived in force to defend their sheriff, and producing their charters the case was dismissed.

In the matter of taxation the city obtained a valuable concession from Edward III to the effect that they should be assessed not as a borough, but as a county. The advantage of this consisted in the fact that when Parliament made a grant of money to the King it was usual to impose a smaller rate on counties than on boroughs. Thus in 1334 a tenth was granted from boroughs and a fifteenth from counties. Not content with this concession, in the year aforesaid the citizens struck a bargain with the King to compound for the sum of 1,100 marks, which he accepted "albeit inadequate". It was customary for an additional 10 per cent. to be raised on all King's taxes levied in the city by way of "Queen's gold", an allowance for the benefit of the Queen Consort. On this occasion, however, because they had compounded the tax for 1,100 marks, the citizens did not see why they should pay an additional 110 marks for Queen's gold, holding that such a compounding arrangement should include everything due. The Queen, not getting her allowance, complained to the King, who sent writ after writ to the city demanding payment, all which they put aside and quietly ignored. At last the Queen prosecuted the citizens in the Court of Exchequer, where the Barons, after searching the Red Book of the Exchequer, decided in her favour. Even then the citizens would not give in, but continued haggling until the Queen, weary of the controversy, agreed to accept 80 marks in settlement. Edward III was a very good friend to the citizens on account of the support they afforded him when he deposed his father from the throne. Among other favours he bestowed upon them the bailiwick of Southwark for £10 a year, enabling them to effect arrests and to hold courts there, and to levy fines and tolls. Southwark originally formed part of the bailiwick of Surrey, but in 1289 Edward I separated it from that county and conferred its " ferm " at different times on various of his friends. Edward III in his first year gave it permanently to the citizens because they complained that fugitive felons from the city habitually took refuge there, where the jurisdiction of London could not reach them. They had possessed the government of Middlesex from early times, paying the Crown £300 a year for the privilege, but from this sum the thrifty citizens took care to get a rebate of £7 on account of the free soke or court held at St. Paul's by the Bishop of London. The citizens had also possessed their own hunting-grounds in the Chiltern Hills and in Middlesex and Surrey from time immemorial. The early origin of these rights is attested by a charter of Henry I confirming them, in which it is said that they shall have them as fully as their ancestors had done. They also possessed right of warren at Staines, on land at Stepney belonging to the Bishop of London, and at Greneford in Middlesex on land belonging to the Bishop of Chester. At different times they refused permission to both these prelates to enclose their land in order that the city's privileges might not be jeopardised. In 1379 they appointed an official known as the Common Hunt to administer their hunting and fishing grounds, an office which was not abolished until 1807.

By the terms of their charters the citizens were not liable for military service outside the city, and this, perhaps, proved the most illusory of all their privileges. The 14th century was a period of foreign wars, partly in Scotland, but more especially in France, and from its beginning to its close we find the city continually furnishing contingents to swell the armies of the Kings, and generally at their own expense. It is at moments such as these that the Letter-Books become alive with real interest, for on many such occasions they do not fail to supply a complete record of the names of those who volunteered for service and of those who gave money towards defraying the cost. But like all such records, not specially intended for the benefit of posterity, they stop short just where the interest would have been supreme. What a glorious tradition, for example, would it be could we have had a list of those Londoners who actually fought at Poitiers or at Agincourt. Such omissions are not due to any lack of appreciation on the part of the compilers of the Letter-Books of the importance of these events as they affected the national honour and the national renown, for they thought it worth while to transcribe in their books the letter in which the Black Prince described the battle of Poitiers, and the anxiety and excitement which pervaded the city on the eve of Agincourt are well known. The explanation is simply that there was nobody present at these battles whose business it was to compile such a list, and details of the kind would only be known from the talk of returning soldiers. It is curious to note, on almost every occasion when contingents were supplied for foreign service, the insistence of the citizens on obtaining Letters Patent from the King to the effect that the aid then given should not be drawn into a precedent. These documents appear to be the only consolation they received for the violation of this clause in their charters, for it never deterred the King from renewing the demand on the next occasion.

One of the city's most valued privileges was the

conservancy of the Thames, the Mayor for the time being acting as chief conservator, and his jurisdiction extended from Staines to Yantlet Creek, near the mouth of the river. This included the right to destroy all kidels, or weirs made of sticks and basket-work, placed in the river for the purpose of catching fish, if their mesh were too small, or their position a danger to shipping. The Thames fish was at this period a valuable source of London's food supply, and the city watched its preservation with a jealous eye. Those kidels which were not of the standard size would catch the young fish and so endanger the industry, and when any were seized they were publicly burnt and the owner fined £10. In 1381 the size of the mesh was ordered to be 1½ inch east of London Bridge and 2 inches west of London Bridge, in both cases the measurement to be reckoned transversely between the knots. In 1385 a serjeant was appointed to seize all defective nets and to have half the forfeitures for his remuneration ; but after working for a year he pointed out that he had received nothing, because all nets and other apparatus seized had been promptly burnt by order of the Mayor. Accordingly after this they paid him 100s. 0. a year for his trouble. In the reign of Henry IV a lively affair occurred which not only shows this jurisdiction in operation and displays the magnanimity of the Mayor, but helps to dissipate the idea so widely held that the middle ages were a long nightmare of oppression of the weak by the powerful, in which the poor, ground down by agelong subjection and misery, no longer possessed the spirit to stand up in defence of what they considered their elementary rights ; whereas the fact is that throughout the period the autocratic attitude of the King and the nobles was about equally matched by

the habitual turbulence of the people. But to our tale :
A sub-conservator of the Thames seized sixteen nets
belonging to fishermen of Erith, Barking, and Woolwich,
intending to take them to London for examination.
Immediately the bells of the churches on the shores
of the river were rung to call the people to arms,
who, to the number of 2,000, armed with bows,
arrows, swords, bucklers, and clubs, and using doors
and windows in place of shields, as we are told, put out
in boats and pursued him to Barking, shooting at him
as he fled. Unable to proceed farther, the sub-conservator landed and deposited his booty with the constables
of Barking ; but the mob, following in his wake, landed
and rescued their nets, with which they returned in
triumph. The ringleaders were afterwards arrested and
brought before the King's Council at Westminster,
but when they humbly apologised, the Mayor, who had
appeared as prosecutor, not only agreed to forgive them,
but magnanimously allowed them to continue using the
same nets until the following Easter, by which time
they were to have new ones made in accordance with
the standard of the city.

In the midst of these privileges, however, there was
one drawback from which the city suffered, probably
to a greater extent than any other part of the country :
this was purveyance. By their earliest charters they
were exempt from the impost known as prisage, and
perhaps it is as well to define the difference—not a great
one—between the two forms of thinly veiled robbery.
Prisage, then, was the requisition of goods for the
King's use with no intention of payment, while purveyance was a similar requisition where a receipt or tally
was given in order to cheer the owner with the faint
hope that perhaps at some time or other he might possibly

be paid. Prisage was not taken without a system ;
for example, from a ship laden with wine the rule was
one tun from before the mast and one tun from behind
the mast. On several occasions the Lieutenant of the
Tower stopped ships belonging to the citizens on their
way up the river and levied this due, but the authorities
were always able to contest the matter successfully.
The King's purveyors, on the other hand, could walk
the city at their pleasure, bearing their white wand of
office, and mark with the broad arrow whatever goods
were required for the King's use. In early times the
citizens possessed little means of defence against this
practice, but throughout the 14th century they carried
on a perpetual agitation to get payment for the requisi-
tioned goods, not without a considerable measure of
success so far as it is possible to judge. In 1359, in
reply to their complaints, the King instructed the citizens
that nothing should be given up to any purveyor unless
he showed his commission, and at the same time he
sent them a list of those who were duly authorised to
act in this capacity. By this it may be seen that the
King's baker was one, with two assistants ; there was
a purveyor of corn, two of flesh, and two of fish ; one
of poultry, three of oats, and one of hay. Each of these
had three or four assistants, and one purveyor of oats
remained with the King, while his seven assistants roamed
the provinces to obtain supplies of that cereal. Strangest
of all, there was a purveyor of the scullery with one
assistant, but what he actually obtained for the King is
not apparent. By Statute of 1362 the detested name
of purveyor was changed to that of buyer, and it was
ordered that all payments for goods taken were to be
made in cash.

Another expense to which the city was liable was

when they sent members to Parliament. These assemblies were held almost every year, only lasting for a few days each time, and more particularly in the early part of the century were located in all parts of the country in accordance with what happened to be the convenience of the King. Sometimes this infliction fell twice in one year, as in 1336, when one Parliament sat at Westminster from the 11th to the 20th of March, and another at Nottingham from the 23rd to the 26th of September. The expenses of these affairs had to be paid by the city, and in 1314, when a Parliament assembled at York and the two city representatives were absent for about a month, the cost totalled 35 marks. To meet this sum a penny in the pound was levied on all citizens who had been assessed for the last fifteenth.

It is no wonder that kings sometimes took it into their heads to look into the city's financial affairs when it is considered that the sheriffs, whose office lasted for one year, were in many cases still in arrear with their accounts at the Exchequer as much as ten years after their term was up. The sheriffs were the chief collectors in the city of all monies due to the King, including the " ferms " of Middlesex and Southwark, and various customs and dues. When these accounts were in arrear the whole body of citizens became liable to the King for their settlement, while the sheriffs were sometimes arrested and imprisoned ; but to inquire more deeply into their doings was not an easy or profitable undertaking, as may be seen by an effort of the sort made by Edward II in 1314. As a preliminary he ordered the sheriffs to suspend all their clerks and officers until he had inquired into their conduct since the beginning of his reign. He then sent four Justices to the Guildhall to examine the affairs of the sheriffs, under-sheriffs, and all their assistants ; but on their arrival the Mayor, sheriffs, aldermen, and the most prominent citizens appeared in force and politely requested the would-be investigators to leave, pointing out that their conduct was an infringement of the city liberties. In face of such a display of force the Justices retired, and the King probably thought better of it, for no more is heard of the matter. There seems to have been no good excuse except the general financial laxity of the time for the sheriffs to be so continually behind in their settlements with the Exchequer, for although, as was the case with all other official positions in the city, any citizen elected was compelled to serve, they were not without certain emoluments which may have, to some extent, repaid them for their trouble. Any victuals confiscated for breaches of the regulations became their property. Thus in 1375 we find them receiving corn which had been forfeited by a merchant who broke the law by purchasing a quantity direct from the country instead of allowing it to come to open market in London. The sheriffs in 1376, one of whom was John North-ampton, agreed that in the event of any confiscated victuals being adjudged to them during their term, one moiety should be given to the use of the commonalty. Anything found straying within the city also became their property, a right which led to some friction in 1387. The beadle of Portsoken ward, having seized a horse which he had found straying, delivered it to the Prior of Holy Trinity, who was *ex officio* alderman of the ward, instead of to the sheriff. For this breach of custom the beadle was imprisoned in Newgate, which so incensed the Prior that he obtained a writ of *certiorari* against the Mayor and sheriffs. This, as the Letter-Book comments, was " contrary to his oath as an alderman ". The case was partly tried before the Chancellor, but adjourned, and after dinner the same day the Mayor, sheriffs, and aldermen waited upon the King's Council at Blackfriars to put their case before that body, when some of the lords who were present persuaded the parties to a reconciliation. The Prior then apologised, admitted the right of the sheriffs, and the beadle was released.

From earliest times the office of Mayor was regarded as one of great honour and prestige, and the rank of the occupant was equivalent to that of an earl, while the aldermen are often referred to as the Barons of London. It is true that at times there were to be found men who preferred to shirk their expected elevation to the chief magistracy, and in such cases the plan adopted was to collect at Guildhall on election day a crowd of people who were paid to shout persistently the name of another alderman, so that their clamour might cause him to be chosen. But perhaps the most extraordinary incident connected with the mayoralty occurred in 1368. At that period it was customary to elect the Mayor on 13th October, although he did not enter upon office until 28th October, thus giving him an opportunity to put his private affairs in order before commencing his duties. In the year mentioned one Walter Berneye was elected, but when 28th October arrived he failed to put in an appearance to be sworn in and presented at the Exchequer. The reason for his absence remains unexplained, but in the emergency thus created the citizens elected another, Simon de Mordone, on the spot, and he thereupon assumed office and rode to Westminster. Afterwards the absentee was condemned to pay his substitute 100 marks by way of damages, with the proviso, however, that if, on examining the

ordinances touching these elections, it should be found
that such payment was illegal, the money should be
refunded.   In London the position of the Mayor was
such that only one man took precedence of him, and
that was the King.   Thus in 1415, when Henry V
summoned the Mayor to the Tower to listen to his
speech dealing with his forthcoming invasion of France,
it is recorded that the Mayor sat in the centre, with the
Archbishop of Canterbury and the Bishop of Winchester
on his right, and the peers of the realm on his left.   The
determination of the Mayors to maintain this prerogative
is illustrated by an incident occurring in 1464, when
Matthew Phillipe, the city's ruler at that time, was,
with the aldermen, invited to dine with the serjeants of
the coif at their hostel in Ely Place, Holborn.   By
some inadvertence the Earl of Worcester was shown to
his seat before any other guest, and thereupon the
Mayor, deeply offended because in the city he ought
to take precedence of everyone, immediately left, accompanied by most of the aldermen.   Proceeding to his
house in the city he ordered a sumptuous feast to be
prepared for himself and the aldermen, which was
served within a remarkably short space of time.   Meanwhile the master of the lawyers' feast, regretting the
misadventure that had befallen, and in an endeavour
to make amends, sent his servants to the Mayor's house
laden with the choicest dainties that had been prepared.
These, however, arriving during the Mayor's dinner,
and seeing him served with dishes as fine as anything
they had brought, retired in confusion.   Throughout
the middle ages the city's ruler was known simply as
" Mayor ", and does not appear as " Lord Mayor " in
charters and documents before the reign of Elizabeth.
It is thought by many that his modern appellation was

assumed when Edward III granted him the right to be preceded by a serjeant bearing a mace of gold or silver embellished with the Royal arms, or as one chronicler informs us, a mace of silver gilt with the Royal arms at one end and the city arms at the other. It is more likely, perhaps, that the form " Lord Mayor " was of gradual growth, and indeed as early as 1283 we find the scribe who wrote up the Letter-Book, imbued apparently with the feeling that the usual appellation " Mayor " was deserving of some additional form of respect, referring to him as " *domino Maiore* ". It first became customary to elect the Mayor yearly in John's reign, although the same man might and often did by re-election serve for several years in succession. Owing, however, to the great and increasing expenses of the office a new rule was made in 1318 to the effect that no man should be compelled against his will to serve for more than one year in succession. Occasional notices are found in the Letter-Books of sums of money voted to outgoing Mayors on account of great and unusual expenses incurred during their term, and on one occasion Matthew Paris records that the King seized the revenue of the Mayor—£40. It seems probable therefore that this was the salary at first received by the city's ruler.

The Mayors of London constitute for the most part a succession of bold and public-spirited men who, in defending the rights and liberties of their city, did not fear to stand up to anyone, king or other. There is the well-known instance in 1264 when, after the battle of Lewes, the Mayor and aldermen were required to swear fealty to Henry III at St. Paul's, and the Mayor addressed the King as follows : " My lord, so long as " unto us you will be a good lord and King, we will

" be faithful and duteous unto you ". The chronicler considers these words outrageous, but no doubt the Mayor won greater popularity thereby. On another occasion, accusations having been made by various London citizens against the Provost of Wells, the Mayor did not hesitate to order his arrest, and he only regained his liberty by a present of £100 to the city.

It is a necessary concomitant of a paternal form of government that the people will either prosper or suffer according to the qualities of their ruler, and this was true of London in the middle ages, when with a strong and public-spirited Mayor the city was free to pursue its affairs with a minimum of outside interference, but if perchance their ruler were actuated by partisan or personal motives the whole population suffered for his misdeeds. The latter state of things is illustrated by the events described in Chapter V, and another instructive example may be observed earlier in the century. It was at the Iter held at the Tower in 1321 that John de Gisors, who had been Mayor in 1312–13, was convicted of bestowing during his mayoralty the freedom of the city under a false date and in return for a bribe on a man accused of murder in order to enable him to exercise the privilege of a citizen by remaining at liberty on bail until the Iter should assemble. Although at the date of the Iter the mayoralty was held by a different man, nevertheless the city was taken into the King's hand, the Mayor dismissed, and a Warden installed in his place ; and when, later in the same year, the citizens received permission to elect another Mayor, it was under more restricted conditions than hitherto. For the remainder of his reign the King retained the power to remove the Mayor at will, a power which he exercised two years later, when, for no apparent reason, he deposed

Hamo de Chigwelle, and appointed Nicholas de Farndone in his stead. He replaced the former in office in the following December, in the meanwhile carrying him about in his train, virtually a prisoner. So far as concerns the offence which was the origin of the trouble. and in spite of the verdict of the jury given at the Iter of 1321, the report of the granting of bail in January 1313, as recorded in Letter-Book D, is, to say the least, somewhat intriguing. The entry does not state who were present upon the occasion, but remarks that mainprise was granted "reluctantly" because the accused had obtained a writ out of Chancery ordering the court to grant it. If the sheriffs only were present, the word "reluctantly" must be taken as an indication of their fear that the matter was not altogether regular, that the accused had obtained his writ out of Chancery by his new and falsely acquired freedom ; but if the Mayor were present in person, it can only mean that he had granted the freedom in all honesty and now realised that he had been tricked. For the honour of the city it can only be hoped that the latter interpretation is correct.

In considering the unique position which London attained in the middle ages, with its unequalled privileges and its self-government, it is pertinent to inquire as to the public spirit of the citizens themselves, or at any rate of the trading community in whose hands the conduct of city affairs more particularly rested. An example of their insistence upon purity in the conduct of their government is found at a period so early that it is safe to assume that few if any other cities in Europe would have acted similarly at that time. It was in 1273 that, several bakers being arrested for selling bread below the proper weight, a sheriff accepted a bribe of

60s. o. from one of them to suppress the case against him, while the others were prosecuted. The record proceeds : " Whereupon this Peter (the sheriff) being " accused thereof in full Husting, confessed that he " had received 60 shillings of the said baker, not to " produce him with the other bakers ; and accordingly " he was deposed from his office, and the same was " immediately promulgated throughout all the city. . . " and it was found, upon inquisition made by certain " great men of the city, charged by their faith in God " and by the oath which they had made unto his lordship " the King, that the other sheriff, Robert de Meldeburne " by name, had given his assent to taking the 60 shillings " before mentioned, and had been there present in form " aforesaid ; and therefore, the same as his fellow " sheriff, he was deposed, and they were both amerced " unto his lordship the King ".[1]

A similar anxiety on the part of the citizens to see that their own Exchequer was properly administered may be observed in 1310, when, on the retirement of the Chamberlain, six auditors were publicly elected to examine his accounts. The Chamberlain was the city's cashier, through whose hands their revenues passed, in the form both of income and expenditure. The result of this audit appears to have been unsatisfactory to the body of the citizens, for we find them in the following year, at an assembly at Guildhall with the Mayor and aldermen present, electing one David de Cotesbroke as their " comptroller against the Chamberlain " with the special duty of overseeing all their financial affairs. As the freedom of the city was conferred upon the new official at the same time it is most probable that he had been brought in from outside for the purpose. An

[1] *Chronicles of Mayors and Sheriffs*, p. 167.

instance of the reputation of the city as a mercantile and financial centre is afforded in 1377, when the first Parliament of Richard II refused to vote supplies for the war with France unless the King consented to appoint independent treasurers or wardens to see that the money was properly expended. He thereupon selected for this purpose two of the most prominent citizens of London—John Philpot and William Walworth.

The potential greatness of London appears to have been recognised at a very early period, for Fitzstephen, writing in the 12th century the earliest description of London which we possess, and quoting from an early Latin poet, says, in words which to-day sound prophetic :

" Brutus, there lies beyond the Gallic bounds
" An island which the western sea surrounds ;

. . . . .

" To reach this happy shore thy sails employ ;
" There fate decrees to raise a second Troy,
" And found an empire in thy royal line
" Which time shall ne'er destroy, nor bounds confine."

INDEX

914.203
P39